Paul 'Stalkie' Stalker Chi

Star of Channel 4's *Imp*

YOU CAN RAISE YOUR GAME!

Live happy. Be fulfilled. Here's how.

Published by Second to None Ltd trading as The Raise Your Game Partnership

www.rygp.co.uk

First edition
ISBN 978-1-9999524-0-2

Print Management by Biddles Books, King's Lynn, Norfolk PE32 1SF

TESTIMONIALS

WHAT PEOPLE ARE SAYING ABOUT
PAUL STALKER AND 'YOU CAN RAISE YOUR GAME!'

"Paul's approach to motivation is as far as I know unique in the UK and the world ... An inspiring and stimulating read ... Paul is an amazing guy, with some wonderful ideas"

– **Julian Richer**, Founder, Richer Sounds, philanthropist and author of 'The Richer Way'

"You Can Raise Your Game methodology is both very different and very powerful. Stalkie makes people think about their lives in a direction that no-one probably has had them thinking before. I have worked personally with Stalkie for the past 15 years and he is still Raising Our Colleagues' Game today."

– **Sir Charles Dunstone**, Co-founder Carphone Warehouse, Former Chairman Dixons Carphone, Executive Chairman TalkTalk Group

"I have used Stalkie's material to help transform and rehabilitate some of the country's most dangerous category A prisoners"

– **Clive Ludlow**, Prison Officer, Belmarsh Prison, Britain's most secure jail

"I think this information will help me communicate better with my family and also help me with doing time in prison"

– **Zubair Khan**, LM6038, Lifer, Belmarsh Prison

"Paul was diagnosed with a very serious form of cancer. His spirit and fight were outstanding. He really did raise his game"

– **Professor Ghulam Mufti**, Professor of Haematological Oncology, King's College, London

PRIVATE CLIENTS SAY:

"You Can Raise Your Game! has been a personal revelation for me and given me the courage and mindset to achieve the work life balance I've craved for years"

"You Can Raise Your Game! coaching methodology has opened my creativity, tapping into something different in me, helping me to personally progress and develop"

"I feel I have developed as a leader. I'm more able to motivate and get the best out of my people, as well as having the difficult conversations with them"

"The teambuilding and motivational tools I've learnt have positively galvanised all my 270 staff behind the company"

"Stalkie stretches you. He has a wealth of knowledge. He's been there and done it but his coaching style draws the answers from within you rather than prescribing what to do"

"Stalkie is great at drilling into the nitty gritty, defining the root problems and then coming up with solutions to resolve them"

"Thank you for getting me out of bed in the morning with a passion to make every day count"

"The whole You Can Raise Your Game! experience is uplifting. You come away feeling energised and motivated"

"I've learnt to communicate so much better in every aspect of my life, with my family, at work, and I'm way more confident socially. Hey, it's not rocket science, but the penny just dropped when I was training with these guys"

YOU CAN RAISE YOUR GAME!

WITH **PAUL** 'STALKIE' **STALKER** AND
THE **RAISE YOUR GAME** TEAM

WITH HUGE THANKS TO WRITER AND
RESEARCHER **CHRIS HUMPHREYS**

ADDITIONAL THANKS MUST GO TO
ADE WHEELDON FOR LETTING US SEARCH HIS SOUL
NEIL WATERS FOR OPENING HIS HEART

LOVE AND THANKS

You Can Raise Your Game! is the result of three decades of inspiration, ideas and experience provided by many special role models, mentors and friends. I think of it as a community of knowledge-sharers with an intrinsic desire to help everyone fulfil their human potential and live an outstanding life for as long as we grace this planet.

Business leaders, thought leaders, role models and creators of magic:
Patch Adams, Muhammad Ali, Maya Angelou, Robert Anthony, Albert Bandura, Jonny Benjamin MBE, Andrew Bernstein, Usain Bolt, Bournemouth AFC, The Boys' Brigade, Baroness Karren Brady CBE, Sir Richard Branson, Bristol Cancer Help Centre, Brené Brown, Buddha, Jack Canfield, Dale Carnegie, Sir Ian Cheshire, Sir Winston Churchill, Donald O. Clifton, Stephen Covey, Marie Curie, Leonardo da Vinci, Dr. Rosy Daniel, Charles Darwin, Walt Disney, Sir Charles Dunstone, Thomas Edison, Albert Einstein, Sir Mo Farah CBE, Sir Alexander Fleming, Henry Ford, Anne Frank, Viktor Frankl, Randy Gage, Mahatma Gandhi, Stephen Hawking CH CBE, Napoleon Hill, Beryl Hillier, Steve Jobs, Martin Johnson CBE, Neil Laybourn, Patrick Lencioni, George Lucas, Martin Luther King Jr., Clive Ludlow, Dame Ellen MacArthur, Malala Yousafzai, Nelson Mandela, Bob Marley, Abraham Maslow, Mother Teresa, Professor Ghulam Mufti, Sir Isaac Newton, Alfred Nobel, Rosa Parks, Allan and Barbara Pease, Tom Peters, Michael Phelps, The Prince's Trust, Rachel Remen, Julian Richer, Anthony Robbins, Eleanor Roosevelt, Martin Seligman, William Shakespeare, Dawn Stalker, Brandon Stanton, Alan Turing OBE, Desmond Tutu, Nick Vujicic, Denis Waitley, Neil Waters, Ade Wheeldon, Jonny Wilkinson CBE, Will.i.am, Oprah Winfrey, Sir Clive Woodward, Paul Zak, Zig Ziglar.

Collaborators who brought this book and app alive:
You Can Raise Your Game! and the RAISE AR app have become a reality due to a handful of key people:

Chris Humphreys, Dawn Stalker, Rudy Kazal, Attila Vaszka and the edirect team, Andy Oxley, Jenny Clay

DEDICATION

*I'd like to dedicate this book to Dawn,
my wife, the light of my world*

WELCOME TO
YOU CAN RAISE YOUR GAME!

Dear Friend,

People tell me that my success is down to my insatiable desire to learn and my persistent determination to act, but I know it is also through the support, faith and expertise of many remarkable people who I am blessed to call my friends and mentors.

Some of these people are internationally recognised entrepreneurs, business gurus, thought leaders, motivational coaches and positive psychologists; most, however, are unsung, 'everyday' heroes whose attitude, care and love can serve as the most profound lesson to us all.

Together, we explored the belief that everybody has various degrees of self-imposed limitations and we are all bound to encounter challenges and change in life.

At one end of the spectrum we can default to handling these limitations and challenges using a blame/procrastination/victim mentality and idly suffer the consequences.

At the other end of the spectrum we can default to a welcome/action/hero mentality. As stimulus-response beings, the choice is ours. Given the right mindset tools and the determination to act upon them, we can all raise our game to fulfil our highest potential.

It was in 2002 that I first began distilling and formalising the knowledge and principles that underpinned the turnaround in my own emotional and physical well-being, into a set of **'Raise Your Game'** educational coaching tools. Since then, this methodology has had transformational and stunning results wherever I have taught it around the world – to corporate leaders and their teams, to high performance sportspeople, to disengaged children, to substance abusers, addicts and life-serving prisoners.

Now, with my revised and super-current **'You Can Raise Your Game!'**, you too can become the architect, builder and owner of the most fulfilled and happy life you could wish for, both for yourself and those you care for.

You can be safe in the knowledge that when life throws up its various challenges, self-inflicted or otherwise, you too can dig deep inside yourself to overcome them. And when opportunities for growth arise, you can seize them quickly and confidently.

You Can Raise Your Game!

Paul 'Stalkie' Stalker

YOU CAN RAISE YOUR GAME!

WHAT'S 'APPENING WITH THIS ICON THROUGHOUT THE BOOK?

Wherever you see this **App Alert** icon and abstract design together (like this page you are reading now), you can simply scan the whole page through your **Raise AR** app with your iOS or Android smartphone and access unique videos and exercises to bring the pages of this book alive. Every **App Alert** image and abstract design will lead you to a new video on our **Raise AR** app.

1. Download the free **Raise AR** app from your App Store or Google Play. This requires WiFi or 4G connection to be downloaded and for video streaming.

2. Open the app and reveal the Augmented Reality image reader.

3. Make sure the **App Alert** page is on a flat surface as shown in these illustrations.

4. Point your device between 15-20cms distance from the page at the **App Alert** images. You will see Stalkie talking direct to you via video!

5. Lightly tap the video twice on your phone's screen and you will be able to take the phone away from the page to view.

For direct links to download the app and further information, you can also visit www.rygp.co.uk

CONTENTS

01

GET TO KNOW ME AND MY BOOK

APP ALERT!!

Realise your potential and live an outstanding life

Better still, by using the simple tools in this book, you will not only be able to learn to fix yourself – you will also have the power and capabilities to help those around you improve their lives.

My aim, my burning desire with **You Can Raise Your Game!** is to help and support you to identify your purpose, to set and achieve goals that will serve your life and others' lives best, whilst cherishing the journey and the relationships along the way, no matter what point you are starting from.

MY AIM

When you experience an emotional hiccup or a major wobble at work, rest or play; when you have trouble relaxing your mind and body; when you can't seem to move forward due to indecision, self-doubt, fear or ill health; when you wonder whether you're good enough or strong enough to succeed; when you have stared an outstanding opportunity in the face and avoided it or screwed it up; when your relationships are going haywire; when you have inflicted a lifestyle upon yourself that is spiralling out of control and alienating the very people that you love and care for the most...

...I will show you how to make a positive difference to your life.

I'll never forget sitting at school when I was nine years old and dreading the request from my teacher, who regularly asked us to write the day and date in our workbooks. All we had to do was copy what she had already written.

What I wrote always looked right to me, but day after day I got it wrong. And day after day the teacher would ring my mum and tell her I couldn't even write the date properly. Mum would take me to the optician and tell them I obviously couldn't see clearly. Little did we know about dyslexia in those days, or ADHD. So, like many a kid with learning difficulties and a hot-headed temperament, I spent most of my schooldays wondering why learning stuff was so hard and boring.

I was also small and physically under-developed until well into my late teens, which gave my peers plenty of ammunition to use against me. And as for the girls? They just weren't interested in me.

My teenage years saw me pin-balling around various failed relationships and jobs until I stumbled across a signature strength that was to serve me well. Some might call it the gift of the gab, others might call it a cocky self-belief; I'd prefer to say that I had a verbal ability to build rapport, communicate and persuade. Particularly when it came to using the telephone to sell things to strangers, many of whom later became my friends.

When I built a business around these principles, boooom! At the age of 28 I sold part of my company, which elevated me to millionaire status. Apart from the trappings that wealth and a fun social-climbing lifestyle brings, I also had a loving family, a gorgeous wife, a young daughter and a baby boy on the way, I had bundles of energy and I slept well at night. I was the successful boss of what I thought was Stalkie LTD – Living The Dream.

So, who on earth was I trying to kid?

The resounding slaps I was about to receive to my smug face not only took me to the very physical and emotional edge of my existence but also collapsed the rest of my life's infrastructure with it.

In short, within a matter of weeks, the investment shareholders in my business parted company with me, my most valuable relationships buckled and cancer took an overwhelming grip on my health. I went from the business boardroom and my lovely family home to The Priory Clinic where I was to spend the estimated 12 weeks that my doctors said I had left on this planet.

If ever anyone needed to raise their game, to stay in the game, it was me.

Now, I've beaten the cancer and taken my health and fitness to its highest point of endurance, which has allowed me to compete in Iron Man, Tough Mudder, triathlon and extreme swimming and cycling events. I've learnt how to grow a business which I love waking up to every day and is based upon good, sustainable profit and a caring culture (I no longer run businesses in order to sell them, but work with companies that I can turn around, make a difference to and create a legacy).

I have a wife and family of five children I adore and who seem to think I'm okay too. And I have a social and community life where I enjoy some very special, mutually rewarding relationships.

I may have a story to tell, but this is not a self-trumpeting autobiography. I am still flawed in 101 ways. However, the information and guidance in this book include the principles, methods and exercises that I have been fortunate to glean in the company of some truly inspiring people who have taken me from my personal abyss to my near-summit (I say 'near' because we are all a work in progress!).

My cohort of game-raisers includes internationally recognised entrepreneurs, business gurus, thought leaders, motivational coaches, positive psychologists and health and nutritional experts, as well as my unheralded heroes – friends of all ages, cultures and creeds who have overcome adversity or are an undeniable force for good.

Because I'm far better at talking than I am at writing, I've collaborated with my colleagues Chris Humphreys and Dawn Stalker to bring **You Can Raise Your Game!** to fruition.

We all work at The Raise Your Game Partnership where we coach outstanding individuals, executives and teams across a variety of industry sectors, specialising in colleague engagement, culture and cultural turnaround, people development, internal and external communications and customer relations.

What I am providing in this book, and through my other **You Can Raise Your Game!** resources (such as online videos, tutorials and seminars which you can find out all about at www.rygp.co.uk), is proven to transform lives. Whatever it is that you are searching for – more confidence and self-esteem, a better job, a way to start your own business, the ability to overcome a health problem, to lose weight or stop smoking, to become wealthy, to find a partner in life or to enjoy flourishing relationships with your loved ones – all these things are possible.

Now, I'm not telling you this is going to be easy. The minimum requirements are commitment and action. Anyone can read a book, watch a video or attend a seminar, but if they take no subsequent action they will not improve or change a thing.

You Can Raise Your Game! looks at ways in which you can overcome the complacency that holds so many people back, blocking them from achieving their life's potential.

All the people and events in this book are real, highlighting some of the true-life trials and everyday tribulations that we all encounter. With understanding and application, we can favourably overcome them all.

GETTING TO KNOW ME

Now that you can understand where I am coming from, I'd like to share in more detail a few things that I have encountered in my life.

I didn't come from a wealthy family – quite the reverse in fact – but my parents were loving and kind to my younger sister and I. We were, and still are, balls of nervous, exuberant energy, which wasn't always well directed and focused.

As I have said, my earliest struggle in childhood – in common with so many people I speak to – was school. My teachers didn't quite 'get' me. Whether they didn't seek to understand me, or how to motivate children like me, or whether they wrote me off is open to debate, but let's just say I think there are better mechanisms in place nowadays to accommodate the young Stalkies of this world and how to make us learn more effectively.

Listening, reading and writing were things I simply couldn't do very well, and consequently I got sidelined. So I squirmed in my seat and messed around, doing absolutely nothing that would improve my life or my performance at school.

But one lesson was different – and it's etched on my mind as if it happened yesterday. It was a French lesson and we were learning to say "throw the ball" and "catch the ball" in that language. The young teacher got us to actually throw and catch a real ball while we said

"Lancer la balle! Attraper la balle!"

What a brilliant idea! It was fun and involved a new way of learning. What's more, it worked for me, as I still remember the words to this day!

If other teachers had taken time to speak to me, engage me and find out what motivated me, as my French teacher did, I reckon I could have been taught very successfully.

There were no learning support staff at the school; there was a 'one size fits all' strategy, and I guess I was just the wrong size.

It was only in my post-education life that I found out my 'wrong size' also consisted of dyslexia and ADHD (Attention Deficit Hyperactivity Disorder). Dyslexia is a general term for disorders that involve difficulty in learning to read or interpret words, letters and symbols, but do not affect general intelligence.

ADHD is a group of behavioural symptoms that include inattentiveness, hyperactivity and impulsiveness. According to the UK Adult ADHD Network (www. aadduk.org) 3.62% of boys and 0.85% of girls have the condition, which is often first identified in school-age children when it leads to disruption in the classroom or problems with schoolwork.

Had these two conditions been diagnosed whilst I was at school, and my tuition planned accordingly, who knows what I could have enjoyed learning?

There were two subjects at school that I did enjoy, however, and, through no coincidence, was good at: sport and cookery. And there were two subjects that I really struggled with: English and maths. But I never received any praise or encouragement from my teachers about my performance in sport and cookery. Instead, they cut the time allocated for the subjects I excelled at and made me spend even more time doing extra lessons in those I was useless at! This added to my frustration at school.

I can't help thinking that if I had been able to progress in the subjects I loved, maybe I could have made a career out of them? I'm sure many of you identify with this experience – and the solution is to do it yourself! It doesn't matter that your first try at education may have failed – try again! To start, though, you need to discover your own motivating factors and your individual learning style.

Having coached thousands of individuals, I can testify that everyone is different, and that people learn in different ways.

Some people learn by assimilating information from books, some will learn from listening to their teacher and some will learn through more practical methods. Teaching must be tailored to the individual in order to achieve maximum impact. We all have different strengths, and we must build on these in order to realise our potential. We'll look into how you can discover your strengths and make the most of them later in the book when we find out how the effects of positive psychology can help you **Raise Your Game**.

Another thing that surprises me when I look back on my schooldays is that 'communication' was never mentioned, let alone taught as a subject – yet it affects every area of our lives. If we can't communicate effectively with our partners then our relationships will fail; if we don't communicate in business then we won't make a living or have satisfying careers; and if we can't communicate properly with doctors and other health professionals, asking the right questions in the right way, then we won't get the answers and treatment we need.

I was amazed to discover that this lack of emphasis on communication wasn't restricted to secondary education; indeed, I met a lawyer who told me that he'd never been taught how to use communication as a tool in his working life. This man, who makes his living from communicating with clients, judges, witnesses, juries and colleagues has never been taught how to do it. Why not? This problem is not just limited to schoolkids and lawyers, it applies to many other professions and walks of life.

How to communicate effectively and powerfully is a theme that runs through the pages of this book and is something that I am passionate to pass on to as many people as I can possibly reach out to.

When I was 15, my mum said I could leave school if I could find a job. I had an inner desire to make something of myself but I'd always been told at school that I would never do well and I didn't have the confidence or qualifications to start a career. I couldn't read and write properly and I couldn't even cope with some of the practical subjects like metalwork. It all seemed out of my control.

Mum did her best to point me in the right direction; she tried various things like trying to get me into the Army and an interview with the local electricity board – all without success. But where I did feel I fitted in and was given plenty of encouragement was the Boys' Brigade – more precisely it was the 14th West Kent Battalion of The Boys' Brigade – which, in many ways, was a saving grace, focusing my energy and my attention whenever I proudly pulled on the uniform.

Here was an organisation that didn't judge me on my weaknesses, it allowed me to explore my strengths. And I had fun. Whether it was camping, cooking, canoeing, sport, first aid, music and marching, or helping out at various community events, the officers encouraged us to take responsibility for our behaviour and our actions, and to help others do so too.

The Boys' Brigade had a 'Motto': 'Sure and Steadfast'. It had a 'Mission': 'Faith in Young People'. It had a 'Vision' and a 'Belief' – that children and young people 'are the solution and not the problem' and that they should experience 'Life to the Full'. These were words and phrases that intrigued me, that I wanted to know the meaning of. I thought it was cool to have a code to understand and adhere to and that I could tell people about.

It's profound to think how such things can shape and stick with you – even now when I coach business leaders, I teach them the importance of having a mission, a core purpose and a core set of values that need to be cascaded throughout the business to shape its culture.

I truly believe that The Boys' Brigade not only kept me off the streets, but it also gave me a purpose and a set of ground rules about what was right and what was wrong. It signalled to me that, despite my literacy problems and my constant need to be on the move, I could be a leader who could engage with people and get them to respond to me.

This spurred me on to make a few phone calls to get the job that would allow me to leave school. I called Radio London and also MCA Records in London. To my amazement MCA said I could come and see them! So I travelled by train from Bexleyheath in Kent to Charing Cross in London and, because I didn't have any money left, I walked from Charing Cross station to MCA's posh offices at Hyde Park Corner. There, I was looked after by a lovely lady called Beryl Hillier who gave me a job in the royalties department and called me her 'chirpy little Cockney sparrow'. Thank you, Beryl!

Then came another breakthrough, when a friend bought me a gift; it was a series of motivational cassette tapes by Dr. Denis Waitley, entitled *'The Psychology of Winning'*.

Dr. Waitley is considered to be one of America's most respected authors and speakers on high performance human achievement, propelling individuals to personal and business excellence. In other words, a top-notch inspirer.

These tapes were a revelation and a relief for me. At last, here was somebody talking in a language that I could understand, that I could relate to and be comfortable with. It enabled me to learn successfully for the first time in my life – and I enjoyed it! No tricky words to read, and I didn't need to be in a classroom. Instead of having to listen to people telling me I would never make anything of my life, Dr. Waitley told me I had the means and the power to be somebody.

He talked about setting goals, thinking positively, believing in your own ability to go for those goals and achieve them. The tapes provided a turning point in my life, and I am very grateful to the person who gave them to me. Over the years I really got to grips with the principles and methods discussed – so much so that I now make a living from doing a similar job to Dr. Waitley!

Having set myself a more ambitious future, I then met a guy called Ed Shepherd who was the head of the London office at Exchange and Mart (a hard-edged, no nonsense newspaper popular for selling vehicles and other domestic and commercial items). Through him, I got a job selling advertising space with Exchange and Mart. This was like a light switching on inside my head. I was amazed to discover that I could actually earn money, a lot of money, just by talking! It was a skill I already had, but nobody had mentioned this at school.

So by now I felt I was going places in my career and I decided – at the tender age of 19 – that I could build my own business. Whilst I had plenty of enthusiasm, and I'd learned about motivation and the importance of setting goals from listening to Dr. Waitley's positive psychology tapes, I was short on business skills.

I could talk to, and persuade, people – I found that communicating with complete strangers on the telephone held no fears for me. I had found my principal strength and I was in my element at last.

I learned by making mistakes (NB: this isn't a practice that I preach when providing advice for my many corporate and business clients!), and I took bad financial advice (ditto!); hence, the business soon failed. What I was a gold medallist at was buying, selling, motivating and communicating. But I was a non-starter at running a business.

Now here's a beautiful thing: Since my early days of stumbling across those powerful Waitley tapes, technology has advanced somewhat! There is now a whole world of 'open source' material by some of the world's greatest thinkers, motivators and inspirers that is readily available online for everyone to access. One of my aims throughout this book, via my website and in all my work, is to point people towards this fantastic and enlightening library of life-enhancing knowledge. For example, a quick trip to www.deniswaitley.com will open the door to much of Dr. Waitley's wisdom, available to download across all platforms.

No amount of positive thinking was going to get over my naivety in running a company. However, I learned some prudent lessons at this point that still hold true:

1. Whatever you're doing – whether it's playing sport, fighting an illness, raising a family, buying a house or running a business – good advice is absolutely paramount.

2. Then you must understand that advice. Get a second opinion and some explanations. Keep asking questions until you clearly understand.

3. Get the right team around you in order to provide all the skills you lack.

Being young, and taking on board these lessons, I bounced back from that failure and started another business. This time, I built up a publishing company that generated its revenue from selling advertising space over the telephone in a variety of business directories, charity events programmes, consumer magazines – in short, anything that was printed.

I still made plenty of errors, such as hiring staff on the basis of friendship instead of competence, and failing to learn enough about the financial side of things. But the culture and atmosphere in the business was electric, with rooms full of young people who were having fun, enjoying their work and making money. It was a formula that soon attracted the interest of various investors and, at the ripe old age of 28, I sold a chunk of my business to venture capitalists, making me a millionaire in the process – one of my biggest Waitley-inspired goals realised.

As with most businesses that skew their efforts towards raking in the revenue but do not concentrate on putting in the systems and processes to protect and sustain the profit, cracks started to appear. Up to this point my investor partners had been quite happy to leave me to my own devices but when revenue slowed, costs increased and profits declined, my investors started to turn the screw.

Never one to shirk responsibility, I became obsessed with working to deliver the required targets, to cut costs and restore the profitable balance to the business. In retrospect, I wasn't smart in the way I went about it. I took it too personally and I took on too much, putting myself under a great deal of stress.

Whilst I faced up to my responsibilities at work, what I didn't face up to was that my health and my personal relationships were suffering.

On the surface, everything was going well and to everyone around me my life must have looked great. But since I had been working 12-14 hours a day to rectify the financial shortfall at work, the business became my sole focus, and I was paying the price in more ways than one.

It was after a weekend away with friends and family that I happened to discover a lump on my neck. At first I attributed this to carrying my daughter on my back in a harness, but it didn't go away. I went to an osteopath, because my back had begun to hurt as well; his advice was to see a doctor immediately. I tried to ignore it, but my sister and my PA eventually coaxed me into an appointment with a GP.

At the surgery, the doctor examined me and said that he needed to refer me to a specialist, whom I saw the following day. I'll never forget the smell of disinfectant in the room, the milky green-coloured radiator which obviously didn't work properly as the room was so very cold, and the Formica table with the peeling edges. The specialist looked at me and said *"I think you've got cancer, Mr. Stalker"*.

It was said completely without feeling and without compassion – totally cold. My sister Jo, who was accompanying me for support, burst into uncontrollable tears.

The doctor showed no emotion when he spoke to me. He didn't try to explain himself; he didn't mention treatments, or what the next step might be. I felt as though he didn't really care about me: I was just another number as he made his way through the day. Communication, you see – it's vital. I didn't know whether I was coming or going, what to say or do next.

What I do know is that the next nine days were the darkest of my life. I was forced on to a never-ending treadmill of hospitals, tests and treatments. I had a biopsy on the lump, a blood test and a CT scan, which involves injecting the body with a chemical to show up anomalies in the blood, as your whole body is passed through a tunnel-like scanner.

At the end of those nine days my worst fears were realised.

The specialist told me I had Hodgkin's Disease (also known as Hodgkin's Lymphoma), an uncommon cancer that develops in the lymphatic system.

His words were mind-blowing, devastating, numbing – in fact, there probably isn't anything in the English language to adequately sum up the feelings that course through your mind and body when you're dealt those words. All I could say in reply was:

"So, I'm going to die then?"

The specialist said this wasn't necessarily the case – but all I'd learned about how you respond to situations suddenly took on a completely different meaning.

The late, great Dr. Stephen Covey – another of my favourite educators who has inspired millions of people with his understanding of the power of universal principles – says in his book, *The 7 Habits of Highly Effective People'*, you can be proactive and 'create perspective expanding experiences' by visualising situations that you might currently fear. I hadn't ever imagined that I would be in this position, but I was determined to find a positive mindset to counter this awful news.

We'll learn more about the phenomenal effect that positive psychology can have on your health and other areas of your life throughout **You Can Raise Your Game!** But, for now, consider this startling information that the Bristol Cancer Help Centre brought to my notice during my treatment: At London's Royal Marsden Hospital (www.royalmarsden.nhs.uk) they carried out an investigation into the beliefs of people who had been diagnosed with cancer. Beliefs included: *'I'm going to get over this', 'Maybe I can beat this', 'I hope I've got a chance' and 'I know I'm going to die, because I've got cancer'.*

Even though all of these patients had the same disease, 80% of those who believed they were going to live, lived. In contrast, 80% of those who believed they were going to die, died. The difference positive psychology and belief can make when overcoming an illness has never fully been qualified but my personal belief is that it cannot be denied.

"Whatever your mind can conceive and believe it can achieve."

– Napoleon Hill

Before all this happened to me I thought my diet was healthy enough, but now I started making an effort to treat my body with the respect it deserved. After all, if your body fails, where do you go from there? To that end, I started eating better – less fast food, more simply cooked fish and vegetables, more fruit.

Still on the merry-go-round of hospital appointments and different treatments, I started chemotherapy; but part way through the course I was told that my body was not responding in the way that they hoped. In plain English, the treatment wasn't working despite all the changes I'd made to my lifestyle and diet. This was yet another devastating blow. What now?

Since listening to that first set of Denis Waitley tapes, I had become a huge fan of other positive psychologists, motivational speakers, and those who study human excellence, such as Napoleon Hill (www.naphill.org), Anthony Robbins (www.tonyrobbins.com) and, as mentioned earlier, Dr. Stephen Covey (www.stephencovey.com). This was the time I needed to practically apply the power of positive psychology. Their motivational writings were about to help me rebuild myself and Raise My Game.

"Your mind is stronger than your body. Believe."

"Your mind is stronger than your body. Believe."

– Paul Stalker

I really thought I had taken my illness seriously enough, but that proved to be quite wrong. The skills I'd learned from all those tapes, and the books I had read, were now put to good use as I began setting myself new goals.

The specialist told me the reason my body was not responding to treatment was that I had poor quality blood. Knowing I had to make even more changes, I set about discovering everything I could about cancer, diet and treatments. My dear and compassionate friend Julian Richer prompted me to pay a visit to the Bristol Cancer Help Centre where he was an advisor.

It has a marvellous team of people working there, and a library full of books and videos containing everything one could possibly wish to know about the disease.

I became convinced that juicing – taking fresh organic fruit and vegetables and squeezing the goodness out of them and into me – was the thing that could greatly improve my diet, and provide those benefits to my blood that I desperately needed. So, I started juicing with a vengeance. Every day. And I still do nearly every day.

As a quick illustration of just how powerful beliefs can be in your life, take this example: When my consultant observed the terrible toll chemotherapy was having on my body, he believed there was nothing more he could do. His general attitude was, "that's it". He thought I was going to die of this disease. After the initial shock, I started to become very thankful for life. I started making suggestions to myself along the lines of 'this is not going to happen'. Eventually, I wrote a plan of how I would beat it.

I started by writing down exactly what I'd do on the first birthday of my son Jack, who hadn't yet been born; I visualised being there with him, the cake, the presents, and all the friends and family who'd turn up to help us celebrate. I carried on this process by imagining all the things we could do together – when he was 3 years old, 5 years old, 10 years old. I had to be there with him! As I finish writing this book we have just celebrated Jack's 20th birthday.

Through this process of visualisation, I created the reasons to try to secure help with my life-threatening condition. This started sowing the seeds of belief that I could get well and, as if by magic (although I now realise that it was my Reticular Activating System at work – which we'll discover more about in the *'Ignite Your Self-Belief'* chapter of this book) I was motivated to source doctors who thought differently to my original consultant. This was my catalyst for survival, and the start of my efforts to beat the disease. In this process, I had combined immense gratitude for the life I had with the belief that I was going to carry on living it and enlarge it. And it worked.

Through this mix of conventional and complementary medicine, the sheer hard work and self-belief on my part, and the support of my loved ones, I beat Hodgkin's Disease. By being proactive, and planning how I was going to beat the illness, I had succeeded. I was given the 'all clear' eight months after the weekend that I had carried my daughter on my back.

I was Raising My Game.

Apart from being a profoundly life-changing experience, beating cancer has been one of my greatest personal achievements; it made me realise that the development of human potential is a right we all have. We're only here on this planet for a short time, so we should make the most of it and, as The Boys' Brigade taught me, *'experience life to the full'*.

I was determined to spread the word about how we can all control and plan our lives, how we owe it to ourselves to look after our bodies and how we can all maximise our relationships through learning powerful and empathetic communication skills.

For the thousands of diverse delegates who have witnessed me in action at my keynote speeches, seminars and live events in the UK, USA and beyond, I hope they don't forget the high energy, no-nonsense, fun manner in which I share my story of transforming fear into power, barriers into benefits and near tragedy into something way better!

I've learned that communication is one of the fundamental keys to a happy and fulfilled life. Through communicating effectively with others, the riches this world has to offer will become apparent (and I don't mean riches solely in a monetary or material sense). The way we communicate, the way we behave and treat others, directly influences our quality of life. It impacts upon the way we feel about ourselves, our relationships, our work, our play and it will create our legacies.

By staking my **Raise Your Game!** principles at the core of my own business, my Raise Your Game team and I have experienced a good deal of business success, adapting my model and methodology to the specific needs, cultures, systems and processes of numerous workplace environments, often with stunning results. These include sprawling multi-national retailers and household brands such as B&Q, Carphone Warehouse, and Iceland Foods; banks and financial institutions such as JP Morgan and Liverpool Victoria; and a host of niche market and boutique trades including luxury tour operators, yacht builders and organic cheesemakers, as well as fostering organisations.

The years I had spent getting to grips with all those books (you'll remember that reading had been a challenge in itself for me) were about to be put to good use. I decided to set up a new business that would give me the means to support people through passing on the life-changing lessons I had learned – and so I started www.paulstalker.com with myself at the helm, supported by my highly effective 'Raise Your Game' team.

I'm not saying my post-cancer life has all been plain sailing, as you'll discover from some of the stories relayed elsewhere in this book.

There's the matter of the tricky divorce and re-marrying some years later, which involved four of my own school-age children and a stepdaughter. And there's the matter of signing a deal to sell a slice of my business to investors, who promptly sent 'experts' into my firm who clearly had a different agenda for the expansion of my precious company... then things got turbulent. But then again, raising your game is about dealing with awkward experiences and growing stronger as a result.

"There is no quick fix in life. You must nurture your body and mind without fail every day to produce the ultimate you."

– Paul Stalker

THIS IS JUST THE START...

You can't simply read the content of this book and expect changes to suddenly happen. You need to do the exercises, find out about yourself and then take action. Action supersedes everything.

Think of yourself as a sunflower seed with the potential to grow into an enormous, magnificent and beautiful flower. To get from that tiny seed to a glorious bloom, standing many feet tall, the flower must be given the right conditions.

Your development needs the right conditions too. Improving your life is no quick fix. Think about the natural principles of farming; if you don't water regularly crops die. They need fertile ground, plenty of sunlight and TLC too. There is no one-off quick action you can take – you can't water once and then go back in three weeks – you have to water every day.

Of course, in the world of farming, if you don't look after a crop the disastrous end-result is very visible, but with people it may not be so obvious. Remember here that you must nurture your body and mind, without fail, forever, to produce the desired results. Your development needs to be cultivated. If you try to ignore these natural principles, the principles will eventually have their way whether you like it or not.

Along the way, just like the sunflower, there will be many 'offshoots' appearing in your life. You may want to learn to drive, or play an instrument, try a new hobby, get fitter, or re-train for a new career.

In order for these shoots to develop, you have to nurture them by practising. This means that you will have to add hard work, energy and training to the right conditions. Just like the sunflower, other seeds will come from your centre – your family, your friends, your colleagues – and then the process will start all over again.

Now, I consider myself to be a lucky man, not only to have survived cancer but also to have finally found my true vocation in life. The series of events which have made up my life to date have led me to believe absolutely in some simple truths: You must plan your life, take action, cherish and learn from every minute of the journey.

If you have challenges in your life, or feel that you merely exist, please read this book. Working together, we'll make sure **You Can Raise Your Game!**

02

FEAR INTO POWER

Using fear as your friend

We all have them. Some of us deny them, some of us can't contain them. But whether we like it or not, emotions influence our very being.

If your desire is to truly **Raise Your Game!**, the primary emotion I need you to understand and to harness is FEAR.

Now, when I say fear, I'm not necessarily talking about a fear of things that go bump in the night, of spiders and creepy-crawlies, of heights or horror movies, government corruption or terrorism – I'm talking about the 'day to day' type of fear that can hold you back in your career, your relationships, your health and well-being: the type of fear that can prevent you from reaching the next level in your life, from achieving your goals and your dreams.

This is the type of fear that makes you doubt whether you're good enough, whether you'll make it: the fear that allows you to think of a bucketful of reasons to justify to yourself and others why you haven't 'gone for it'; the fear that has made you so worried about the consequences of poor performance and of taking risks that a host of great opportunities have simply passed you by.

Let's parcel up some of these everyday fears and see if they apply or have ever applied to you, and to what extent:

THE FEAR OF FAILURE

In a recent YouGov survey conducted on behalf of Linkagoal (a goal-based social network which you can find more about on www.linkagoal.com), the fear of failure was cited by 31% of adults as their biggest overriding fear in life.

It was the biggest roadblock to either achieving their goals at all or to encouraging them to revisit their goals.

The fear of failure pays no regard to gender (men were measured at 31%, women at 30%) and, horribly, is increasing as society evolves: millennials (the generation of people born between the early 1980s and 2000s) are more likely than any other age group to suffer from it (40%).

APP ALERT!!

THE FEAR OF REJECTION

This is possibly the biggest killer of relationships, including all types of personal, social and business relationships, and certainly your all-important relationship with yourself.

To put your faith, trust and love in another person and to rely upon them to reciprocate wholeheartedly – how's that for a test of your need for emotional security and connection?! (We'll be delving into 'needs meeting' in greater depth in the *'Why Do You Do That?'* chapter later on in this book.) The fear of rejection can turn us all a bit haywire.

THE FEAR OF LONELINESS

This is the fear of 'unwilling solitude' which aggravates an emotional state of emptiness and disconnection, which in turn can lead to insecurity, anxiety and depression – even to addictive behaviour and illness.

It can lead us to avoid entering into a new relationship, or to become tentative and insecure when meeting new people (which means they might not see the best of you).

It can lead us to jealousy, suspicion or to doubt our partner's intentions (maybe they'll cheat on me? Maybe they're just paying me lip service?). It can hold us back from becoming emotionally or intimately committed. It can make us worry about our body image or personality traits.

It can make us act prematurely by prompting us to reject others to guard against them rejecting us first.

Then there's the fear of your boss refusing your request for promotion or a pay rise, so you lose the nerve to go for it in the first place. Or the fear of not being accepted by your new work colleagues, school mates, team or club members, social group...

Need I go on?

Clinical and research evidence suggests that one effect of this fear can be over-neediness, maybe to the point of allowing others to exert control over you.

In many ways, the fear of loneliness is a bedfellow of the Fear of Loss of Freedom.

There are people who avoid serious relationships because they're scared that they won't be able to handle not being totally in control.

Either way, prolonging or avoiding a serious relationship because of fear will not lead to a prolonged state of happiness.

THE FEAR OF CHANGE

In a rapidly changing world – where technology is often the driver of changes in the way and frequency we communicate, the information we receive, the jobs we do, the pursuits we follow – is it a surprise that the fear of change is increasingly common? This is where our comfort zones can become challenged and become far less comfortable places to be.

The fear of change usually results in a resistance mentality, which means we take no action at all. Enter stage left the stagnant person, the stuck-in-a-rutter, who may become removed or disconnected from some of life's great opportunities.

I have had countless coaching clients who have come to me because they are treading water in their personal or business lives, incapable of thinking beyond their routine or what they have always done. I've also had many clients whose aspirations or ideas are outstanding and ambitious but they haven't had the courage or passion to pursue them.

"The fear of change usually results in a resistance mentality which means we take no action at all."

– Paul Stalker

These clients have all shared a common fear of change and have suffered the negative consequences such as frustration, anxiety, self-doubt, low self-esteem, even guilt (the worry that the change they have been contemplating might adversely affect other people in their lives).

How many talented people have rejected the next level in their progression, such as promotion or leadership opportunities, because they feel they're not good enough? Such people often overcompensate for this by becoming perfectionists and stall their speed of progress as a result.

The fear of change is closely allied to the Fear of Uncertainty, the Fear of Being Judged, the Fear of Inadequacy, of Embarrassment, of Expressing True Feelings ... I'm sure you get the picture. And to top it off, the prevalence of fear amongst our younger generations (the millennials) is increasing!

I suppose we shouldn't be too surprised by this fact – after all, this is an era where digital communication is king, in which social media platforms such as Facebook, Twitter, Instagram and YouTube constantly feed us with streams of celebrity culture, 'false news' and bite-size entertainment, and hook us by tapping into our deepest needs, desires and insecurities. It's an era where you can get dumped by text, fired by email... and all via mobile devices that sit alongside us and alert us all day long.

In a relentless, virtual world in which we are encouraged to construct our own online identities (avatars) which may or may not reflect our true selves, one tweet or a dodgy selfie can result in a stream of damaging comments or, worse still, we may post an update or a photo and receive no re-tweets or no 'likes'. No 'likes' is the 21st century hallmark of rejection!

'Nomophobia' – the fear of losing or being without your mobile phone – is not only a recognised word, it is now a phenomenon: the number of people afflicted with nomophobia was revealed in a study by SecurEnvoy (www.securenvoy.com), in which 66% of people admitted having this fear.

Young adults – aged between 18 and 24 – tended to be the most addicted to their mobile phones, with 77% unable to stay apart for more than a few minutes, and those aged 25 to 34 followed at 68%. 59% of us say we are dependent upon social media but that ultimately it makes us unhappy and anxious.

If you'd like to gain further insight into just how addictive social media is becoming and the effect that online media such as gaming can have on our moral code, our strengths and our weaknesses, I recommend reading a couple of pathfinding books:

'Irresistible – Why We Can't Stop Checking, Scrolling, Clicking and Watching' by Adam Alter, an Associate Professor of Marketing and Psychology at New York University's Stern School of Business, and *'Invisibly Blighted – The Digital Erosion of Childhood'* by a team from University College London and Plymouth University Business School. I'm pretty sure these will be the first of many behavioural studies on the subject.

In a physical sense, fear can involuntarily trigger changes in your body – accelerated heart rate, sweaty palms and forehead, a quivery voice, acid in the stomach, a need for the loo. But in an emotional or psychological sense fear can trigger a numbness, an unwillingness or complete lack of desire to act.

Whatever your reasons for choosing to read this book, I would bet that fear has been a significant factor in the passage of your life up until now. Ask yourself, "what has it cost me, what is it costing me, what might it cost me in the future?"

The good news is you don't have to succumb to it or be governed by it. Have you ever thought how you can work with fear to help you control your destiny?

WHAT IS FEAR?

Before we plunge far deeper into the world of fear and what we can do about it, I'd like to give you a short explanation of where fear has previously compromised my life.

As a child, fear often reared its head at school. I was ridiculed every time I read out loud in class because I couldn't get my head around how to pronounce the words. But that all seemed like a breeze compared to the day I was diagnosed with cancer – this fear of the unknown, of what on earth would happen next, of taking an unwanted, unexperienced journey.

Yet somehow, by eventually accepting, confronting and channelling it, fear became an emotional anchor in defying the odds and beating cancer. If I hadn't learnt how to understand, embrace and use my fear, I'm pretty sure I'd be dead by now and would have missed out on the life I adore.

The evolutionary theory of emotion, (which started with Charles Darwin in his 1872 study, *The Expression of the Emotions in Man and Animals*), suggests that fear has both positive and negative consequences regarding the way in which you focus your attention. Fear can govern your life in one of two ways:

The first is that you react to it **negatively** by consistently visualising the negative pictures in your mind. This will prevent you from taking action, it adds to procrastination and, in many cases, is the catalyst for a downward spiral.

In contrast, the **positive** side means that you feel the fear in a situation but just go for it – you go for the job interview, you ask the girl/boy of your dreams out, you get married, you get up on the stage and speak or sing in front of a crowd, you get strapped into the rollercoaster seat and so on.

"If you don't leave your comfort zone you will never discover what life has in store for you."

– Paul Stalker

Individuals who react in this positive way towards fear often become addicted to the feelings associated with overcoming a difficult situation and use it as a catalyst for extraordinary achievement. From the extreme sports addict to those who have overcome debilitating phobias, there are a host of high-profile achievers who have successfully danced with their fears:

Just like Elvis Presley, Muhammad Ali also had a fear of flying which he first faced in order to compete and win a gold medal at the 1960 Rome Olympics; Walt Disney feared mice; Gustave Eiffel (the French civil engineer and architect of the Eiffel Tower) had a fear of heights; Marilyn Monroe and Laurence Olivier had stage fright; Tiger Woods and Richard Branson have a supreme fear of public speaking.

During his early life, the *"awful strain of public speaking"* and a fear of crowds was so punishing for Mahatma Gandhi that he even avoided speaking at friendly get-togethers and dinner parties. When he qualified as a lawyer, Gandhi panicked and left the courtroom on his first appearance, feeling humiliated after freezing and not being able to think of any questions to ask.

In time Gandhi found the purpose and the leverage to face his anxieties and fears. His desire to free India from the restraints of the British Empire motivated him to stand up for what he believed in and enabled him through his brilliant orations to spark millions of fellow Indians into action. Through personal sacrifice, continuous threats and spells in prison he triumphantly led the non-violent protest movement and helped to create a climate for Indian independence.

"Be stubborn … because you have considered the maximum number of people who will benefit and wish to serve them by solidly banging the drum for what you know to be true," he wrote.

If you choose the negative response to fear, you may never achieve your desired result.

"Remember that only you are ultimately in control of your destiny."
– Paul Stalker

Are you the sort of person who faces a fear, even though you may be apprehensive at first, taking in the signs and using them to your advantage, thereby becoming stronger for your next challenge? This can be described as 'stacking up your self-belief'.

Or are you the sort of person who buries their head in the sand or just walks away from a fearful situation and thinks "it's all too much!", justifying to yourself why you haven't faced it. Remember, the choice is always yours!

Throughout my days of living with cancer, fear was a companion that I learned to acknowledge and validate – without ever allowing it to dictate the outcome of my life.

I educated myself to remove all the negative thoughts that flooded my mind in the early weeks of my diagnosis and replace them with a strong visual picture of my future life without cancer. By setting daily goals for myself, by adopting an attitude and demeanour based around my ever-increasing knowledge of positive psychology, and by treating my body with respect in terms of diet and exercise, I was able to act authentically and build the foundations on which to protect and improve my life.

The words 'act authentically' are crucial here: In 2010, a team of researchers from the Pepperdine University School of Business and Management wrote an absorbing review of studies on courage, which concluded that you'll never be able to conquer your fears without being honest with yourself about them.

> *"Living in an authentic manner – meaning acknowledging and appropriately expressing one's actual feelings, thoughts, and desires – requires acknowledging one's fear and risks and moving forward anyway when the cause merits action."*
>
> – Alizabeth Lord Jetter*

APP ALERT!!

Fear can present itself in many different scenarios, other than life or death ones. The following case study, based on one of my clients who suffered some very common fears, highlights the consequences you can suffer unless you decide to do something about them.

When he first came to England, John Pierce needed a job. He saw one advertised; it was exactly what he wanted. He thought about it again and again, and eventually dialled the number, but as the phone was ringing, he put the receiver down. I asked him to describe the thoughts that were going through his head at that time. *"I had a string of fearful doubts such as 'am I really what they want? I'm sure there is someone more qualified than me going for the job... will I really be able to take on the responsibility? Do I really have the skill set?' The fear became all-consuming for me, to the point where I couldn't think of anything else."*

After several restless days and nights, John decided not to apply. In the end these irrational emotions consumed him, causing him to believe that he really wasn't good enough and damaging his self-esteem in the process.

Please understand that there is a ratio of risk to reward in every situation. Going for a job has no downside, and no risk; if you don't get the job you are no worse off, but you have gained the experience of an interview, learnt how to improve your technique, and will think about how to present yourself better next time around. The conclusion is obvious: why the fear? Experience only has an upside – there's no downside.

Quote taken from 'A Qualitative Exploration of Courage', presented to the School of Business and Management Pepperdine University by Alizabeth Lord Jetter.

In this scenario, John did actually raise his game. He made the call – he really did do well. He could have said to himself, *"Well done, John. You did it! You made the first move. A bit late, but I found the courage and did it. All I need to do now is remember my success so that, anytime I want to, I can do it again. I can apply for a new job – the world is my oyster."*

John's episode doesn't end there. The following week he woke up and, for some inexplicable reason, he thought *"I've got nothing to lose. I'm going for it!"* He called the number in the ad, only to be told that the vacancy had been filled. John subsequently discovered that the person who had got the job was someone he knew, called Phil. A red mist appeared as John was filled with anger, regret and sadness.

He was so annoyed with himself that he started to really beat himself up, resulting in a negative dialogue with himself: *"If only I had courage – why did I take so long to act? What's wrong with me? I know I could have done a better job than Phil. I'm just a loser. I don't deserve a good job if I can't even be bothered to ring in time."* His negative thoughts went on and on.

This positive affirmation would have been brilliant in the context of applying for the next job. What he should also be thinking is, *"I did pick up the phone and call, but how could I do even better next time? Call quicker! That's what I have learnt."* By taking positives out of the experience, the likelihood is that John would have been so pleased with himself that he'd be spurred on to call the other job ads straight away.

FEEDING FEAR

"Fear is the main source of superstition, and one of the main sources of cruelty. To conquer fear is the beginning of wisdom."

– Bertrand Russell*

After failing to get the job, John much later found himself in a very unpleasant situation. Whereas his initial phone call had been made on a whim rather than out of necessity, he now found himself painfully out of work. Slowly but surely John's savings diminished and he found it harder and harder to pay his bills and enjoy his life.

APP ALERT!!

Then came an opportunity to apply again for a job in the same company as Phil, albeit in a much junior position. To avoid hitting rock bottom and even losing his house, John went for the interview and subsequently took the job. Much to his disappointment, John had to sit and watch Phil get promoted through the company, whilst still believing that he was far more talented and could have done the job better himself. It was painful to bear.

Each time John thought about Phil, negative feelings infused his body – and he let these feelings remain, instead of 'taking the power back' (a concept that you'll find out all about in the chapter dedicated to this principle). Knowing he had skipped that first interview with the company, John felt remorse, hate and anger, much of which was directed towards his poor unsuspecting colleague, Phil.

*Bertrand Russell (1872-1970) was a British philosopher, mathematician, historian, writer, political activist, pacifist and Nobel Laureate.

49

The reason John came to see me was that he remained in his lowly position for years, whilst Phil climbed the career ladder, and as a result of his bitterness, John's behaviour deteriorated further. He started to gossip, telling his colleagues how bad he thought Phil was at the job, desperately trying to tear him down. John was developing a blame mentality towards the company and towards his other colleagues for his lack of career progression. He never tried to take the power back by proactively seeking a better position or a job elsewhere.

Instead, John stayed in the same role, meeting his needs in a negative fashion by gaining affection and connection with the colleagues he gossiped with (see, the importance of 'needs' and their influence again?).

These people provided him with a feeling of significance and variety in his boring day-to-day existence, because their own negative attitude made them gravitate towards John and justified his backstabbing.

We all know people like this, don't we? But can you honestly say you'd love to be one of them, or that you enjoy their company?

Many people hold themselves back in their lives because of fear. Often, they don't actually realise it because they're too busy convincing themselves that they've been dealt a bad hand, preferring to blame others – their partner, their parents, their friends, their boss – for their situation.

In reality it is they who have the problem, because they are not facing up to a particular fear. Moreover, they're not big enough to admit it to themselves. Are you one of these people? If so, the consequences are bleak – unless you deal with it.

FACING FEAR

"Fear is the mind-killer. Fear is the little death that brings total obliteration. I will face my fear. I will permit it to pass over me and through me. And when it has gone past I will turn the inner eye to see its path. Where the fear has gone there will be nothing. Only I will remain."

– Frank Herbert*

Will is an old friend of mine. We went to a party with a large group of our friends where there was a nice relaxed atmosphere and a really good night ensued. That night Will spotted a lady called Julia and couldn't stop enthusing about her to us all: *"Have you seen her? She is gorgeous! I'd love to speak to her"*. *"Well, what's stopping you?"* I remember joshing him (even though I knew he'd have to bat above his average if he was to catch her imagination!).

Fear could have stopped Will. That shadowy fear of rejection, in fact. What if Julia ignored him or blew him out? What if she laughed in his face? What if she didn't fancy him? What if we thought it was a huge laugh and made fun of him?

However, I have seen this fear of rejection transformed into enthusiasm and connection, *because fear can be turned into power.*

Instead of shying away, Will used the power of focus in the following way: Firstly he imagined how his banter would make Julia laugh; he pictured their first dance together; their first physical contact and their first kiss; he visualised their next date together and thought about them walking hand in hand, and dancing and laughing together.

*Frank Herbert was a critically acclaimed and commercially successful American science fiction author.

As a result of this empowering technique, Will's body language followed suit: he stood tall, head held high and shoulders back and walked over to Julia in a confident manner, constantly affirming to himself that she was going to say yes to a drink, a chat and a dance. Go on, Will!

Bingo! This really worked for Will, and as it transpired, for Julia too. He got just the response he was wishing for, and they continued chatting and dancing for the rest of the evening. They never looked back in their relationship and have been together ever since. Of course, Will was nervous of rejection, but he couldn't face having to think about what might have happened. For Will, the pain of not knowing would have been bigger than the rejection itself.

Will's story is a great example of what we call 'The Triangle of Communication' – something that we will explore in greater detail in the *'An Attitude of Gratitude'* chapter. It also confirms the potency of *visualisation and positive self-affirmation.* To explain:

In his book, *'Extreme Fear: The Science of Your Mind in Danger',* veteran science journalist Jeff Wise explores the neurological underpinnings of the brain's fear response to better understand how to take charge of fear, shedding light on the science with stories of people who have faced threats, adversity and extreme pressure and how they have managed to come through intact.

His conclusion is that we can learn from such brave souls and train ourselves to be more courageous, using positive psychology techniques such as visualisation.

For example, Wise tells us about Navy psychologist Marc Taylor who surveyed Olympic athletes about whether they practised positive mental skills such as silently voicing affirming thoughts.

Taylor has found that athletes who routinely did this were significantly more likely to survive the intense pressure of elite competition and reach the medal stand. *"If a coach can work with a promising young athlete to pay attention to his or her internal dialogue, and to stop negative thinking,"* he says, *"it can really change their performance."* You can check out Jeff's blog at www. jeffwise.wordpress.com

APP ALERT!!

When you find yourself in a challenging situation, what do you do? This depends on how you deal with your feeling of fear. Will chose to use his as an asset rather than a liability – he used his confidence to speak to Julia with passion, fun and persistence.

It is true that he risked rejection, but he could still have taken the positives out of that situation; looking at the risk to reward ratio, if she turned him down then he would still be one rejection closer to a 'yes'. He would have been no worse off, because he didn't have a girlfriend at that time anyway.

If it had all gone wrong, he could have learnt what not to say, refined his banter and tried a different approach on the next lucky lady. When Will thought like this he psyched himself up, took a quick swig of beer and went over to Julia. As a result, he doesn't have any of those 'what if?' feelings that can eat away at you for days, months, or even years after.

THE DO'S & DON'TS OF DEALING WITH FEAR

Do you listen to your emotions, and also your fears? Do you think of fear as your enemy, like John, or do you roll with it and think of it as your friend, like Will?

Whatever your fear, it can be controlled, and used to your advantage. Fear is an incredibly strong emotion, and everyone deals with it in very different ways. Here are my five do's and don'ts of how to deal with it, before it deals with you:

1. Don't Avoid Fear

My amazing colleague and friend Ade Wheeldon, whom I had the pleasure to coach and work alongside for a number of years, was born into a dysfunctional family who tried their best to love him but were unable to do so.

As he was living in an environment where alcohol, drugs and verbal violence was commonplace, this resulted in Ade being taken into care from the age of 11 and placed into a number of children's homes where he fell in with some bad company.

"It's fair to say that the homes were run on a culture of fear and I needed to grow up street-wise at a very young age to avoid being bullied – it was best to fit in with the crowd, which started when I was 13. We hung around amusement arcades drinking cider," says Ade.

By the age of 16, he got his girlfriend pregnant and vowed to make it work out for his young family, but she left him soon after the baby was born. *"Although I loved her, I was still a kid myself and couldn't really look after myself let alone a baby. The feeling I had at that time was absolute fear. I already feared that I was too far gone to fit into society.*

"I compared my insides to people's outsides – everyone else had the good parents, the good prospects, they seemed to have things under control and know what they were doing but I was afraid that I wasn't enough and would never be accepted. When my baby daughter was taken away, the feeling of failure intensified and my behaviour deteriorated."

That behaviour led Ade into a dark world. *"I was a 'face', always with a drink in my hand and I felt part of something for a while."*

All through this existence, Ade pushed away the few people who cared for him, such as his sister and his girlfriend. *"I wanted a 'normal' life, to be loved, to have a family and to work, but I was fearful of losing them, of being rejected and of being useless to them.*

"So ironically I decided to take control and push them away myself instead so I couldn't be hurt any more. I was actually afraid of changing my ways and of loneliness, but instead I blamed everyone else for my behaviour, I terrorised sympathy and self-pity. It was me versus all of them. I chose to avoid my fears and carried on acting like a victim. I was drifting away from them thinking that my input wasn't truly felt or valued and I veered towards other routes to meet my needs."

Ade's story of avoiding fear may seem extreme, but it's a profound example of the downward spiral that occurs when you feel powerless to deal with it. He chose to escape his situation through alcohol and recreational drugs abuse, but this resulted in him feeding his fear further.

Whilst Ade chose alcohol and recreational drugs others may choose to overeat or gamble... it's also a specific example of a general rule – like attracts like. When you're in conflict with yourself and choose a course of behaviour that might not best suit or serve you, you'll soon attract others treading the same path, who will happily collude with you and help you justify your behaviour, taking you further away from where you want to be.

2. Don't Ignore Fear

Let's continue with Ade's story, as he decided to continue ignoring his fear:

"During this time, I didn't really know who I was trying to please the most. Was it myself, my carers, my family, my girlfriend, my new 'friends'? Ignoring my fears had left me sad and soulless, ending my relationship with the people in my life that I loved and cared for, including the child that I had always wanted.

"I was staying in squats and getting beaten up in violent halfway houses and I'd got to the stage when I knew, through what I had previously witnessed, that the ending wasn't likely to be good. I remember a mate who was one of the good-looking lads I used to admire, and he was now walking through town in a ripped sleeping bag while his body was falling to bits.

"I really felt like my destination was the graveyard, but I still took substances so that I didn't have to deal with my reality.

"I ended up in hospital for five weeks with an infected leg which would have had to be amputated if I'd left it any longer. But while I was in hospital I stole money from the payphones and went out during the day on my crutches to burgle houses to get money for my next fix.

"I hated waking up confronted by life, by knowing that people were getting up, kissing their family, going to work and making something of themselves while I couldn't even sign on the dole because I was using a load of false names to avoid the police catching up with me. Then they did... I had a long crime list and I ended up in Lewes Prison for nine weeks."

One of the key messages that will recur throughout **You Can Raise Your Game!** is that in deciding to opt for short-term pleasure (the alcohol, the drugs, avoiding the difficult conversations and ignoring the consequences), Ade had also opted for long-term pain in all the relationships that mattered to him.

Ignoring his fear resulted in Ade being incarcerated, petrified and unable to sleep. Granted, this is not an everyday story, but I hope the message resonates with everyone reading this book.

We'll return to Ade later. It makes compelling reading.

3. Don't Be Regretful Because of Fear

We all know people who live with their regrets. They justify why they didn't face their fear by saying that the job, person, situation etc. was silly – *"the job isn't worth having anyway"*, *"the questions were too difficult"*, *"he's just a twit, nobody likes him"* is the sort of thing you might hear them say.

If you let bad situations continue, just as Ade did, you may end up with constant feelings of regret. It's a very difficult emotion to live with. If you've ever felt annoyed or upset with yourself for not making the most of your opportunities, you will know how infuriating, saddening and even depressing this can be.

Moreover, if you are fearful of applying for that dream job, sorting out your relationship with your partner or trying something new, you could feel regret because you will have just existed, instead of living life to the full. You will never know whether you have reached your full potential.

This is the result of choosing to ignore or deny your feelings and emotions, and it's especially true if you deny the emotion of fear – there will be repercussions every time.

I'm not saying this is a majority verdict, but how many of our older generation, those in their twilight years, do you know who still talk about the coulda, shoulda, woulda's in life? How much happier they'd have been if they'd divorced, or travelled, or played an instrument, or not smoked or drunk too much, or taken more risks, or saved or invested their money better...? Harsh to bring up our older friends here? Bet it's true!

This is what I call the Rocking Chair Test – think and act now before you're in your rocking chair and slippers by the fire, regretting what you haven't done in your life, because you were too afraid.

NOW, LET'S MOVE ON TO 'THE DO'S' WHEN DEALING WITH FEAR...

4. Do Understand and Face Fear

Dr. Brené Brown is a research professor at the University of Houston Graduate College of Social Work. She has spent the past two decades studying vulnerability, courage, worthiness and shame, and is the author of five bestselling books on these topics (read more about Brené's pioneering work at www.brenebrown.com).

In her book, 'Daring Greatly', she deduces that the belief in our own unworthiness drives us to fear-based lives, in which we fear letting people see who we *really* are and potentially exposing our true selves. This means we tend to avoid courage and we also avoid vulnerability – two qualities that can greatly improve our lives!

Where fear is concerned, the best approach is to use it to your advantage. Turn it into power! Know now that you will be faced by fear in your everyday experiences, but you must stand strong.

Facing your fear will at the best remove it completely, or at least allow it to fade knowing you've encountered it. Avoiding fear makes it even scarier, prevents us from moving forward, causes further anxiety and will have damaging consequences. If you fell off your bike as a kid, weren't you always told to get straight back on it?

Understand the reason for your fear and accept it, welcome fear and go with it, treat it as a motivator, know you are learning from every situation, use it as a tool for improvement.

APP ALERT!!

5. Do Dance with Fear!

You recognise it, you understand it and the time to deal with it is upon you. What practical steps can you take to focus on dealing with it?

If you are faced with fear, you kick into 'fight or flight' mode – your body will assess the situation before telling you to either fight the fear, or run away from it. If you choose to ignore the fear altogether, then you will never gain anything from it. So, when you feel fear, and get those butterflies in your stomach, you must devise the best strategy for dealing with the situation. Amazingly, fear will improve your life! Try these:

- Take time out – this is a time to think clearly, to avoid false crutches such as a stiff drink or any other form of 'pick-me-up'. Take a cuppa, a bath, a walk, sing, meditate or pray if that's what you enjoy doing.

  Taking a walk for example, particularly amongst nature, not only allows you to exercise and take in nourishing oxygen but also replaces feelings of fear and anxiety with more pleasant feelings such as calm, hope and happiness. A closeness to nature reduces blood pressure, heart rate, muscle tension and the production of stress hormones.

Meditation and mindfulness techniques such as sitting quietly, observing the moment, recognising and feeling your body's pulses and going with them will also synch your emotional and physical focus.

- Remove feelings of apprehension (such as a faster heartbeat or sweaty palms), not by fighting it but by accepting the feeling, placing your hand on your stomach and closing your eyes. Breathe normally, then take one slow, deep breath in, and imagine that all the anxiety is now in your lungs; as you exhale, you are blowing it out of your body. Repeat until the anxiety is removed.

- Visualise a place that you associate with safety and calm, with happy memories and positive feelings. Think of past glories; recall a time when you managed to overcome a difficulty, and focus on that. Paint a graphic picture in your mind of that occasion and how wonderful you felt when you had succeeded.

- Visualise the positive end result (the 'win') that you desire when facing your fear and how fantastic that will make you feel when you've actually made it happen. I'll examine visualisation techniques further in the *'Ignite Your Self-Belief'* chapter of **You Can Raise Your Game!**

- Rehearse what you would say to a friend who was encountering a similar scenario to you, then listen to yourself and act on your own advice.

- Imagine what the worst outcome could be as a result of your positive actions towards dealing with your fear. I doubt whether they outweigh what you have already decided is your best path?

- Share your fear and get support – fear has a habit of causing us to feel disconnected from other people. According to *'The Longevity Project'** one of the key predictors for longevity of people who have experienced trauma in their lives is the strength of their social relationships, of how friends and family have helped them to make a realistic assessment of their issues and being supported through them. In short, sharing fears takes away a lot of their scariness.

- If you can't talk to partners, friends and family and the fear is overwhelming, there are a number of helplines, charities and online support agencies which you can contact for impartial, professional advice.

- Celebrate your success when you've dealt with your fear. Treat yourself to whatever gift or pastime that makes you feel great. Lock in that feeling of success and store it for the next time as an incentive to act swiftly when another fear needs dealing with.

* *'The Longevity Project (surprising discoveries for health and long life from the landmark eight-decade study)'*
is a book based on research by **Howard S. Friedman**, Distinguished Professor at the University of California in Riverside and **Leslie R. Martin**, Professor of Psychology at La Sierra University, and Research Psychologist at UC Riverside.

In 1921, a remarkable study began tracking the loves and lives of 1,500 Americans from childhood to death. The study continues today, with research teams led by Howard Friedman keeping tabs on the remaining few who are still alive and analysing massive amounts of data to establish what it is precisely about these 1,500 individuals that led some to stay well and others to fall ill or die before their time. (www.howardsfriedman. com/longevityproject)

TOP 10 TIPS TO HELP YOU MAKE FEAR YOUR FRIEND

1. Am I going to be enough? Will I make it? Ask yourself what fear has cost you in the past and what it might cost you now and in the future – is it the perfect partner, the job you've always wanted, the skill or hobby you've wanted to perfect?

2. Are you avoiding fear? Plumping for short-term pleasure will often result in long-term pain. But short-term pain can equal long-term pleasure.

3. Do you have a negative or positive reaction to fear? Write down the possible negative and positive outcomes to facing your fear and decide whether you want to use the fear, or ignore/avoid it. Ask yourself what could happen in 1, 5, 10 and 15 years as a result of your decision.

4. You will experience the real you when you're faced with real adversity. Only then will you discover where your true strengths lie. We all have an inner peace, an inner core. If you listen to your heart, let yourself go and just do it, it will be alright!

5. You don't regret what you do, you only regret what you don't do. Regret is permanent. Don't live with regret until it's too late to do anything about it. Do the very things you think you're unable to do.

APP ALERT!!

6. Reach your thresholds. To fail is to learn and gives you an opportunity to grow. When you really want something in life, you'll often need to break through your personal pain barrier.

7. Making the most of your opportunities is dependent upon not worrying about the consequences of failure. Don't let opportunities drift by or you'll never know which of them will provide the next golden nugget.

8. Be honest with yourself – there is always a bucketful of reasons for you to justify to yourself and others why you just haven't gone for it. Honesty is the best policy if you wish to avoid paralysing your talent, creativity and resourcefulness.

    Be honest and tell yourself all the reasons why you're going to go for it and take action.

9. Avoid nerves or the risk of poor performance by visualising the positive outcome, rehearsing the scenario and how this will make you feel. Set yourself for the task ahead by taking time out; use breathing exercises to achieve the focus – what you focus on, you feel.

10. Over-thinking and over-theorising are the barriers to improvement. Action supersedes everything.

"Inaction breeds doubt and fear. Action breeds confidence and courage. If you want to conquer fear, do not sit at home and think about it. Go out and get busy."

– Dale Carnegie*

APP ALERT!!

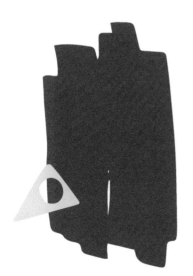

***Dale Carnegie** (1888–1955) was an American writer and lecturer and one of the 'daddy' developers of courses in self-improvement. He was the author of *'How to Win Friends and Influence People'* (1936), a bestseller that remains popular today. Dale Carnegie's four-part book contains advice on how to create success in both business and personal life.

03

AN ATTITUDE OF GRATITUDE

APP ALERT!!

How gratitude can propel you to great heights

"Piglet noticed that even though he had a Very Small Heart, it could hold rather a lot of Gratitude."

– A.A. Milne

CHECKING OUT YOUR ATTITUDE

In my experience, if people have a troublesome episode or a duff day at work – generally when things are against you – they tend to be in a bad mood as a result. For most people, for example, work is a necessity. It's something you have to do. It can be tiring and fruitless and, as a result of that, you can end up feeling down.

The fact is, you can and you do choose how things affect you in your everyday life. From the time you wake up in the morning to going to bed at night, you choose how you act and react to things happening around you.

YOUR CIRCLE OF INFLUENCE

How you react to circumstances has a direct bearing on the people around you, especially those who are closest to you – the very people that you really don't want to upset, because you care about them. When you take your bad mood out on family and friends, you often feel great regret and embarrassment later. It hurts more.

Whether it's at home, in the workplace, or in a social situation, your frame of mind has an effect on a large number of people. I want to hit this point home with you by asking you to complete the following quick exercise:

"Gratitude is the source of light for the soul. Think about what you have rather than what you haven't and this will transform your thinking forever."

– Paul Stalker

Stalkie's
'CIRCLE OF INFLUENCE' WORKOUT

Make a list of all the people that you come into contact with throughout your day. Write your list here:

How many people have you listed? Now think about the number of people they in turn come into contact with. Your 'mood board' – what Stephen Covey calls your circle of influence – is pretty substantial!

_____   _____

_____   _____

_____   _____

_____   _____

_____   _____

_____   _____

_____   _____

_____   _____

BEING GRATEFUL

"Gratitude can transform common days into thanksgivings, turn routine jobs into joy, and change ordinary opportunities into blessings."

– William Arthur Ward*

*William Arthur Ward** (1921-1994) was one of America's most quoted writers of inspirational maxims, articles, poems and meditations. He was also one of the first recognised motivational speakers and educators, but his words remain timeless.

I truly believe that most people have an innate sense of what attitude and behaviours would serve us best in our daily lives, but we don't always default to them. For many people, the easier path is to be selfish, self-centred and 'all about me' with a good deal of daily moaning thrown in for good measure.

There are so many external factors that can obstruct us from living in line with our values – call it 'overwhelmed by the heat of the moment', 'fearful of the consequences', 'taking the easy way out' – that I think it's vital to empower ourselves with knowledge and techniques that allow us to always choose the right path of action.

Continually looking for something bigger and better in our lives – the greener grass, the bigger house, the better car, the expensive trips and dining out, the 'nip and tuck' – won't necessarily improve the quality of your life and make you happier, if the real problem is a lack of balance in mind and perspective.

We all know people who have the big home, the car, and a good level of health but who never have anything positive to say, don't we? The thought of giving any thanks for what they have is alien to them as they sit at the bar with a double gin moaning about their job, their relationships, their family, their football team, their dog, whatever. Isn't it deflatingly dull to be in their company – particularly when they are living the life that many can only dream about? Would you rather give thanks, empower your mind and fill it with glee – or be a bitter bore?

One of the most fundamental principles I'd like you to understand is that gratitude is an essential component of adopting the right attitude.

There's a high chance that as a child you were cared for, fed and given clean water. Many people in the world are not so lucky. If you think about those who live in some of the world's extreme conditions and trouble spots, you are lucky and wealthy beyond belief. With a roof over your head, clothes on your back and food on the table, you are among the top 10% richest people in the world! That kind of helps put your own off-days into perspective.

APP ALERT!!

I'm sure those people who live in a war-torn environment just want to get on with their daily lives, to make homes, enjoy and care for their families, and socialise with friends. In short, they would like to be free to enjoy the lives that have been gifted to them. It is rare that you think about these things every day, and you can be guilty of taking your good fortune for granted. When you remind yourself of these things you might choose your attitude with greater care. You'll also realise how little reason there is to be grumpy, sad or impatient.

Have a quick look at www.givingwhatwecan.org/get-involved/how-rich-am-i

Giving What We Can is a 'community of givers' whose mission is to inspire people to donate significantly and as effectively as possible to charities. They've also got an algorithm on their website that allows you to put in some simple details about yourself (where you live in the world, what your household income is and how many dependents you have) and it will calculate just how rich you are in relation to other people in the world. You'll be amazed. And grateful.

Do you choose to take things for granted or to be grateful for them? Let's see where you are right now:

Stalkie's 'GRATITUDE' WORKOUT

Sit down and think about all the things you are grateful for in your life. It could be that you have a great partner, a loving family, nice holidays, a warm house and possessions, good health, a fun social life, or it could be that you are just grateful for life.

Now grab some paper and write a list of everything you are grateful for – from the big to the small – try not to stop writing for at least five minutes. Please play full out!

If you want to Raise Your Game don't stumble along in life until you're forced to make a change due to an 'external' circumstance such as losing your job, or illness, or a bereavement. By then it may be too late! You may not have developed the attitude and behaviours to deal with it for your own good and that of your loved ones. Now that's worth thinking about!

Gratitude plays a vital role in adopting the right attitude. So, when you are facing a difficult situation, make your first thought relate to something you can be grateful for, before you respond. If things aren't going well, think about what you have got rather than what you haven't, before you moan about your hardship; in this way, you will learn to reframe the situation and put it into perspective.

Seek to rise above the situation and take the power back. Draw upon like-minded people who are naturally attracted to a similar empowering attitude as yours. I don't believe it is a coincidence that it will most likely bring you more of the same. It is a social scientific phenomenon – a Principle of Attraction.

APP ALERT!!

THE SCIENCE OF GRATITUDE

Research has shown that a gratitude mindset can have some startling benefits towards living a life of satisfaction and fulfilment. These include improved general well-being, increased resilience and preparedness for the events that life can throw at us, fruitful social relationships, reduced stress and less propensity towards depression.

The more grateful you are, the greater the likelihood that you will have a stronger immune system, lower blood pressure, good quality sleep. You'll be more alert, compassionate and giving, with a greater capacity for joy and positive emotions.

To distil various aspects of the huge body of gratitude-based research into an easy read would fill a book in itself, but the headline news is that a feeling of gratitude activates parts of the brain such as the ventral and dorsal medial pre-frontal cortex, as you can see in the image of the brain on the next page. These areas are involved in feelings of reward (the reward when stress is removed), morality, interpersonal bonding and positive social interactions, and heightened empathy – the comprehension of what other people are thinking or feeling.

The process of displacing negative thinking with positive thinking has the capacity to trigger neurotransmitters and neurochemicals – the organic 'feel-good' molecules such as serotonin, dopamine, nerve growth factor and oxytocin that participate in neural activity. Unleash these and they'll perpetuate the feelings of closeness, connection and happiness:

- Dopamine is a monoamine neurotransmitter. It plays a key role in the functioning of the limbic system, which is involved in emotional function and control. It is also involved in cognitive processes associated with movement, arousal, executive function, body temperature regulation, pleasure and reward and other processes. Dopamine motivates us to take action toward goals, desires and needs, and gives a surge of reinforcing pleasure when achieving them. Procrastination, self-doubt and lack of enthusiasm are linked with low levels of dopamine.

- Serotonin is a monoamine neurotransmitter that plays a regulatory role in mood, sleep, appetite, body temperature and other processes. Serotonin flows when you feel significant or important.

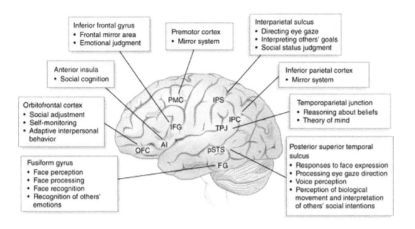

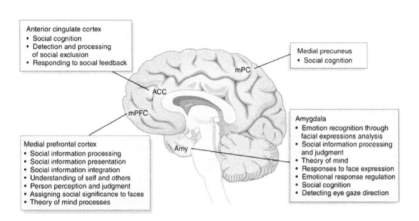

Loneliness and depression occur when serotonin is absent. Unhealthy attention-seeking behaviour can also be a cry for what serotonin brings. Barry Jacobs, Professor Emeritus, Princeton Neuroscience Institute (https://dof.princeton.edu/about/clerk-faculty/emeritus/barry-leonard-jacobs) explains that most antidepressants focus on the production of serotonin.

Reflecting on past significant achievements allows the brain to re-live the experiences. Our brain has trouble telling the difference between what's real and imagined, so it produces serotonin in both cases. It's another reason why gratitude practices work. They remind us that we are valued and have much to value in life. If you need a serotonin boost during a stressful day, take a few moments to reflect on past achievements and victories.

- Nerve growth factor (NGF) is a neurotrophic factor and neuropeptide primarily involved in the regulation of growth, maintenance, proliferation and survival of certain sympathetic and sensory neurons (nerve cells). Numerous biological processes involving nerve growth factor have been identified, two of them being the survival of pancreatic beta cells and the regulation of the immune system.

- Oxytocin is a hormone that is made in the brain, in the hypothalamus. It is transported to, and secreted by, the pituitary gland, which is located at the base of the brain. It is classed as a nonapeptide (a peptide containing nine amino acids), while its biological classification is as a neuropeptide. It acts both as a hormone and as a brain neurotransmitter.

Oxytocin creates intimacy and trust, and builds healthy relationships. It's released by men and women during orgasm, and by mothers during childbirth and breastfeeding. Animals may reject their offspring when the release of oxytocin is blocked.

Oxytocin increases fidelity; men in monogamous relationships who were given a boost of oxytocin interacted with single women at a greater physical distance than men who weren't given any oxytocin. The cultivation of oxytocin is essential for creating strong bonds and improved social interactions.

Often referred to as the 'cuddle hormone', a simple way to keep oxytocin flowing is to give someone a hug. Dr. Paul Zak,* known as 'Doctor Love' through his research into oxytocin (www.pauljzak.com) explains that inter-personal touch not only raises oxytocin, but reduces cardiovascular stress and improves the immune system.

*Dr. Paul Zak's two decades of research have taken him from the Pentagon to Fortune 500 boardrooms to the rain forest of Papua New Guinea in a quest to understand the neuroscience of human connection, human happiness, and effective teamwork. His academic lab and companies he has started develop and deploy neuroscience technologies to solve real problems faced by real people.

Zak's latest book, *'Trust Factor: The Science of Creating High Performance Companies*, uses neuroscience to measure and manage organisational cultures to inspire teamwork and accelerate business outcomes. His 2012 book, *The Moral Molecule: The Source of Love and Prosperity'*, recounted his unlikely discovery of the neurochemical oxytocin as the key driver of trust, love, and morality that distinguish our humanity.

Paul is the founding Director of the Center for Neuroeconomics Studies and Professor of Economics, Psychology and Management at Claremont Graduate University. He has a number of outstanding TED talks under his belt which you can find online but for starters see his 'Moral Molecule' presentation on YouTube.

Free to stream, TED talks are short videos from expert speakers on education, business, science, technology, creativity and global issues.

Now a word about brain training. We know the brain changes with experience, so the more we experience gratitude, the more the brain will serve us by tuning into the positive things around us. However, this isn't something that comes naturally because we are more programmed to notice threats or negative elements in the environment.

It therefore requires determination and practice to (1) prime the brain towards the positives and (2) drill the positives in. Drilling the positives in means holding on to those thoughts and feelings long enough to allow the brain to process them and then create a structural change to store them. By expanding its storage system of positive experiences, the brain will help us to experience those feelings more readily and for longer periods of time.

If you wish to read more about this, I recommend the research done by Dr. Rick Hanson (www. rickhanson.net), psychologist, educator, author and expert on the essential inner skills of personal well-being, psychological growth and contemplative practice – as well as about relationships, family life and raising children. His bestsellers include *'Hardwiring Happiness: The New Brain Science of Contentment, Calm, and Confidence'* which shows you how to tap the hidden power of everyday experiences to change your brain and your life for the better. One of his key findings is that focusing on an experience for 20 seconds is long enough to create positive structural changes in the brain.

You can watch Dr. Rick in action during his excellent TED talk on the subject of Hardwiring Happiness on YouTube.

What else has research revealed about the power of gratitude?

- **Grateful people are more hopeful and more healthy**

There are many studies that confirm this, but a favourite of mine was published in the *Journal of Religion and Health*[1] which found that those who were more grateful for who they are and what they have were more hopeful and also physically healthier.

Gratitude reduces a multitude of toxic emotions, ranging from envy and resentment to frustration and regret. One of the authors of this piece is Robert A. Emmons, Ph.D., who has conducted multiple studies on the link between gratitude and well-being. His research confirms that gratitude effectively increases happiness and reduces depression.

Robert is the world's leading scientific expert on gratitude. He is a professor of psychology at the University of California, Davis, and the founding editor-in-chief of *The Journal of Positive Psychology*. He is the author of the books *'Thanks! How the New Science of Gratitude Can Make You Happier'*, *'Creating Emotional Prosperity'*, and *'The Little Book of Gratitude'* (www. greatergood.berkeley.edu/profile/ robert_emmons)

1. Krause, N., Emmons, R.A. & Ironson, G. (2015). Benevolent Images of God, Gratitude, and Physical Health Status. *Journal of Religion and Health, 54*(4), 1503-1519.

Grateful people experience fewer aches and pains and they report feeling healthier than other people. They exercise more often and are more likely to attend regular check-ups with their doctors, which is likely to contribute to further longevity.

• Increased self-esteem

A paper in the *Journal of Applied Sport Psychology*[2] found that athletes who expressed more gratitude toward their coaches and also in general had higher self-esteem two and six months later compared to those who weren't as openly thankful. Whether you're an athlete or not, self-esteem is an essential ingredient in peak performance.

Other studies have shown that gratitude reduces social comparisons. Rather than becoming resentful toward people who have more money or better jobs – which is a major factor in reduced self-esteem – grateful people are able to appreciate other people's accomplishments.

2. Lung Hung Chen & Chia-Huei Wu. (2014). Gratitude Enhances Change in Athletes' Self-Esteem: The Moderating Role of Trust in Coach. *Journal of Applied Sport Psychology, 26*(3), 349-362.

• Grateful people sleep better

This gave me a fabulously warm feeling when I first found out about this study which was published in *Applied Psychology: Health and Well-Being*[3]. It concluded that writing a gratitude journal improves sleep, suggesting if we spend just 15 minutes jotting down a few grateful thoughts before bed, we may sleep better and longer. It's something that I've been doing for years, and that I've passed on to colleagues, clients, family, friends – basically anyone who'll listen to me.

My kids even have a jar each which they fill with their grateful thoughts so that they can always remember them. It works!

3. Digdon, N. & Koble, A. (2011). Effects of Constructive Worry, Imagery Distraction, and Gratitude Interventions on Sleep Quality: A Pilot Trial. *Applied Psychology: Health and Well-Being, 3*(2), 193-206.

- **Gratitude increases helpfulness and empathy**

One study in the journal *Psychological Science*[4] found that those who expressed more gratitude were also more likely to help out others. So "positive and helpful behaviour" are in turn linked to greater happiness. Empathy also apparently increases when people are thankful. A 2012 paper in *Social Psychological and Personality Science*[5] found that higher levels of gratitude were linked to greater empathy and lowered aggression. "Gratitude motivates people to express sensitivity and concern for others," the researchers wrote.

4. Monica Y. Bartlett & David DeSteno. (2006). Gratitude and Prosocial Behavior: Helping When It Costs You. *Psychological Science, 17*(4), 319-325.

5. C. Nathan DeWall, Nathaniel M. Lambert, Richard S. Pond Jr., Todd B. Kashdan & Frank D. Fincham. (2012). A Grateful Heart is a Nonviolent Heart: Cross-Sectional, Experience Sampling, Longitudinal, and Experimental Evidence. *Social Psychological and Personality Science, 3*(2), 232-240.

- **Gratitude increases mental strength**

For years, research has shown gratitude not only reduces stress, but it may also play a major role in overcoming trauma. A 2006 study in *Behaviour Research and Therapy*[6] found that Vietnam War Veterans with higher levels of gratitude experienced lower rates of Post-Traumatic Stress Disorder. A 2003 study in the *Journal of Personality and Social Psychology*[7] found that gratitude, or recognising all you have to be thankful for – even during the most challenging times that you may ever face – was a major contributor to resilience following the US terrorist attacks on September 11, 2001.

6,7. Both studies cited by Amy Morin in her article '*What Mentally Strong People Don't Do – 7 Scientifically Proven Benefits of Gratitude*', April 3, 2015, Psychology Today website.

There is much scientific grounding to my findings in **You Can Raise Your Game!** – not just in the realm of gratitude – to place alongside my 30 years of personal anecdotal evidence of this stuff. And, as we'll determine in the *'Why Do You Do That?'* chapter of this book, I'm grateful that there is a growing wave of academic and scientific research and resources revealing the empirical evidence behind positive psychology.

THINKING DIFFERENTLY

"Often people ask how I manage to be happy despite having no arms and no legs. The quick answer is that I have a choice. I can be angry about not having limbs, or I can be thankful that I have a purpose. I chose gratitude."

– Nick Vujicic*

Some people have a naturally positive, optimistic attitude towards life. Others have a naturally negative, pessimistic one. In order to change from a negative attitude to a positive one, the key is to reframe a situation, which involves thinking about it in a different way – from an alternative perspective – and to seek the positives in it.

APP ALERT!!

*Nick Vujicic was born in 1982 in Melbourne, Australia. Without any medical explanation or warning, he came into the world without limbs. Whilst growing up, Nick dealt not only with the typical challenges of school and adolescence that we all have to deal with, but also with bullying and self-esteem issues. He also suffered with depression and loneliness as a result of his physical challenges. He describes his main haunting question as:

"Why was I the one born without arms and legs?"

Nick, however, learned how to deal with his disability and others' perception of it, gradually accomplishing more on his own. As a result of encouragement by one of the caretakers at his high school, at 17 he plucked up the nerve to start speaking publicly about overcoming adversity, firstly with small groups of students and then with wider groups including businesses. By the age of 19, he had built a dream to empower other people by giving speeches around his own life story. He found:

"the purpose to his existence, and also the purpose in his circumstance".

Nick has now travelled to over 60 countries around the world sharing his story with an estimated 400 million people, from US Presidents, Heads of State and Fortune 500 companies to life-serving prisoners, refugees and child prostitutes.

He is the founder and president of an international non-profit organisation, Life Without Limbs (www.lifewithoutlimbs.org) and owns the motivational speaking company, Attitude Is Altitude. To see Nick speak about his life, or on topics such as gratitude, hopefulness and coping with adversity, is an inspiration in itself. So please either have a look at his website (www.nickvujicic.com) where there are examples of him in action, or plug his name into YouTube and you'll have a great choice there, too.

His best-selling books such as *'Life Without Limits', 'Unstoppable', 'Limitless', 'Stand Strong'* and *'Love Without Limits'* are also a definite Stalkie recommendation.

To me, Nick is the ultimate example of how to reframe a most disadvantageous situation and turn it into a positive force for personal and social good.

THE TRIANGLE OF COMMUNICATION

So far we've demonstrated the power of focusing on the good stuff, of saying the right things in both your internal and external dialogue; now let's look at adopting strongly positive physiology.

At this point, I want to make you aware that your physiology can profoundly affect your attitude. Your non-verbal indicators such as how you stand, how you hold your shoulders and head, whether you walk quickly or slowly, with a purposeful stride or a reluctant dawdle – all these can count towards a positive or negative attitude.

Ironically, this is something that Nick has had to contend with and has completely overcome, but for us lesser mortals, it's a fundamental component in achieving our potential.

Focusing on the good will automatically make you stand and walk tall, put your chest out, breathe better, smile and generally look more positive. You will say more positive things to yourself and to others, and generally feel better about life.

Even when you don't have anything positive to focus on, just changing your body language will have an amazing result on the way you feel. This simple shift in behaviour can also happen when you apply it to your family, your college or school, in your social circle, your teams and clubs – any group environment that could benefit from a more constructive, dynamic atmosphere.

Try this when a colleague or family member is putting a downer on things! Get them to stand up straight, stick their chest out and smile. This will immediately change how they feel, and have a direct effect on their attitude.

It's infectious, as we'll now prove together:

Stalkie's 'POSTURE' WORKOUT

To demonstrate just how easy it is for your posture to affect how you feel, try these exercises:

1. *Put a pencil horizontally in your mouth, and try to frown. It's a very difficult task.*

2. *Look down, slump your shoulders, breathe shallowly and try to be happy. It's impossible.*

3. *Stand up straight, shoulders back, thrust your chest out, look to the sky with a big grin on your face. Try to feel depressed. You can't.*

All three exercises show how your physical body can override your thoughts. Your brain is wired to receive messages, and your body is part of this. To have the right attitude, adopting the correct body language is fundamental. What you focus on can also have a powerful influence on your attitude. Try this:

4. *Sit comfortably and don't focus on the colour blue. Don't think about anything blue – the sky, the sea, football strips, rivers and streams, your favourite sweater – nothing blue. Sit for a few minutes not focusing on anything blue...*

Now be completely honest – did anything blue go through your mind? Of course it did. We always have to focus on something, and the power of suggestion is very strong, as you have just discovered. Your focus will always make a difference, whether it is positive or negative, so – focus on the good stuff!

Focusing on the good stuff, saying the right things internally and externally and having positive body language: these three things are all interlinked and each impacts upon the others. Get all of them right and you'll be on fire!

You can remember these three things as the Triangle of Communication (depicted below) and use it every day to improve your life. This is something that we will be exploring further in the *'You Can Be An Influencer'* chapter of **You Can Raise Your Game!**

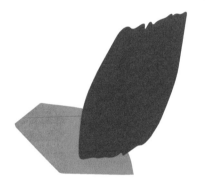

APP ALERT!!

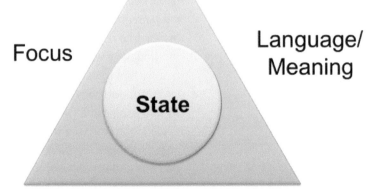

Focus

Language/ Meaning

State

Physiology

"PATCHING IT UP"

The Positive Effects of a
Positive Attitude

*"At the age of 18, I made up
my mind to never have a bad
day in my life. I dove into an
endless sea of gratitude from
which I've never emerged."*

– Patch Adams

One of my favourite films is 'Patch Adams' which was based upon the real life story of Dr. Hunter Doherty 'Patch' Adams, who is known not just for his work as a physician through the famous Gesundheit Institute which he founded in 1971, but also as a social activist who has devoted his life to changing America's health care system, promoting an alternative health care model not funded by expensive insurance policies.

His personal USP is the attitude which he has adopted to address all the problems associated with the politics and delivery of health care. For example, every year Patch organises a global group of volunteers who dress as circus clowns and travel to various countries to bring humour to patients and orphans in care institutions. These missions supply aid, educational programmes, building projects and community development around the world in communities in crisis from sickness, war, poverty and injustice.

Patch's mantras include *"laughter, joy and creativity are an integral part of the healing process"* and *"spread joy indiscriminately"*. To give you an insight into the genius of Patch's methodology would take, well, a feature film to explain! But I can't let this opportunity go without reproducing some words of further explanation from the man himself about his initial interaction with patients and his philosophy of healing:

"When a person comes to me, unless the problem is an arterial bleed, which has to be addressed that second, the first goal is to have a friendship happen out of that relationship. So we spend three to four hours in the first meeting. We might go for a walk. If you like to fish, maybe we will go fishing. If you like to run, we run together, and I'll interview you while we are running. By the end of that time, I hope we have a trust, a friendship starting to develop, and from there we can proceed.

"From the start, it was obvious to me that we had to have fun in what we were doing. Forget the patient, it had to be fun for us. Life has to be fun! I saw what life was like when I was serious. I had ulcers and I wanted to kill myself. That was me as a serious person. That failed.

"As a healer I hate this idea that the healing interaction is a draining one. If friendship, as it is for me, is the most important thing in the world, and the healer's life is really a stream of intimacies, when a patient sits with you and tells you the worst stories that could burn you out, they are also giving you the greatest trust. I focus on the trust, respect and love they give me rather than the pain of their story... I'm there to be a good listener first and to be a good friend, and then to do what intuitively and scientifically both come to mind."

Adams recommends that we all spend more quality time visiting our loved ones who are ill or depressed. Spending more time with loved ones – and even visiting people whom we don't know – does a lot to help them feel better emotionally and physically. In addition to encouraging such visits, Patch offers practical advice for making these visits enjoyable and fulfilling for both the patient and visitor. He provides tips for promoting our own healing and advises that we extend our compassion to our communities as well.

Check out www.patchadams.org to find out more about this incredible force of human nature, who chose to adopt an assertive attitude which has allowed him to live an intrinsically motivated, bountiful life.

To illustrate the effect of choosing your attitude, I often compare it to owning an 'emotional bank account'. The attitude that you take dictates whether deposits are made to this bank account or withdrawn. A deposit will be made when a positive attitude is taken, or the positive reframing of a situation has been successful.

'Gesundheit' by Patch Adams, M.D., with Maureen Mylander. Publisher: Healing Arts Press,1998.

Let's imagine for a moment that it's raining, and the day's outing you arranged with the family has been ruined. You moan about living in England, say the weather is unpredictable, and complain that it's never possible to plan anything in advance. This attitude and behaviour is an example of how you are making withdrawals from your emotional bank account. By perceiving a rainy day in the most pessimistic way possible, you are handing over the control of your feelings and emotions to a completely unpredictable event: the weather! How daft does that seem?

Put a child in the same situation, and they won't moan or want to cancel a day out – it's just rain. It makes you wet, and then you get dry again.

In order to reframe this situation positively, you need to view it from a different perspective: this country does not suffer from drought; rain makes our grass green, and our crops, plants and flowers grow. Plus, your kids can't have fun jumping in puddles without rain! In this way, you are investing in your emotional bank account. You are thinking of all the positives.

My wife doesn't always thank me when I've been out in the rain with the kids and the dogs and we all come back soaking wet from puddle jumping – but she'll know we've all had a great time. Go try it for yourself!

We all have examples of not running our emotional bank accounts well. When I go to watch my beloved AFC Bournemouth play football, there is a 'fan' (who shall remain nameless, but 'hello' to him anyway!) who sits in very close proximity to me and always expects our beautiful boys to play well and win, so that he can come away having had a good afternoon. When the team plays badly or loses, he shouts at the players, abuses them, thinks that they never make an effort and they're pampered and overpaid – he leaves them in no doubt that they've ruined his day.

'Fan' never invests in his team; he does not encourage them when things are not going their way, and he just expects them to do well so that he can have an enjoyable afternoon. 'Fan' keeps making withdrawals, without any investment. His emotional bank account is definitely in the red, and he is in danger of alienating people and leading an unhappy life as a consequence.

When you invest in someone or something, it must be without expecting anything in return. When you invest wholeheartedly, it will come back to you – often tenfold. Do you only invest for a return? Would you only do a favour for a friend if they promised a favour back?

APP
ALERT!!

GRATITUDE IS THE SPRINGBOARD FOR ATTITUDE

When you start your day with a few minutes of gratitude, it becomes the springboard for your attitude. Continue in the same way, and it is likely that your day will get better and better. This is true no matter what obstacles are put in your way, when you are grateful and choose your attitude. By keeping gratitude in your thoughts, you will make sure that every situation you encounter is processed in your mind in a positive way. This is the turning point.

Remember that you will never get this day back. These minutes and hours are unique, so make the most of them. For every 60 seconds spent in anger, frustration and upset, you have a lost a minute that could be filled with love, laughter and fun.

If gratitude was a virtue, it would be the daddy of them all. The more you express gratitude for what you have and what you have experienced, the more you'll have to be grateful for.

It's up to you to either take life's occurrences for granted and roll with the consequences (good or bad), or take them with gratitude and clear-cut ownership.

APP ALERT!!

Stalkie's Summary
TOP 10 TIPS TOWARDS AN ATTITUDE OF GRATITUDE

1. Do you find yourself mindful of others, what they've got and what they've achieved – then you compare that to your own life and feel distinctly second best? Is that you? Then **FORGET IT RIGHT NOW!** It's destructive, it's disruptive and it's not pretty. **STOP!**

   Do you want to be a drain, sucking the life out of people you come into contact with? Or a radiator, energising and delighting them?

2. The way you react to circumstances has a direct bearing on the people around you, especially those who are closest to you – the very people that you really don't want to upset, because you care about them. When you take your bad mood out on family and friends, you alienate them and will suffer the regretful consequences.

3. Sit down, think and make a note of all the things you are grateful for in your life. It could be that you have a great partner, a loving family, nice holidays, a warm house and possessions, good health, a fun social life. Do this every day. Keep a daily gratitude journal.

4. When facing a difficult situation, make your first thought something you are grateful for, before choosing your response. Reframe the situation and put it into a new perspective.

5. When you focus on your gratitude, reinforce this with your internal and external dialogue, and adopt a strong physiology. Using this positive Triangle of Communication will serve you best in any given situation.

6. For a positive attitude to work effectively, action needs to be taken. Like an emotional bank account, if time is taken to make an investment, the interest and dividends will grow. If nothing is invested, there will be no return. Gratitude is a currency that we can mint for ourselves, and spend without ever getting into debt!

7. Pay the gratitude forward. When you come into contact with people, think 'how can I make your day?' It may be something very simple, like a quick chat, a 'thank you' or listening to them with sincere interest. It may be something tangible like a card, a letter, flowers, or a big hug. Adopting an attitude of helping people spreads optimism and good feelings.

8. The more people you cheer up through your attitude, the more they will make your day in return, and the better you will feel. This 'principle of attraction' is a social scientific phenomenon.

9. Of course there will be times when there is tragedy and sorrow in life, and it will be hard to find a positive view of them. BUT, you still have the choice to dig deep into your reserves of gratitude and move forward.

10. Scientific research tells us that grateful people are healthier, happier, more helpful, empathetic and resilient, sleep better and have higher self-esteem than those who are not. Surely you fancy some of that?

APP ALERT!!

04

TAKE THE POWER BACK

*How to choose your response
in any situation*

So you haven't managed to get everything done that you wanted to do today: why did everyone choose today to message you and take up so much of your time, and why did the kids leave the house in such a mess anyway? It's not as if they care about you being busy or thank you for running around after them all the time.

So you feel overwhelmed and stressed out by your workload: why does your boss expect you to do so much and how come your colleagues are not pulling their weight, so you have to do it all yourself? And when you had a moan at your boss about some of your colleagues, why didn't your boss say he'd sort the problem out? Day off here we come! Either that or you'll just let your standards slip at work for a bit and shut yourself off from your colleagues until your boss notices you're not getting enough support from them.

So you've run up a lot of debt on your credit cards, it's the end of the month and you're strapped for cash: why do your friends insist you keep on going out with them and make you blow your cash on shopping, booze, food and socialising? And now your lifestyle, diet and late nights are making you feel tired and grumpy, so you're struggling at work, you can't afford to go to the gym, you look awful and the only way to forget about it is to give in to your mates, go out even more and get drunk.

So you get caught by a speed camera: why did your partner delay your departure, making you late, so you had to drive too fast and why do the police authorities insist on putting a speed camera on such a clear bit of road?

So your partner has decided to take you out for an evening: why do they always insist on choosing such a dull film and restaurant and not bother asking you where you want to go? And now they'll think they've banked some brownie points by taking you out, so they'll no doubt want something in return.

Any of this sound familiar?

If you allow your feelings and behaviours to be governed by what other people think and do for you, if you allow your power, your 'remote control,' to rest in the hands of others, then I can guarantee that you will struggle to achieve true happiness.

Who or what are the power dangers in your life?

- Is it a person – your boss, your parents, partner or friends? Are they domineering or draining you?

- Is it an emotion or feeling – such as fear, anxiety, lack of confidence, laziness, or is it that you can't seem to live up to your values? (I'll talk about this in detail in *'Let the Real You Shine Through'* chapter of **You Can Raise Your Game!**)

- Is it an institution – such as your workplace, school or college, the government (have you been Trumped or Brexited?), religion or philosophy?

"When you blame others, you are handing your life's remote control over to them. You become powerless."

– Paul Stalker

- Is it your health, or a pattern of lifestyle that you've drifted into – such as lack of sleep, lack of exercise, comfort eating, alcohol or substance abuse?

- Is it money – you don't ever have enough of it, you're struggling to keep your head above water, you have to graft so hard to earn it, or you have plenty of it but it doesn't seem to bring you happiness?

- Or is it that old chestnut, 'time'? Why is it never on your side? You just don't know where it goes; you never seem to get everything done, or to manage your time effectively. Perhaps you're always late or under pressure, or maybe your partner questions what you actually do all day?

Well, **HOLD ON RIGHT THERE!**

Choosing your attitude and reflecting it in your behaviour has a profound influence on your life and the people around you. It may seem obvious, but it's a discovery that has led countless people – including thousands who have attended my seminars and live events – to enjoy a more complete existence in our home, work and social lives.

It's amazing to equip yourself with the mindset to allow your relationships to prosper, to brush aside life's little niggles and to overcome tough challenges **WHEN YOU TAKE ACTION!**

Personal power is all about having faith in your ability to take action. It's about using your power to choose what you want to do in life and nailing it with passion and integrity. After all, ladies and gentlemen, boys and girls... we only get one chance of doing life!

Whatever the extent you feel your personal power rests outside yourself, let's inspect how and why this can happen. Then we'll explore how you can choose your response to any situation and raise your game.

BLAME MENTALITY

"When you blame others, you give up your power to change."
– Robert Anthony*

*Dr. Robert Anthony is a behavioural psychologist, psychotherapist and personal performance trainer.

In addition, Dr. Anthony has authored over 15 books, which have been published in 22 countries. His flagship books, '*Beyond Positive Thinking*' and '*The Ultimate Secrets of Total Self-Confidence*' have sold over a million copies. You can check him out at www.abundance-and-happiness. com/dr-robert-anthony.html

I'm sure we've all had at least a little dabble at blaming others, or 'circumstances' for our predicaments. But if this becomes a default mentality, or a habit, you're on a slippery path towards indulging your negative emotions and behaviour.

Blaming someone else for your problems won't fix them. It won't make you feel better in the long run. It will alienate the people that you blame. It will alienate the people that you moan to – unless they enjoy a good moan as well, in which case you can wallow in your 'poor me' attitude together, reinforce each other's blind spots and watch as your problems dig deeper into your mental and physical health.

I'm going to give you two examples of the consequences of what a blame mentality and an inability to take your power back into your hands can lead to. Both are real life stories. One example is clearly more hardcore than the other, but both scenarios happen every day and affect the lives of people that you are sure to recognise.

Firstly, you've already read about Ade in the *'Fear into Power'* chapter of this book.

As we saw, Ade's emotional difficulties led him to violence, drug dealing and substance addiction, which took him first to hospital and then to prison. And every step of the way he blamed circumstances beyond his control for his predicament. He ticked a lot of the boxes of things we all find easy to blame, the very things I mentioned at the top of this chapter.

"My mind automatically went into blame mode whenever something occurred outside of me. That's how I was wired at the time, it was a hole I couldn't get out of."

Ade blamed his parents, his family, his friends. He blamed his emotions (fear, anxiety, not living up to his values of wanting a job, a family, to be loved). He blamed the institutions (social workers, police) and of course he blamed the lack of money and the impact of drugs upon his health. He had the complete blame set – lock, stock and barrel – until he could blame no further. You'll find out about Ade's remarkable turnaround later in this chapter.

Now I'd like to introduce you to Patsy who is also based upon a personal coaching client of mine. Patsy is married to Simon who is a successful executive and they have two young children. She is currently having a break from work to concentrate on looking after her family.

As part of her weekly routine, Patsy likes to meet up with her friends for a coffee and they naturally talk about their respective families. However, it only takes a few sips of Americano before Patsy's blame game surfaces, usually moaning about her burdensome workload and that she never gets any time to herself.

Typically, Patsy would start her conversation on a high, before moving on to mention how much she was doing: shopping, ironing, DIY, caring for the kids – and the fact that she gets no help from her mum, her sister, her in-laws and Simon is too busy to give her any recognition or thanks.

"They take me for granted, and don't show me any love or appreciation! They expect it all to be done for nothing in return!"

To so many people, including her friends, these are normal events in their everyday lives – and yet to Patsy, they had become her sole focus, culminating in a 'poor me' state of mind.

Patsy believed her parents always favoured her brother and sister over her and treated her unfairly. Her husband never took her out, bought her things or helped around the house (which he did, but she conveniently forgot). Time was never on her side, which meant she felt like everybody's skivvy and never had time to enjoy herself.

By constantly saying these things, both to herself and to her friends, Patsy now believed her own words, even though the reality was quite different. She really wanted more for herself than she was prepared to give to others, and became divorced from the truth.

In time, this attitude led to resentment on the part of her closest friends who were coming to the opinion that Patsy didn't really want to genuinely help people – she didn't want to support and love her family unconditionally and she was never prepared to offer a hand to her friends when they needed a bit of practical or emotional support either. Her family probably knew that whatever they did they'd get moaned at, so why bother even trying?

Sadly, Patsy had become a victim of her own choices. She did not take responsibility for her actions or reactions. She would always opt for the path of least resistance, blaming others and justifying to herself that she was hard done by. Not a pleasant rut to be stuck in.

This behaviour can lead to depression, breakdown and mental health issues, as you are no longer responsible for your own actions if you blame others.

"When you give less than you wish to receive in life, you will divorce yourself from happiness."

– Paul Stalker

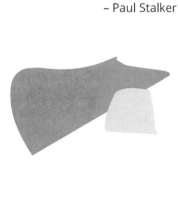

APP ALERT!!

Whilst it can be difficult for anyone to accept their shortcomings in life, it's also difficult for many of us to conjure up the confidence and tact to face up to people like Ade and Patsy and challenge them about their behaviour. This can lead to isolation on their part or the need to surround themselves with other Ades or Patsys – to start their very own self-destruction club!

If that's your bag, great. But don't be surprised if a 'poor me' attitude – or 'terrorising sympathy' as Ade calls it – will finally alienate the loved ones and friends who care for you.

FEELING POWERLESS

If you delegate to someone the responsibility for making you happy, angry, sad or optimistic, then you have handed your power to that person.

The problem with both Ade and Patsy is that they sincerely and genuinely believed it was the people and things around them who caused the problems, rather than themselves. Every bad mood, every piece of bad luck and every depressing incident they were involved in was automatically blamed on the other people in their lives.

This type of behaviour is self-destructive, but its root cause is low self-esteem which had rendered them both incapable of taking responsibility for their actions.

So, how could Ade and Patsy take steps to empower themselves before they were completely cut adrift? In Patsy's case it was through a friend's intervention and through coaching.

One day at their usual coffee morning, one of her friends plucked up the courage to talk to Patsy about her moaning and advised her to take control of her actions. Patsy was amenable to her friend's advice and took it on board – to a certain extent. She interpreted it as an excuse to take more control over the other people in her life, rather than choose her own measured responses to situations. Unfortunately this backfired.

LOSING CONTROL

From her warped perspective, Patsy expected Simon to demonstrate how much he loved her by changing the date and location. But by demanding more from him without even acknowledging he had done something nice by booking the dinner in the first place, she had achieved nothing! And there's more…

It started when Simon, Patsy's husband, booked a table for them at a restaurant for a treat. Patsy, however, saw this as an opportunity to assert 'control' over Simon and test how much he cared for her. Firstly, she told Simon she was unable to make the date, and that she didn't particularly like the restaurant he'd chosen. She was hoping for a response such as, *"don't worry darling – I'll find another restaurant that you like, and we'll go when it suits you."* Instead, Simon replied, *"no problem, we won't go then."*

Why didn't she just say yes to his well-meaning offer?

Patsy had always found it difficult to love others, mostly because she was unable to love herself. So, in order to make herself feel better, she craved attention, and resorted to a form of blackmail to get it. Simon was totally oblivious to this hidden agenda, and didn't play ball.

When she told Simon she was fed up that he didn't choose the right restaurant or rearrange the evening, she seemed to view it as a debt – as if he owed it to her to take her out to dinner, even though she never suggested they enjoy an evening out together.

APP ALERT!!

Her friend persisted, and tried to help Patsy understand that her actions would never get her the results she wanted. She told Patsy that she needed to take a long hard look at her own behaviour, and not that of other people. She explained to Patsy that the act of only making herself feel good when others do as she wants is a very negative way of travelling through life and that, unless she changed, she could lose Simon forever and end up a single parent.

Terrorising love and pushing others to their limits is not the Stalkie way forward. Patsy needed to take the power back and have peace of mind with who she is, rather than seeking to obtain love from how others react to her. Throughout this episode, Patsy was never really in control of her own feelings: she put her remote control in the hands of Simon.

It was this advice that persuaded Patsy to attend one of my life-coaching seminars with her friend. Exposing herself to the principles and exercises that you will read about in this chapter and the chapters on 'Fear into Power', 'An Attitude of Gratitude', 'Let the Real You Shine Through', 'Ignite Your Self-Belief', 'Why Do You Do That?' and 'Praise Your Game Now!' allowed Patsy not only to understand the reasons behind her behaviour but it also gave her the tools and leverage to change her outlook.

When your feelings, such as confidence and self-respect, are only associated with the things that others think of (and do for) you, believe me, you'll never be truly at one with yourself. No matter how powerful you may think you are – no matter what personal qualities you possess – you cannot control what other people think or do. Patsy's friend recognised this, and knew that Patsy needed to empower herself rather than others. However, she also realised that taking the blame for your own behaviour is a bitter pill to swallow.

TAKING RESPONSIBILITY

APP ALERT!!

"People who believe they have the power to exercise some measure of control over their lives are healthier, more effective and more successful than those who lack faith in their ability to effect changes in their lives."

– Albert Bandura*

Some people feel foolish and beat themselves up when they realise that they don't choose their own responses to situations. Others simply think you just can't 'choose your responses'.

My answer is that it's so much easier to blame others and think they are wrong, rather than look within and admit *"I have been weak"*, *"I have been stupid letting others control me"*, or *"I am really the one to blame."*

"Taking responsibility for our actions and responses often requires determination and discipline, which is why many people are resistant to it."

– Paul Stalker

*Albert Bandura is a brilliant psychologist who has been responsible for contributions to the field of education and to many fields of psychology.

His personal website contains a lot of academic and personal insight, with various links to video footage of his public speaking and experiments:
www.albertbandura.com

How many times do we hear comments such as *"the kids are really driving me crazy"*, *"my boss really winds me up"*, or *"this weather's depressing me"*? In my book, comments such as this can always be translated into *"I am preferring not to take responsibility for my feelings and actions"*.

If blaming the weather was an Olympic sport, us Brits would dominate the medals, wouldn't we? CHOOSE YOUR RESPONSE TO IT! Rain is going to happen. Put up your brolly and get on with it. It's the same for all of us. Similarly, you can look for a new job if your boss genuinely has a bad character. Take the kids somewhere interesting if they're driving you mad.

It is all about choosing a response that you are happy with – one that empowers you, and one that means you have taken responsibility, allowing you to regain control.

STIMULUS RESPONSE

"When we are no longer able to change a situation, we are challenged to change ourselves. Between stimulus and response there is a space. In that space is our power to choose our response. In our response lies our growth and our freedom."

– Viktor E. Frankl*

*Viktor Emil Frankl M.D., Ph.D., was an Austrian neurologist and psychiatrist as well as a Holocaust survivor. His book *'Man's Search for Meaning'* chronicles his experiences as a concentration camp inmate.

In a rare video clip from 1972, Frankl delivers a powerful message about the human search for meaning — and the most important gift we can give others. You can see it at: www.ted.com/talks/viktor_frankl_youth_in_search_of_meaning or alternatively read more about this remarkably inspiring man at www.viktorfrankl.org

If you get some pepper up your nose, you sneeze. The pepper is a stimulus, the sneezing is a response. Imagine that a friend jokingly pretends to poke you in the eye – you'll involuntarily blink, even though you know they're not really going to hurt you. These are examples of reflexes, which are automatic responses to stimuli over which you have no conscious control.

All humans are stimulus-response beings. However, there are responses that you can control, and which are not automatic. With these, you have a space between the stimulus, i.e. what happens to you, and your response. In other words, between someone speaking harshly to you (the stimulus) and you getting angry (the response), there is a gap.

Interestingly, where children are concerned, the gap between stimulus and response has not fully developed until the age of around 3–4 years. Children respond instantly to stimulation by a comment, a situation or an action.

Assuming you're an adult reading this, my advice is MIND THE GAP! Use it meaningfully to choose how to respond to each stimulus. You can choose to allow your anger to develop, or to exercise patience. In every moment, this choice exists – there is always a choice.

These principles are very easy to understand, but quite challenging to put into practice.

You are socially conditioned to respond in a certain way; so, when the weather is grey and overcast, a lot of folk will moan. If a son or daughter behaves wrongly, they are conditioned to expect to be disciplined. A conditioned response to bad customer service in a restaurant is "let's not make a fuss – it will be alright".

Taking the power back requires bravery and strength, and it demands us to be truthful with ourselves, which is often painful.

APP ALERT!!

THE ADE WAY

Taking responsibility and understanding stimulus response was at the very heart of an epiphany in Ade's life. I'm sure you'd like to know how on earth he managed to 'take the power back':

During the nine weeks of his stay in Lewes Prison, and without a single penny to bargain with, Ade was unable to feed his heroin and alcohol addiction. He had no other choice than to ride out his addiction which left him in agony, petrified and unable to sleep. He was, however, relieved to have been removed, temporarily at least, from the environment that he blamed for his fall from grace.

During this time, he was made aware that, at the end of his sentence, he could be granted a drug treatment order which involved six weeks of probation and residential treatment, if a place was available.

When the time came to stand before the Judge at the end of Ade's sentence and to either be released, detained or granted the drug treatment order, there were no places available at the rehab unit for two weeks. As the Judge told Ade of his decision to release him (back to his previous life, no doubt), something clicked inside:

"I just found myself pleading with the Judge to keep me detained IN prison for a further two weeks until a place at the rehab unit became available. The plea came straight from my subconscious self; if I'd have thought about it, rationalised it, I wouldn't have had the nerve to suggest it. I now realise that in a few seconds my mind had prompted my destiny and re-shaped my life." Right there, he had taken the power back. The Judge agreed to Ade's request.

During his stay within the drug rehab centre (the 'stimulus'), Ade gained enough headspace (the 'gap') to choose his response to the treatment. He connected deeply with one of the mentors on the programme and was gradually re-introduced to his mother, his sister and his girlfriend who all visited and supported him.

"I realised it was always me at the scene of my life's crimes and I needed to take the responsibility for my own actions. I had a choice. I had a purpose and I had an amazing girlfriend who I didn't want to lose. I must be ok if I had managed to attract her! The levels of trust between me and my mentor, and me and my girlfriend seemed to remove the fear that I would be left alone."

Ade soon gained another purpose as he was offered a trial as a plasterer, which he stuck at for a few days, then a few years, and now he has his own highly successful business in which he employs his previous boss!

And Ade also bought in to the principles and rules of Alcoholics Anonymous' 12-step recovery programme – a free treatment programme for people suffering from alcohol abuse and addiction in which participants follow a set of recovery steps to achieve and maintain abstinence from alcohol. The programme uses a spiritual approach that includes a belief in a higher power.

That higher power might be God, or it could be defined as something or someone that resonates profoundly in each participant's mind – Ade, for example, describes his higher power as 'the universe', which is a collective conscience that we all tap into. You can read more about the AA's 12 steps and the 12 'traditions' or guidelines for living and working together in and outside the AA programme at www. alcoholics-anonymous.org.uk

A central objective of the 12 steps is for members to pass on what they've learnt on their journey to others, which Ade says, *"was key for me as it not only overcomes my self-centredness but gives me accountability. I can't go back once I teach others, can I?! I realised that I could never safely use alcohol or drugs ever again. If you give yourself to others and the messages are positive, you'll receive it back with interest."*

Ade chose to pass his message on to thousands of young people via events and workshops organised by The Prince's Trust, a marvellous charity which helps young people between the ages of 13-30, often from challenging backgrounds and circumstances, to get into jobs, education and training (www.princes-trust.org.uk). This is where I first met Ade and was so inspired by him that I invited him to work alongside my team at seminars and events.

Fast forward a number of years and I'm proud to say that I attended Ade's wedding to his delightful and devoted girlfriend Rachael. He has become a father for the second time. He owns one house and is on course to buy a second, and his business is going from strength to strength. But he still has some dodgy tattoos!

We've christened his transformation from addict to entrepreneur *'The Ade Way'*. What's your way? In what aspects of your life do you need to take the power back? Because if Ade and Patsy can do it, then you can too.

APP ALERT!!

AN EXERCISE IN TAKING THE POWER BACK

Stalkie's **'TAKE THE POWER BACK' WORKOUT**

Think of an aspect of your life which you blame on something or somebody else. Write this down. Then follow this up with 'but now I believe' which is your changed behaviour, instead of apportioning blame as you did. Do this five times i.e. five instances where you have blamed something or someone. Here are a couple of examples taken from Ade's perspective:

Example 1: "I used to believe that I would never be a successful dad because of the way my parents treated me."

"My new belief is that my parents unconditionally loved me and their behaviour challenged me to make me stronger in later life. I want to be a role model for my children, to protect and care for them so that they are proud of me."

Example 2: "I used to blame my dealers for making me fearful of being honest and for controlling my actions."

"My new belief is that I now wake up energised that the world is a welcoming place, no one is my enemy and it's ok to participate. I can have honest conversations and relationships with the people whom I love and respect and they can do the same with me."

Okay, it's time for you to have a go yourself:

APP ALERT!!

1. I used to blame...

But now I believe...

2. I used to blame...

But now I believe...

3. I used to blame...

But now I believe...

4. I used to blame...

But now I believe...

5. I used to blame...

But now I believe...

CHOOSE FREEDOM!

When you choose to take responsibility, you will feel liberated. By accepting that, no matter what your boss does or says, they can never control how you feel, you'll no longer need to blame them for making you feel bad. How free would you feel if, whatever your wife or husband, boss or kids did or said, you could think to yourself: *"I am choosing my response, and I am not going to hand over the power to them to control my feelings"*?

Stalkie's Summary
TOP 10 TIPS TO HELP YOU TAKE THE POWER BACK

1. It's difficult in life to accept or admit to your shortcomings – to look in the mirror and see the problem staring right back at you. Step one is to understand how much of your power you are giving away and ask yourself the consequences of this behaviour in the future.

2. Blaming someone else for your problems won't fix them. It won't make you feel better in the long run. It will alienate the people you blame. It will alienate the people you go moaning to and attract fellow moaners who will join you on the path to destruction. Stop it! Now!

3. When your feelings, such as confidence and self-respect, are only associated with the things that others think of (and do for) you, you'll never be truly at one with yourself. By choosing the right response that serves you best in any given situation, you'll soon learn to take the power back.

4. You are where you are today because of you. Start to focus on what you have got, what you have achieved, what you are proud of and gain peace by being grateful and thankful.

APP ALERT!!

5. Exercising control over your life requires discipline and determination but the payback is a more healthy, energetic, effective and fulfilled life than those who lack faith in their ability to effect changes in their lives.

APP ALERT!!

6. Being true to yourself and to your values gives you, and only you, the choice to be happy, optimistic, positive, caring, supportive and fun – and will attract similar behaviour in others, allowing you to be part of a powerfully positive community.

7. Think:

   "I'm going to have a great day today, and I'm not going to let anyone else control it. I am in control of my life."

   Choose to believe in this mantra and expect to attract the results you desire.

8. Minding the gap or taking a personal time-out when you feel under pressure is a great tactic that allows you to focus on the attitude, behaviour and body language that will best serve you (your own 'Triangle of Communication' which we probe in the *'An Attitude of Gratitude'* and *You Can Be An Influencer'* chapters).

9. When you take a time-out check your hydration and your energy – are you thirsty or hungry? If so, redress the balance, regroup, then focus on what makes you feel good.

10. Personal power is all about having faith in your ability to take action. It's about using your power to choose what you want to do in life and nailing it with passion and integrity.

05

LET THE REAL YOU SHINE THROUGH

*Helping you become
authentic*

If you were to die today, would your last thoughts and feelings be of contentment and satisfaction? Would you be happy with the way that you have conducted your life, with the things you have left behind?

If you consider all the various aspects of your life, work, relationships, parenting and family, social life, hobbies, clubs and teams – the whole shooting match – are you proud of all your achievements in these areas?

When I was told that it was likely I was going to die of cancer, I spent what seemed like days replaying moments in my life, wondering whether I could be proud of my life and thinking about what I already stood for. Had I been a good person, a good husband, parent, friend and boss?

Hand on heart? I marked myself no more than 5 out of 10 in a lot of the areas that count the most. It was reminiscent of my old school reports. Fair enough, I'd made some money in business, had quite a lively social life and was (mostly) happily married with a young daughter whom I didn't spend that much time with, and a baby boy on the way too. But if the truth be known, my recent behaviour up to the point of my diagnosis had taken all the things that I treasured up to the point of collapse. To die now wouldn't give me any type of legacy to be truly proud of.

I woke up to the realisation that I had clearly valued my work life over and above my health and my family. In business, I knew what targets and goals to set and the strategies and behaviour required to reach them. My main motivation was extrinsic – the accumulation of wealth and possessions. Why had I allowed this mindset to take me to the brink of death?

I realised now that I'd never really thought about what I stood for, what my values were. And if I didn't know my values, how could I ever know whether I was being true to myself at all? It was as if I had been living out of synch with myself.

VALUES

Ironically my near-death sentence was the very leverage that I needed to discover what values I held dearest, and this in turn activated my brain to focus upon them and help me visualise how I could build my future life around them. I consider that this was a vital component in focusing my energy on survival, on fight rather than flight.

Through a combination of my own profound experience and reading avidly about the amazing resilience of the human mind in crisis, I can vouch for the power that creating your own personal value system can bring to your life, and how it can direct you to understanding what you want out of life.

An exceptional doctor called Rachel Naomi Remen* encapsulates my thoughts entirely on this. She says: "It has been surprising to see how often people do not realize that their deepest values are as personal as their fingerprints. Not knowing this, many of us have sacrificed certain things in order to have other things that we have been told are more important. Some of the things we have let go of in order to be seen as successful may be far more important to us personally in the end than some of the things we have held on to or even fought for.

"Sometimes it takes a wake-up call like cancer to bring us back to ourselves. The crisis of illness may shake us free of the life that we have created and allow us to begin a return to the life that is our own.

"Often what then turns out to be important is not a surprise at all. One patient, a CEO diagnosed with cancer, told me, "I always knew what mattered. I just never felt entitled to live by it before."

*Rachel Naomi Remen, M.D.
is Clinical Professor of Family
and Community Medicine at
the University of California San
Francisco School of Medicine
and Founder and Director of the
Institute for the Study of Health
and Illness at Commonweal.

Her bestselling books include
*'Kitchen Table Wisdom: Stories
that Heal'* and *'My Grandfather's
Blessings: Stories of Strength, Refuge
and Belonging',* published in 23
languages. Dr. Remen has a 60-
year personal history of Crohn's
disease, and brings the unique
perspective of both physician
and patient to her work.

Read more about Rachel at
www.rachelremen.com

The phrase *"I always knew what
mattered. I just never felt entitled to
live by it before"* struck a real chord
with me. I needed to establish what
mattered most to me and entitle
myself to live by it.

We might be born with basic
biological and physiological human
needs such as air, food, water
and warmth (I'll talk much more
specifically about 'human needs' in
the *'Why Do You Do That?'* chapter of
this book), but we are not born with
a set of values.

Thinking about your life and what
you stand for will lead you to
discover just what your values are.
You may find that you have values
such as pride, loyalty, love of family,
friendship, integrity, reliability,
optimism, helpfulness, thirst for
knowledge, truth, understanding of
others, patience, joy-bringer – the
list could be as short or as long as
you want.

But it is vital that you find out, so you know what your brain is focused on. When you know what your values are then you are more self-aware – you will know what is important to you, what you want to avoid and so on. This knowledge can be a new beginning for you, just as it has been for me.

My absolute plea – and I cannot emphasise how important this is, so excuse me if I sound like a broken record – is that I don't want you or anyone else in your life to wait for the wake-up call, like I did with my cancer, before you choose to use this information in your life. Whether it's cancer, heart disease, anxiety, depression, or the increasingly modern plague of diabetes, you cannot cheat your body into serving you for the best! But you can adjust your mindset and lifestyle to make sure that your mental and physical health is properly cared for.

We'll be doing a lot of exercises together in this chapter, just like the ones that made a difference to my life – the sort of thing that I now incorporate into a lot of my coaching, seminars and live events.

APP ALERT!!

If you can determine your values, change them for the better and act upon them, you will be sculpting a fulfilling life not just for yourself, but for your family, friends and colleagues. The payback from becoming a role model is exponential – it will grow in direct proportion to the effort you make.

When I was ill and confronted myself, I knew that I valued my friends and family, I loved going to football and having a few beers with my mates, and that I was driven to succeed in my work, but apart from this I was fairly stumped. In my heart though, I knew I was a caring, loving person and that I wanted to make the most out of the rest of my life whether I was fully restored to health or not.

What followed was very powerful and moving for me. I did an exercise that really challenged my ideas and emotions; something that I'm going to implore you to do too. First, let me tell you how it came about:

In 1888, a French newspaper ran an obituary for the Swedish chemist, engineer and inventor Dr. Alfred Nobel, a man of enormous wealth and reputation who was most famous for inventing dynamite. The piece, when translated, read:

"The Merchant of Death is Dead.

"Dr. Alfred Nobel, who became rich by finding ways to kill more people faster than ever before, died yesterday."

One man who read the obituary was Dr. Alfred Nobel himself. The paper had confused Alfred for his brother Ludvig, who had just died. Thanks to this error, Alfred Nobel got a rare opportunity to see how the world would portray his life and remember his legacy – in his case, one of perceived greed and destruction.

APP ALERT!!

Six years later, when Alfred finally passed away, his heirs and peers were shocked to find that, in his revised final will and testament, he had dedicated his vast wealth to the creation of prizes to award those who had done their best to benefit mankind in the fields of physics, chemistry, medicine, literature and peace.

The first Nobel Prizes were awarded in 1901 and continue to this day. Past winners include luminaries such as Nelson Mandela, Mother Teresa, Martin Luther King Jr., Albert Einstein, Sir Alexander Fleming and Marie Curie.

It's a fair bet that Nobel's legacy is more recognised globally for the Nobel Prizes rather than his invention of dynamite – just put his name into a search engine and see what comes up.

Given my condition of health, I imagined what *my own* obituary would be like.

I came up with words that I would want my friends, family, colleagues and 'community' friends (people from my club, gym, church) to use if they had to describe me to a journalist who was writing about me. The answers would show how I would like to be remembered.

I wanted my family to say I was caring, supportive, loving, loyal, always there for them, exciting, energetic, generous, funny, passionate, trustworthy, a good cook and a role model.

I wanted my friends to say I was kind, inspiring, honest, comforting, fun, a good laugh, the life and soul of the party, someone who knew right from wrong.

I wanted my work colleagues to say I was hardworking, supportive, knowledgeable, led from the front, inspirational, positive, courageous, passionate and a good listener.

I wanted my community friends to say I gave my all for the cause, I was supportive, fun, happy, friendly and optimistic.

The list of words and phrases I produced above were my desired values. This is how I would like to be seen. These were the words that I soon honed into my very own personal mission statement:

"To make friends, spread love and happiness, and have faith."

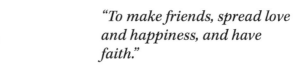

APP ALERT!!

117

Have you ever thought about writing your own mission statement? Imagine you are the boss of your own company and your job is to successfully market and sell brand 'you'!

Stephen Covey describes this in 'Habit 2' in his book *The 7 Habits of Highly Effective People*. Habit 2 is called 'Begin With the End in Mind®' and he says:

"In one's life, the most effective way to begin with the end in mind is to develop a mission statement that focuses what you want to be in terms of character and what you want to do in reference to contribution of achievements. Writing a mission statement can be the most important activity an individual can undertake to truly lead one's life.

"That mission and vision statement is more powerful, more significant, more influential, than the baggage of the past, or even the accumulated noise of the present...

"...Personal mission statements based on correct principles are like a personal constitution, the basis for making major, life-directing decisions, the basis for making daily decisions in the midst of the circumstances and emotions that affect our lives.

"When we create a mission statement of our own and choose to live by it we can flow with changes. We don't need pre-judgements or prejudices. We don't need to figure out everything else in life, to stereotype and categorize everything and everybody in order to accommodate reality.

"In order to write good mission statements, we must first begin at the very center of our Circle of Influence, that center comprised of our most basic paradigms, the lens through which we see the world. Whatever is at the center of our life will be the source of our security, guidance, wisdom, and power.

"As we go deeply within ourselves, as we understand and realign our basic paradigms to bring them in harmony with correct principles, we create both an effective, empowering center and a clear lens through which we can see the world. We can then focus that lens on how we, as unique individuals, relate to that world.

"Creating a mission statement is not something you do overnight. It takes deep introspection, careful analysis, thoughtful expression, and often many rewrites to produce it in final form. It may take you several weeks or even months before you feel really comfortable with your mission statement, before you feel it is a complete and concise expression of your innermost values and directions.

Even then, you will want to review it regularly and make minor changes as the years bring additional insights or changing circumstances.

"Your mission statement becomes your constitution, the solid expression of your vision and values. It becomes the criterion by which you measure everything else in your life."

(www.stephencovey.com)

Stalkie's
'DISTILLING YOUR VALUES' WORKOUT

Imagine a journalist is writing your obituary for a national newspaper and asks a close friend, a family member, a work colleague and a person from your football team/ choir/club/church to describe you.

What would you like them to say? Choose five words you would like them to use.

- Close friend:

_____

_____

_____

_____

_____

_____

_____

_____

- Family member:

_____

_____

_____

_____

_____

_____

_____

_____

- Community friend:

_____

_____

_____

_____

_____

_____

_____

- Work colleague:

_____

_____

_____

_____

_____

_____

_____

_____

_____

APP ALERT!!

What you have just written down are the emotions and behaviours that you personally value. These can form the basis of your own personal mission statement.

Stalkie's
'PERSONAL MISSION STATEMENT' WORKOUT

APP ALERT!!

What would you like your personal mission statement to say? Take time now to prioritise your values into a short sentence which you would be proud for everyone to know and that you would willingly commit to live in accordance with.

Personal Mission Statement Draft:

_____

_____

_____

_____

_____

_____

_____

_____

_____

_____

_____

Now read your values and your mission statement over again and ask yourself this question:

IS YOUR BEHAVIOUR MOVING YOU TOWARDS YOUR VALUES?

"Remembering that I'll be dead soon is the most important tool I've ever encountered to help me make the big choices in life.

"Almost everything – all external expectations, all pride, all fear of embarrassment or failure – these things just fall away in the face of death, leaving only what is truly important.

"Remembering that you are going to die is the best way I know to avoid the trap of thinking you have something to lose. You are already naked. There is no reason not to follow your heart."

– Steve Jobs*

***Steve Jobs**, co-founder of Apple Inc. passed away in 2011 after battling pancreatic cancer for nearly a decade. He was 56 years old.

Please think about everything that you have just written. If your friends had to tell the truth, is this what they would say about you? Could you, hand on heart, show everybody your mission statement and be confident that they would recognise these qualities in you? Would there be any changes to the words you have chosen?

Often your behaviour doesn't reflect the way in which you would like to be remembered. These exercises are pivotal in enabling you to assess your values and also to see how they are reflected in your behaviour.

When I undertook these exercises a few years ago, I took it a step further and asked my colleagues at work to honestly come up with words that described my behaviour. When asking them to do this, I reassured them that there would be no unfavourable consequences, it was an exercise in trust.

They said I was:

- Strict
- Patronising
- Scary
- Led from the front but not collaboratively
- Inspirational (thank goodness!)

Reality-check time! Until you hear what people describe you as, you can't be sure of yourself. I'd probably been thinking how wonderful I was at work, but my colleagues had given me plenty to contemplate.

I'm pretty sure that most people wouldn't like to be told how they are really seen, and most would be too embarrassed to give people such true feedback (unless they knew there would be no comeback and that their feedback would be acted upon). It's sad, but in most people's reality, we don't learn the truth and live a lot of our time in a state of 'artificial harmony'* with our loved ones and colleagues which means we lose sight of our values and the brilliance of achieving them through the correct behaviour.

This honest feedback from my colleagues was a "wake up and smell the coffee, Stalkie" moment, but it focused my attention on what behaviour I needed to adopt in order to become the friendly, loving, happy, caring, inspirational, passionate, faithful, healthy person I desired to be.

*Coined in **Patrick Lencioni's** excellent book, *The Five Dysfunctions of a Team*', the term 'artificial harmony' relates to relationships which appear healthy but lack commitment. Team members prefer to fake their buy-in to group decisions rather than commit to constructive, passionate debate. On the surface people are being nice and respectful to each other and there are few signs of team dysfunctions such as conflict, shouting and anger.

But beneath the surface there are fragile egos, vulnerability, limited trust, a shortage of courage and a fear of conflict. In reality, this artificial harmony defeats all the benefits and positive advantages of teamwork and is often the reason that businesses suffer from disappointing results.

When I help businesses to overturn poor performance, I often refer to the model that Patrick Lencioni promotes in 'The Five Dysfunctions of a Team' so that they can experience the deep satisfaction, growth and accountability that naturally result from true teamwork.

To see how Patrick's methodologies are brought to organisations and the people within them, you can explore his website www.tablegroup.com

Let's delve further into my exercise and see what else I learnt. My colleagues had been admirable in their honesty, but I was keen to know more, such as why they thought I was scary and patronising, for example – so I asked them.

They replied that I didn't let them finish making a point and I would be quick to rebuke them if they did one thing wrong, but slow to praise them even if they did ten things right. My own desired values were 'supportive' and 'positive' but my colleagues described me as quite the opposite!

If I was to follow through on these perfectly valid opinions, I would need to agree upon a new improved set of behaviours. For example, when a colleague did a number of things right, I should acknowledge it and congratulate them. When a colleague did something wrong, I would not let it fester, always remind them of the good and separate the errant behaviour from my empathy for the person.

Rather than never letting my colleagues finish a sentence, my new behaviour would be to be a good listener – to seek to understand, then be understood (Stephen Covey's Habit 5).

Such discussions enabled the whole values 'thing' to become quite clear to me. Although I genuinely did value supporting people, my behaviour undermined this. I now know the behaviour to adopt when it comes to supporting my colleagues.

When I thought further about this and was candid with myself, I realised I had been guilty of these traits not just at work but outside it too – it was something that I needed to address with my wife and family as well.

Living in line with your values means that you back them up with your behaviour. If you love, care and support then the love, care and support you get back will flourish. Give the emotions you wish to receive.

Creating an environment where your values can be appreciated by others, and vice versa, gives a real opportunity for honesty, love and personal growth to thrive in all your relationships – whether at home, socially or at work. It is tremendously fulfilling to live life in this authentic way.

APP ALERT!!

MOVING CLOSER TO YOUR VALUES

In order to move closer to your values and reinforce them with your behaviour, look back at the words you used to describe how you would like to be remembered, then ask yourself some questions based on these values and emotions.

When choosing the questions, focus on the people, relationships and things that matter most in your life. Ask yourself whether your behaviour and actions when dealing with the people and things that matter most to you truly reflect your values. **Remember: what you focus on, you feel.** I want you to focus on behaviour and actions that will serve you best from this point on.

Also be aware that some questions are better asked in the morning, and others at night. Why? In practical terms, some questions will provoke a quick action on your part; ask these in the morning and you might be able to fit them into your day's activities. Also, going to sleep may help reinforce or preserve certain emotions that you evoke through certain questions:

"We are learning that sleep seems to help us process and consolidate information we acquire while we are awake,"

says **Allen Towfigh**, M.D., a New York City-based board certified sleep medicine doctor and neurologist who pioneered the Sleep Medicine Fellowship Program at Cornell University,

"Going to bed after an argument will likely cause your feelings to be consolidated more effectively than if you went on to remain awake for that same eight-hour period."

(www.drallentowfigh.com)

There are no hard and fast rules for these questions, but to give you a steer, these are some of the questions I asked myself when I was reassessing my life's priorities and my values:

- *Who do I love and when did I last tell them how much I appreciated their love?*

- *Who am I proud of, and when did I last tell them?*

- *Who do I have faith in and respect, and when was the last time I let them know?*

(My answers to the above questions were unanimously 'my wife, my family, close friends and work colleagues'.)

- *What am I grateful for, and what can I do to perpetuate that gratitude?*

(My main answer here was life itself and, of course, my health – something I could perpetuate with my new health, diet and fitness regime.)

- *What am I excited about and when did I share it?*

(Being alive and having the chance to create a new destiny for myself and those around me.)

- *What acts of kindness and positivity am I going to implement every day?*

- *What am I going to do to always lead from the front?*

- *How am I going to give more to my team?*

Whatever the answers to your own specific questions, now go and do it! Follow them up and make it happen. Demonstrate and share your love, gratitude, pride, excitement, faith and respect. Then continue doing it.

I also believe that you shouldn't gloss over the types of behaviour that may not have been serving you well up to now. Don't be afraid to ask how and why you managed to set yourself up for a fall in the past; remind yourself of the uncomfortable consequences that certain aspects of your behaviour might have already brought to your life. Ask what would happen if you continued along this destructive route.

The outcome is to create leverage so that you look for the good and focus on behaving in line with your values, while avoiding the very opposite.

For my part, I don't mind telling you that I didn't fully act upon my questions – I talked the talk but didn't always walk the walk.

I was fabulous at following through with my work colleagues which resulted in a far more collaborative, trusting and productive team environment. I was great at following through with my friends and family members whom I grew far closer to as a result. Also with my health, which has led me to achieve things that I never thought possible, including competing in Iron-Man, triathlon, cycling and sea-swimming endurance events around the world.

Our personal development is always under construction. It took me a considerable amount of re-evaluation and re-education of my behaviour before I could say I became true to myself and happily flourished in all aspects of my life. Like any form of exercise, regularly repeating these exercises will make you stronger every time you do them.

BEING TRUE TO YOURSELF

Doing these 'value' exercises made me realise that I often used to choose the path of least resistance in my life, the one that took the smallest amount of energy. Does that resonate with you too?

It's easy to bumble along isn't it? Are you reading this book for its curiosity value or because you are open to improvement and are willing to commit to change and live an outstanding life?

Many people that I coach come to me as a result of their default negative attitude, which means they find it difficult to radiate to others but find it easy to drain their family and friends of their humour, goodwill and faith. It is because of this behaviour that they are unhappy – as are their families and their colleagues – but they struggle to understand why. The more this continues, the more immune they become to people's feelings.

If you don't really think about emotions at all, and see little point in caring for yourself and others unconditionally (because you can't see what good it will do you, or you can't find the courage to take the first step towards changing your outlook), you'll never know how rewarding an abundance mentality can be in comparison to the consequences that will no doubt come your way. My chapter on *'Take The Power Back'* explains in more detail why opting to take the easy path to short-term pleasure often leads to a far more difficult journey involving long-term pain.

Caring for others is a natural principle. If you forget to water a plant, it is likely that it will die. If you do not care for your loved ones, friends, colleagues and customers they will, in time, leave you. Whatever kind of business or lifestyle you have, these principles apply.

There is a great power to be found in caring for others and giving unconditionally. If you do something for another person without pay or even the expectation of a reward, you'll have much to live for.

I'm reminded of one such Eureka! moment in my life, for which I am eternally grateful to Tony Robbins and his team: I paid several thousand pounds to attend a Tony Robbins Life Mastery course (justifiably described as 'an immersive experience in a magical setting, dedicated to your growth'). Early in the proceedings, my team leader asked me to hand out drinks to all the co-delegates on the course. I immediately had a hissy fit, asked him why and threatened to leave the course. Why should I do it? I hadn't paid all that money and travelled half way round the world to be a butler!

My team leader's calm words stopped me in my tracks. He simply said, *"Maybe that's your learning point, Paul? Maybe you should learn to serve others rather than yourself all the time?"* Bang! I felt as if I'd been hit in the solar plexus by a ninja warrior. The jumped-up diva Stalkie was instantly replaced by the butler-extraordinaire Stalkie. A valuable life lesson learnt right there.

OUR THREE SEPARATE LIVES

In order to maximise the quality of your own life in tune with your treasured values, I'd like you to take into account that we all have three distinct lives. This is an absolute gem of knowledge that I have borrowed from time spent with the supreme Dr. Stephen Covey.

Dr. Covey says that we live three separate lives. Here is a breakdown of what each means:

- **Public Life** is seen and heard by our colleagues, associates and others within our circle. This is when you are conducting your daily life in public, when you are out and about shopping, at the pub, restaurant, school, sports club, church, or at work dealing with customers, suppliers or colleagues.

- **Private Life** is where we interact more intimately with spouses, family members and close friends. This is when you demonstrate and show your truer feelings (good or bad) because you feel close to them and secure to do so.

- **Secret Life** is where your heart is, where your real motives lie (the source of your 'Primary Greatness'). This is where you are one on one with yourself, when you are on your own, putting your head on your pillow and reflecting upon your day, your life and what you stand for. Only you will know whether you have acted with courage, with integrity and love. This is not about what others think of you; these are the times when you know whether you are truly comfortable with yourself and your behaviour.

The key takeaway here is that we need to be self-aware enough to spend time exploring our secret life since that is truly who we are and who we want to be.

APP ALERT!!

By carefully examining the importance of the hidden you, you will experience just how essential it is to find ways to live in harmony with your values. During times of challenge or achievement, pause and ask yourself, *"What do I think? What do I believe is right? Am I being true to my values?"*

If you are living according to the values that matter to you, then you will feel contented when you're alone with your thoughts.

If, however, there is an emotion that you value such as honesty and you have betrayed it by being dishonest in some way, then most people would be eaten away by this and feel discomfited and unhappy. Alternatively, you may try and convince yourself that the occasional little white lie is okay, in which case you start deluding yourself because you don't want to face up to the truth.

I'm living (still, thankfully!) proof of this. In the run up to having cancer, I had constructed a life that was bearable, mainly due to my perceived success in the workplace. In reality, it was an extrinsically motivated success and was based around meeting my needs negatively (we'll look far deeper into this in the chapter on '*Why Do You Do That?*') – my significance, my contribution, my connection were all work-related and measured by the accumulation of wealth, which I liked to show off in my public life. Was I behaving in accordance with my values? No.

My private life had been heading for the rails for some time, without me having the courage to take a grip of it. I was living the life of a 'married single', spending more time 'working away' or at the football with my mates than giving time over to my wife and daughter. I avoided the awkward conversations I needed to have at home and preferred to live at odds with what I knew was right.

My emotions became numbed as I self-justified my lifestyle and blanked out any thoughts of what the medium and long term looked like for me and my family. Whilst my public and private lives were mainly being scripted by the pressures of delivering success in the workplace, I couldn't even face my secret life. I lost all perspective around my self-awareness, my own identity and my empathy or understanding of others.

I had entered the territory where poor mental and physical health can collide with devastating effect; the territory that can house depression alongside psychosomatic illness, alongside self-medicating with drink and drugs, alongside self-harming – I'm sure you get the picture.

My personal tipping point came when I left my marital home. I no longer had the solutions, energy or motivation to deliver the revenue that the investors in my business required all those years ago.

Retrospectively, I can say that my cancer came as a relief, but I wouldn't recommend it to you or anyone as a course of action for anything you wish to improve in your life. I'm here to help you embark upon the improvements that you desire and offer you some powerful tools and principles you can apply to guard against such a crisis.

ANTI-VALUES

Now we need to identify the flipside to your values. This time we're looking at those behaviours that are undesirable to you. These are your 'anti-values', the behaviours you wish to avoid. Understanding these will intensify your appetite to bring your values alive.

Some people find it a hard task to pinpoint these, but just ask the 'hidden' you what you would like to avoid and what emotions or feelings you really hate.

APP ALERT!!

132

Some clues towards this might be feelings of embarrassment, anger, hatred, a feeling of being overwhelmed or out of control, loneliness, boredom, ignorance, or even dishonesty.

Stalkie's 'PERFECT DAY' WORKOUT

Imagine you are creating your perfect day. Examine an average day for you, thinking about all the things that happen and the people you meet, then take out of it all those emotions that irritate or upset you.

Remember you're trying to create a day in your life when nothing at all happens to mar your enjoyment. You will need to think about all the different areas of your life to make sure you capture all those negative emotions that get in the way of perfection.

With this in mind, now write down your answers to these questions (my own sample answers to these questions are given as examples):

1. What feelings and emotions are most important for me to avoid at home?
   (e.g. arguments, negative news, poor focus, last-minute rush)

   _____

   _____

   _____

   _____

   _____

   _____

2. What feelings and emotions are most important for me to avoid at work?
   (e.g. not to focus on what hasn't been done, nor worry about what happens if things go wrong)

   _____

   _____

   _____

   _____

   _____

   _____

3. What feelings and emotions are most important for me to avoid with my loved ones?
(e.g. bad behaviour, focusing on 'problems')

_____

_____

_____

_____

_____

_____

_____

4. What feelings and emotions are most important for me to avoid in my other relationships?
(e.g. talking about people behind their backs, negative cliques)

_____

_____

_____

_____

_____

5. What feelings and emotions are most important for me to avoid in my health life?
(e.g. lack of energy, laziness, avoiding exercise)

_____

_____

_____

_____

_____

_____

When I first did this exercise, I soon discovered the 'anti-values' that I didn't want to spoil my perfect day, that I didn't want to spoil my life. Over time, I have tweaked these – as I say, the best 'you' is always under construction – but they have remained pretty consistent:

- Dishonest
- Unfair
- Patronising
- Scary
- Narrow minded
- Miserable
- Upset
- Angry
- Lazy
- Selfish
- Ungenerous/mean
- Pessimistic
- Faithless
- Unhealthy/unfit
- Ungiving
- Don't keep promises

THE VALUE EFFECT

When you've carried out my workouts with diligence, you will now have two distinct lists – one will list your *desired values*, the other will list your *anti-values*.

When you open your eyes to the role that your values can play in sculpting the future you deserve, the next step is to walk the walk and live your life practically in line with your desired values (whilst avoiding your anti-values in the process).

Come up with a list of practical, deliverable actions or baby steps that will take you towards your values. Promise to yourself that you will take action immediately. Don't be over ambitious, make these actions realistic. These do not need to be a hole-in-one, but they do need to be on course.

Here's a recent example of a list of actions that I chose for myself – every one of them is geared to committing to and reinforcing a value of mine:

- I am going to show appreciation and gratitude to my wife who has been juggling her intense work and family commitments without a word of complaint! I am going to offer to cook the meals every night and will ask if there is anything I can do around the house. We'll talk and have a cuddle.

- I am going to spend some fun time with my youngest daughter, starting by watching the dance that she made up and wanted to show me the other day when I was 'too busy'. I'm also going to tell her how proud I am of her.

- I am going to be less dictatorial in the office. My colleagues and suppliers sometimes know better than me. I am going to have meetings with individual colleagues tomorrow, ask them what their personal goals are and how I can support them to achieve these.

- I am going to intensify my bike-training and book some yoga lessons.

I recommend that you keep a diary to write these actions in. I keep a special book to log all my answers to the exercises that I regularly do – even my family can check it! With this sort of accountability, we can measure and celebrate progress together.

Now you too can do this exercise and find areas of your life where changes in your behaviours will mean that you bring your life into line with your desired values.

Stalkie's
'FIVE AREAS YOU NEED TO ADDRESS' WORKOUT

List the five biggest areas you need to address in order to move closer to your positive values and avoid the negative values.

(If you are living in exact accordance with how you would like to be portrayed – where there is no room for improvement – ask yourself how you can take your life to the next level and what behaviours can help you to do that.)

1

_____

_____

_____

_____

2

_____

_____

_____

_____

3

_____

_____

_____

_____

4

_____

_____

_____

5

_____

_____

_____

_____

By recognising these areas, you are now in a position to do something about them. Remember this Stalkie mantra: *action supersedes everything.*

APP ALERT!!

Stalkie's
'FIVE ACTIONS TO MOVE YOU CLOSER TO YOUR VALUES' WORKOUT

Write down five actions that you are going to complete today to move you closer to one of your values e.g. If you would like to be remembered as loving and you believe that you need to improve in this area, then an action could be to ring your friends and family and tell them that you love them.

Write five action points that you are going to do now:

1

_____

_____

_____

_____

2

_____

_____

_____

_____

3

_____

_____

_____

_____

4

_____

_____

_____

_____

5

_____

_____

_____

_____

Now, take this further. Commit to taking action within the next month: Write down five actions you are going to carry out within the next four weeks:

APP ALERT!!

1
_____

_____

_____

_____

4
_____

_____

_____

_____

2
_____

_____

_____

_____

5
_____

_____

_____

_____

3
_____

_____

_____

_____

In order to make any changes, it's action stations!

Now you are sure of your values, and your mission statement, you will be able to understand why it is that you feel a certain way about events, relationships and situations in your life and how you can adjust your attitude and behaviour to make every day a proud day.

> *"Nothing is given to man on earth – struggle is built into the nature of life, and conflict is possible – the hero is the person who lets no obstacle prevent him from pursuing the values he has chosen."*
>
> – Andrew Bernstein*

*Dr Andrew Bernstein is a philosopher, novelist and educator who lectures internationally on subjects such as Objectivism, the nature of heroism, the history of capitalism, and application of the principle of individual rights to a broad array of topical issues, including health care, abortion, gun ownership, immigration and the war on drugs. Read about him at www.andrewbernstein.net

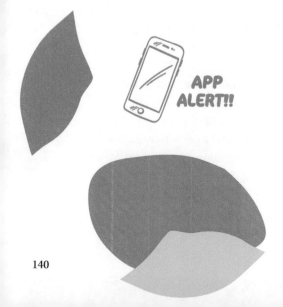

APP ALERT!!

Stalkie's Summary
TOP 10 TIPS TO FINDING THE REAL YOU

1. Have you really thought about what you stand for, what your values are? Determining your values and moving your behaviour towards them will enable you to sculpt a fulfilling life for yourself, your family, friends and colleagues.

2. Writing your own imaginary obituary, using words that you would want your friends, family and colleagues to use if they had to describe you, will point you towards an understanding of what your values are.

3. Write your own personal mission statement as if you are marketing and selling brand 'you'! Use this personal constitution as the basis for making major, life-directing decisions, enabling you to flow with changes.

4. Check and agree upon the words you have chosen in your obituary and mission statement. Then focus on the positive things in your life and ask yourself what you can do to reinforce the behaviour and feelings that will serve you best in moving as close as possible to your values.

5. Establish your 'anti-values', too – the behaviour you wish to avoid. Understanding these will intensify your appetite to bring your values alive.

   Living in line with your values means that you back them up with your behaviour. If you love, care and support then the love, care and support you get back will flourish. Give the emotions you wish to receive.

6. When you are on your own, putting your head on your pillow and reflecting, only you will know whether you have acted with courage, with integrity and love. This is not about what others think of you, these are the times when you know whether you are truly comfortable with yourself and your behaviour. Spend time exploring 'the secret you' as this is truly who you are and who you want to be.

7. Come up with a list of practical, deliverable actions or baby steps that will take you towards your values. Timetable when you will undertake these actions using the final exercises in this chapter.

8. Keep a diary to write these actions in and to log all your answers to the exercises that you do. With this sort of accountability, you can measure and celebrate your progress.

9. Our personal development is always under construction. Like any form of exercise, regularly repeating these exercises will make you stronger every time you do them. The payback from becoming a role model is exponential – it will grow in direct proportion to the effort you make.

10. Creating an environment where your values can be appreciated by others, and vice versa, gives a real opportunity for honesty, love and personal growth to thrive in all your relationships at home, socially, at work and in the wider community.

APP ALERT!!

06
IGNITE YOUR
SELF-BELIEF

*Empowering you for a
positive change*

IGNITE YOUR SELF-BELIEF

How often do you sit down and spend time actually reviewing your life situation? Probably never! The fact is, we spend a lot of our time helping and planning for other people and things, such as our family, work, social events, clubs and societies and so on.

Discovering your life plan starts with asking yourself some searching questions:

- Where are you now compared to where you want to be?

- Are you fulfilled in all aspects of your life?

- Where are you spending your time? Is the balance good?

- Is your behaviour moving you towards your aspirations?

- How's your body's health?

- How's your emotional health? Think about how many positive emotions you have in your life; are you moving towards these, or away from them?

- Are you motivated and energetic?

- How are your relationships?

- What secret fears and niggles do you have?

An honest assessment of the above should then lead you to ask:

- How much pain am I willing to take in my life before I change the aspects I'm unhappy with?

- What do I need to change and how do I do it?

- Am I up for it?

I sometimes have people say things to me like: "go on then, Stalkie – motivate me!" In truth, the only person who can motivate you **is you**. As Dwight D. Eisenhower, the five-star general in the US Army and US President from 1953-1961, said:

"Motivation is the art of getting people to do what you want them to do because they want to do it."

The minute you go to a restaurant expecting them to give you the best night of your life on a plate (so to speak!), or the minute you go out with your friends and expect them to show you a good time, or for your bosses to give you a complete road map that will effortlessly lead you to a destination of job satisfaction and wealth – well, you are heading for disappointment. It just won't happen, because it's your responsibility to make the most of your life.

"Love the day."

– Paul Stalker

To do so, the 'what-ifs?' ('what if it doesn't work out?', 'what if I'm just not good enough?', 'what if I end up looking like an idiot?') must be removed from your life. We're also not at home to you saying you'll do one thing, then ending up doing another. Nope. Not allowed.

Unlocking your self-belief is a cornerstone to becoming what you want to be. If you are honest with yourself and seek to understand the things you need to improve upon, then I can certainly give you the knowledge and the tools for action. When you faithfully follow that action, change will happen as a direct result. It's as simple as that!

APP ALERT!!

WHY TAKE NOTICE OF ME?

My life story is all about overcoming self-doubt and my own limiting beliefs; being told I had around 12 weeks to live and fighting the system against all odds, before flourishing again as an entrepreneur, a business coach to FTSE 100 companies, a peak performance coach to business leaders, sports teams and personalities, and a life coach/mentor to disaffected schoolchildren and life-serving prisoners.

I've had the pleasure of working with many different people from many walks of life, here and abroad; from those suffering with cancer and successfully conquering it.

In the corporate world, I have utilised my belief in my skills to help create cultural shifts in the most demanding of workplaces.

I have worked with inspiring and highly successful business leaders such as Sir Charles Dunstone and David Ross, who founded The Carphone Warehouse together (Charles is now Executive Chairman of the TalkTalk Group); with Julian Richer and his company Richer Sounds; with Sir Ian Cheshire, who was Group CEO of Kingfisher PLC, owners of B&Q and Screwfix; with Iceland Foods, Savers, Debenhams, Thomas Cook, DHL, J.P. Morgan and many others. You can read or watch videos about what these companies have to say about me on my website www.paulstalker.com/case-studies

These incredible people are on my website eulogising about little old me! How did that happen?!

My trump card is to achieve the best performance possible out of their colleagues, from the boardroom to the shop floor and all points in between. This involves getting them enthused in their lives and engaged in their jobs, by teaching them to understand how we, as individuals, work. This results in a happier workforce, meaning happier customers and, as a by-product, sales increase, ultimately affecting the bottom line and profit.

My techniques, systems and advice have worked without fail. My company even offers a 'money back' guarantee – that's how convinced I am that what I talk about works, through my seminars, keynote speeches and training programmes, together with the learning tools I produce.

This may all sound very "slap yourself on the back, Stalkie", but I believe that life is not all about how much money you have, or what position or title you attain, it is about YOU – because your life matters to you. It is your friends, family, colleagues and the people you come into contact with who also matter. None of this would have been possible in my life without unlocking my own self-belief. And if I can do it, you certainly can too. *Because self-belief is learnable*. I had to learn it or God only knows where I would have ended up.

Your current level of self-belief isn't fixed for the duration of your days on this planet. We can all learn and adapt. We were born into this world with no sense of what we could or couldn't achieve. As a child you have endless horizons and you don't comprehend the concepts of doubt and pessimism. Then, as sure as apples is apples, life gradually imposes limitations upon you, to whatever degree you allow it to.

So, that's why I have started this chapter by prompting you to re-examine your life plan. We're going to be discarding many of the limiting ideas you have accumulated about yourself. If you've readily absorbed and felt good about acting upon the information in **You Can Raise Your Game!** so far, you should be well along that route by now. And the good news is that many of the *'Fear into Power'*, *'Let the Real You Shine Through'*, *'Take the Power Back'* and *'An Attitude of Gratitude'* principles and learnings will put you in pole position to ratchet up your levels of self-belief with comfortable ease.

My most rewarding moments have not been those where I've banked the biggest cheque, or won the biggest contract. They have been the times when individuals have come up to me at one of my seminars or coaching sessions and reported on their courage to change and improve their lives, such as "I now have the courage to stop taking Prozac", or "I have got the best relationship with my kids now after 20 years, thank you", or "after 35 years, I've stopped smoking". All these are real moments that have made me proud.

At one of my seminars, one participant owned up to the fact she had always blamed her current situation on her father being an alcoholic. During the time she spent with me, this lovely lady realised that she had to take responsibility for her own life, and not blame him at all. She now has the self-belief to choose her response to everything, and knows she can only change the future; the past is history. So let's also change your future as you wish it to be.

First up, we agree that you can't change history, but let's not discard it.

I bet you've achieved some pretty impressive things in your life already! There will have been times when you've backed yourself with a high level of self-belief and determination, and times when you haven't held such solid belief, but you've still succeeded – wouldn't it be great if you never had to go through the nonsense and rigmarole of doubting yourself?

Let's celebrate. Write down ten things that you have achieved in your life to be proud of – the driving test, the first job, doing the fun run, falling in love, overcoming a fear, speaking in public, helping a friend in need...write them quickly here:

APP ALERT!!

1

_____

2

_____

*Well done! You've proved you can do
these things. True self-belief actually
comes from developing the vision
that you can do so much more – is it
starting that business, being a great
partner and parent, losing weight,
fulfilling that dream trip or hobby?
Whatever, it's doable by you for the
greater you.*

3

_____

4

_____

5

_____

EXTERNAL FACTORS THAT SHAPE YOUR SELF-BELIEF

6

_____

7

_____

8

_____

Self-belief is a set of ideas we have
about ourselves that we consider to
be true. These ideas become our
self-image and are authentic when
we behave in line with them – which
means supporting our ideas through
our confidence in our own abilities
or judgment.

9

_____

10

_____

These beliefs are influenced by past
experiences and desires, taking into
account external factors such as:

Our Environment

Earlier in **You Can Raise Your Game!**, I recounted Ade's story to you. Ade used to believe that the state of his life was down to everyone else. He was initially raised by unstable parents who allowed their lives to be dictated by the company they kept, where alcohol, drug abuse and verbal violence were commonplace. He blamed his life problems on his parents, and they on theirs.

It was this environment that played such a part in influencing Ade's own belief that everyone else was to blame for all his misdemeanours and his destructive lifestyle.

On the flip side to this, my next-door neighbour and friend Neil Waters, who is 48 years old and makes his living as a self-employed professional driver, is one of the most grateful, happy and caring people I have ever known. He looks vibrant, he works hard on his health and his fitness. Sure, he's been through some low times in his life (which we'll probe into a little later), but he has a happy knack of rising above any challenge that comes his way through tapping into his stock of self-belief. Neil readily acknowledges that his mindset owes much to the environment in which he was brought up.

When I asked if I could include his wisdom in this book, he told me:

"I completely believe that you should take nothing for granted in your life. I consider myself blessed that my parents were always there for me. They were loving, caring and supportive but what has always stayed with me is that they were never, ever short of time to talk things through with me.

"The greatest gift they ever gave me wasn't money or belongings, it was the gift of communicating openly, with support and trust – and that's a precious thing that I hope I am passing on to my kids, and that they will pass on to their kids too. It took a few knocks before I realised just how deep I could dig into my reserves of self-worth, but now I know that my foundations are so strong, I'm ready for anything that comes my way... and that gives me peace of mind.

"If you take things for granted, they can lose their value and appreciation. When you appreciate what people do for you, make sure you pass your appreciation on to them and the chain will grow from there. Once people know how great it feels to be appreciated, they are far more likely to openly express their appreciation for others.

"Thanks to my parents and various events in my life, I consider that my self-belief is now rock solid. I've learned that whenever I persistently give more to the 'team' or to 'the planet' (or however you'd like to describe it), good things come back to me in return, without request. This stuff is addictive! There's only 24 hours in a day, of which we'll be asleep for maybe eight hours, we'll spend eight hours or so at work, which only leaves eight hours a day with family and friends. You can't take this time for granted, you must live it to the full."

Life Events and Triggers

As a result of a sickening car accident a few years ago, Neil came very close to losing everything he had worked for – he lost his livelihood, his house, his health, and his partner found it almost too difficult to live with him. The accident had soured his outlook on life.

As soon he was able, Neil went back to driving and over-compensated to make up for the time and money he had lost. He threw himself into his work, spending a punishing amount of hours on the road, eating a bad diet 'on the hoof', piling on weight, sleeping badly, suffering constant headaches, nausea, dizziness and nose bleeds.

He was taking around 15-20 painkillers a day. It was only when he went to stock up on his self-medication that a late-night pharmacist told Neil he looked unwell and insisted that there was no way he should continue driving that night, and that he should see a doctor first thing in the morning:

"The following morning, the doctor discovered that my blood pressure was critically high and that I was a danger to myself and everyone I was driving. He had caught it just in time. It was my proverbial 'wake-up call'. I thought I was strong enough to drive all day and night, to fill my body full of crap, and to hide my worries from my partner and kids.

"The reality was the opposite. By taking my mental and physical health for granted, by chasing the money and not communicating openly, by ignoring the things that I had learned from my parents, I was in danger of becoming no use to my family at all.

"I'd let the accident undermine my confidence and, rather than back myself to deal with it in the way I knew best, I'd switched into a thoughtless, automaton mode. Never again! How can you feel good about the things around you, unless you feel good about yourself first?"

Life will always throw some missiles in your direction, but it's up to you to deal with them authentically, in the manner that you know serves you best. Neil's self-belief had been rocked by a car accident that was unavoidable, which in turn led him to question himself and act out of character. But once he reverted to 'being himself' and to believing in himself again, he was soon able to get back on track. As a result of this trigger, Neil agrees that he is even more aware of the character traits and principles that naturally serve him best and he is stronger because of it.

In Ade's case, it took the radical trigger of imprisonment to traumatise him into dropping the beliefs and mentality that had been responsible for his anti-social behaviour. Based on the knowledge he gained from this experience, his new self-belief is serving him magnificently.

In my case, it took the equally radical trigger of cancer for me to re-evaluate my belief system and emerge from the experience with new empowering belief in myself.

The moral of this is a recurring theme in **You Can Raise Your Game!** If you are seeking positive change in your life, please don't wait for a negative external trigger to shake you up before you resolve to take action. Grasp the nettle now. There is knowledge and there are tools and techniques a-plenty in this chapter and in this book to set you on the way BEFORE life throws a missile at you.

Knowledge and Results

According to the Merriam-Webster dictionary, knowledge is defined as the *'circumstance or condition of apprehending truth or fact through reasoning'*. Knowledge is gained through direct experience, skills and knowledge claims i.e. what you know to be true but is open to discussion and debate. The sources of knowledge are instinct, reason and intuition.

The knowledge you possess will certainly play a critical role in what you choose to do and not to do. But you can be sure that knowledge without application is simply knowledge. *If it is not put into practice, it will be of no benefit.* Test-driving your knowledge will produce results which are personal to you and which will help shape your self-belief further.

There are many examples of the extent to which our self-belief is constructed by external factors, but I can't help referring to the pressure that many kids tend to put upon themselves as a result of their exposure to the culture of celebrity and the role that social media plays in promoting it. Why? Because I am getting more and more requests from parents who are worried and want advice about their kids' self-esteem and confidence issues. Here's a common example based upon a recent client of mine:

Hannah is the eldest of two daughters in the Smith family. By the age of 15 she had encountered difficulties in her confidence and in her relationships because she believed that she was unattractive and overweight. Hannah believed that if she lost some weight, she would be a lot happier and it would lead to greater levels of acceptance by her school friends, too.

APP ALERT!!

To me, Hannah clearly wanted to feel proud of her body, so that she could be confident the boys would find her attractive, while the 'cool' girls would like her more and include her in their friendship groups. Hannah had never been a slim girl, and her weight had always bothered her a little – but now it had become a self-belief detractor.

Liz, Hannah's mum, had always thought her daughter fine just the way she was, although Hannah's recent interest in her weight had prompted Liz to consider what would be best for her child's physical and emotional well-being. She could see that Hannah believed her weight was holding her back from being in the right crowd at school and she was concerned that if Hannah's weight continued to rise, it might damage her health. Or, if she was to go down the other route and lose weight rapidly, this might also bring its own problems. Liz was worried that Hannah's eating patterns were starting to change and she was becoming very picky with her food.

153

Both Hannah and Liz were convinced that what they believed about Hannah's situation was correct. However, their respective beliefs had evolved through two totally different sets of external influences.

Liz had grown up in an environment where health was always considered to be the most important thing; she has, therefore, always been very cautious when it comes to her children's well-being. Her belief that Hannah's weight was a health issue, rather than a popularity one, was based on this. Liz also believed that the images of women that her daughter tended to access via tv, film, advertising and social media were unrealistic and unrepresentative of the real world.

Liz knew that teenage girls often fluctuate in weight, but this knowledge also led her to believe that it was something to keep an eye on from a health point of view. By looking after Liz's health when she was a child, her mother made sure Liz was rarely ill and never missed a day off school. This factor added to her beliefs.

Meanwhile, Hannah had a completely different set of beliefs. Her thoughts on how teenage girls should look were pretty much based on how they were portrayed in the media, and she had grown up in an environment where the thinner girls were more popular with the other girls and the boys. It seemed that they were having loads more fun and were much more sure of themselves.

Hannah believed, therefore, that she too should lose weight in order to be a member of the 'in crowd'. She had only ever known this way of looking at the situation, and believed she urgently needed to lose some weight, otherwise she would never get to where she wanted to be. She wanted to change right now.

Stalkie's 'UNCOVER YOUR SELF-BELIEFS' WORKOUT

The outcome here is to understand how self-belief is built-up by establishing your beliefs about yourself and how you came to believe them.

Write down ten beliefs that you have about yourself – for example,

"I am a very loyal friend"

"I am a hard worker"

"I have a small attention span"

and so on.

These can be positive and negative beliefs. Alongside each statement, write the reasons why you believe these beliefs to be true.

1

2

3

4

5

6

7

8

9

10

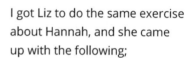

APP ALERT!!

When Hannah did this exercise, these were some of her beliefs;

- *I believe I am fat because when I compare myself with most celebrities and successful people, I am way bigger.*

- *I believe I can't attract boys because they always want to go with slim, attractive and fit girls.*

- *I believe I'm not popular at school because the most popular girls and boys are all ripped and fit.*

I'm sure you get the gist of most of her answers. Not surprisingly, Hannah found this a very difficult and upsetting exercise to do because she could not think of many positive beliefs she had about herself.

I got Liz to do the same exercise about Hannah, and she came up with the following;

- *I believe that Hannah is a very beautiful girl who doesn't need to look like lots of the celebrities featured in magazines, because a lot of them are false, unhappy and being manipulated by fame.*

- *I believe Hannah should concentrate on her health not her weight, and that she must not do anything to harm herself just to lose a few pounds quickly.*

- *I believe Hannah is extremely attractive because she is funny, talented, a great friend and great company. I know a lot of boys think she's great.*

Liz and Hannah's beliefs were completely different, based on their differing environments, past events unique to them, their knowledge, and the results each had achieved.

Stalkie's
'HOW DO YOU VIEW YOURSELF' WORKOUT

APP ALERT!!

The outcome of this workout is to understand the difference between how you view yourself and how your friends and family perceive you.

First, write down ten words that you think accurately portray yourself.

Next, ask a minimum of three friends and family members to come up with ten words that describe you.

1	1
2	2
3	3
4	4
5	5
6	6
7	7
8	8
9	9
10	10

Now, compare the lists – see how similar or how different they are. The more similar the words on the two lists, the more you are behaving as you believe, OR not if there are quite a few differences between the lists.

At this point, I would like to remind you how crucial it is to do all of my *Stalkie Workouts* with your heart. Please, please don't cop out and be anything other than frank and honest with yourself. If you genuinely seek to raise your game in all aspects of your life, you have to have a reality check and a base camp to start your journey from.

You might also be tempted to do the workouts on behalf of your friends and family rather than engaging them to help you – i.e. to complete their parts of the workouts by 'predicting' what they might say about you, rather than getting them to actually divulge what they really think. Please DON'T. This is simply lying to yourself and is a waste of time.

It's understandable that you might feel odd about asking others to become involved in something so personal, but if they are true friends to you, I promise you they will be intrigued and will appreciate being asked to participate. More than likely, once you've shared your new knowledge and intentions with them, they'll wish to become more involved in your journey and even wish to follow a similar path. As my neighbour and friend Neil says, "this stuff is addictive" – the best addiction you could ever wish for.

I've completed these workouts with thousands of people in my time – old, young, male, female, of many different creeds, races and sexual persuasion, from billionaires to those living on handouts, from intellectual heavyweights to those who find it difficult to articulate their thoughts, from philanthropists to life-serving prisoners. And, almost without exception, they have been amazed at the power of this material, learnt new things about themselves and benefited from the education. The thing is to make the process fun, to fully take on board the learnings and then follow through to act upon them.

The Damage of Negative Self-Belief

Hannah believed that her weight was responsible for making her feel negative about herself. But, beneath the surface, her biggest desire was to be accepted by all the 'right' people. She wanted to be proud of herself, and to have confidence. If she could achieve the acceptance of the 'cool' crowd at school, this would be bound to make her feel happy and loved.

She could have quite easily become fixated about her weight, potentially leading to health problems. She found herself in a raw emotional state because she thought she was unattractive, bringing with it the feelings of being unloved, insignificant and insecure.

In this state of mind and body, Hannah was at a crossroads in her young life: She was close to choosing to satisfy her needs in a *negative fashion*, such as self-harming or starving herself, knowing that people would come to her aid and give her the attention, love and significance she craved.

APP ALERT!!

This is the route that Ade had taken in his early life – his negative beliefs and behaviour certainly attracted the attention, love and significance he was after – from like-minded people who colluded with each other on a path to self-destruction and criminality.

This is the route that Neil flirted with too. He went against his positive self-beliefs – of good health, gratitude and appreciation, honesty of communication, never taking things or people for granted – and nearly drove himself to an early grave.

In my own painful experience, when I opted to let fear consume my everyday thoughts and deeds, this triggered me to abandon my health, avoid the people I most cared for and absorb myself in the pursuit of material wealth and status.

DEVELOPING POSITIVE SELF-BELIEF

The Reticular Activating System (RAS)

The Reticular Activating System? What on earth is that and what's it got to do with my self-belief, I hear you ask? The RAS is a diffuse network of nerve pathways in the brainstem connecting the spinal cord, cerebrum and cerebellum, and its role is to mediate our overall level of consciousness.

In other words, it's our 'control centre'. I describe it as a gatekeeper for the signals that are coming in to the brain. It's also one of the most valuable friends you'll ever have!

We all have lots of nerve cells that are reporting data to our brains every second – data about the sounds, smells, tastes, touches, or sights being detected from all parts of the body. But because the conscious brain can only handle between 40-130 messages per second in any meaningful way (these figures depend upon what body of neuroscientific research you read), it needs to filter and prioritise millions of messages and the RAS filters these messages into a manageable flow.

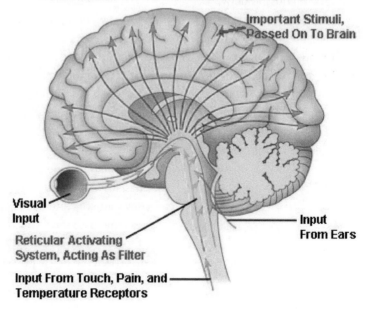

The Reticular Activating System

Important Stimuli, Passed On To Brain

Visual Input

Reticular Activating System, Acting As Filter

Input From Touch, Pain, and Temperature Receptors

Input From Ears

For those of you who prefer graphics and movies to explain this sort of info, there's a really neat video about the RAS that I can recommend on YouTube: just search for Reticular Activating System.

APP ALERT!!

Most nerves run through the RAS and then get sent out to various other parts of the brain for the interpretation of their signals. If it wasn't for this circuitry, your consciousness would be flooded with so much sensory information your decision-making ability would be log-jammed. Pain is a good example of this. Pain signals immediately get sent to the front of your consciousness so they can be analysed and responded to.

But that's just for starters. The RAS is intuitive and learns from your conscious mind what to look out for in your environment. It is the major goal seeking mechanism in your brain. You can tell it what to look for and it will help you find it. Better still, once your RAS is instructed what to look for, whether told consciously or even unconsciously, it will be searching without you even being aware of it. This is one of the untold magical things about the human mind and body.

Your RAS is part of your natural tool kit. It helps you to see the information that you need to. Have you ever noticed, for example, that once you've decided what type of car you're interested in buying, you suddenly start seeing them on all the roads around you? This is your RAS at work, finding and noticing things that are directly connected to what you have been focusing upon.

Your Reticular Activating System also filters things that are unimportant to you, or that you don't need to concentrate on. For example, the noise of trains going by may annoy those who move into a house near a railway line, but after a short time the RAS will activate and seek to screen out the sound of the trains from the mind.

Therefore, *whether your beliefs about yourself are positive or negative*, your RAS will scout around and find more of the very things that you are focusing on and reduce the number of things you are not focusing on. It will always find justification for your beliefs, because your mind wants to prove you right! The implications of this are enormous to each and every one of us.

In Hannah's case, when she only believed the negatives about herself, she could only find evidence to confirm her thoughts were true. She seemed to see 'slim people' everywhere she looked, she would only notice boys with their slim girlfriends, which meant her negative beliefs were 'proving her right'.

Conversely, if she could make the switch and believe positive things about herself, then her RAS would validate these instead. How can such a switch be generated?

An Attitude of Gratitude and Taking the Power Back

All my **You Can Raise Your Game!** principles and the chapters in this book are interlinked. So by reminding yourself of the material we have already covered in the *'An Attitude of Gratitude'* and *'Take the Power Back'* chapters, you'll now know that for Hannah to feel good about herself, she first needed to be aware of how lucky she is and grateful for what she has going for her in her life, rather than allowing negativities to swamp her progress. Once she had found gratitude, she could start instilling the right attitude and progress towards her goals in the way that would serve her best and be sustainable.

Easily said? Yes. Easily done? With discipline, determination and ACTION, also yes.

APP ALERT!!

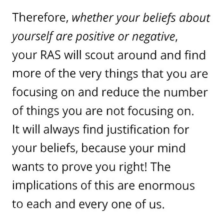

Thoughts and Actions

The power for change and the quality of your life are massively dependent upon the quality of the internal thoughts and questions you have and the ability to take action upon them.

APP ALERT!!

Whenever Hannah went to a restaurant and looked at the menu, she would inevitably ask herself practical and emotional questions such as *"Shall I have a starter? What do I fancy most? That sounds delish, but is it healthy? Should I order dessert? What will people think? Why am I stuffing my face again?"*

Then comes the jumbled thinking and the what ifs; *"I could order the burger and leave some of it to show I'm not greedy, or just order the salad instead? But then I'd probably feel like a pudding..."* Whatever her questions, they were always internal, self-doubting and mostly negative.

If you ask yourself whether you should have a burger and not eat it all in case everyone thinks you're a little piggy, the enquiry is made with a negative presupposition. You'll then end up justifying the thought to yourself and turn it into a reality – you'll actually think that others are looking and judging you when, in actual fact, they're probably not paying any attention to you at all.

Everyday life is bursting at the seams with people telling themselves that they can't do things:

- *Can't lose weight because of my genes*

- *Can't give up smoking because it's an addiction*

- *Can't dump my boyfriend because he'll be nasty to me*

- *Can't tell my girlfriend that I love her in case she thinks I've gone soft and she's got me where she wants me*

- *Can't go for promotion at work because they'll think I'm too big for my boots and I might not be up to it anyway*

THE POWER OF SELF TALK

Is your self-talk helping or obstructing you?

When you talk to yourself – which will be all day long – whose voice do you hear? If you're in negative self-talk mode, you might hear the nagging voice of parents, the threatening voice of people you find intimidating, the voice of anybody that has undermined, criticised or misled you. Or it might be an amalgamation of voices that aren't actually your own. The good news is, you can challenge these voices internally without any fear of reprisals – they're not real, they won't bite. Tell them to go away, ignore them. They can easily be banished, ignored and replaced by something far more like the real you or the you that you want to become.

First of all, you need to become aware of the inner commentary that accompanies your day. Tune into it. Listen to the things that pop into your head and the words you are actually saying to yourself.

- *Can't ask my parents for advice because they'll probably lecture me*

- *Can't go to the doctors because they'll probably tell me I've got something badly wrong with me*

- *Can't apply for that course because I'm not clever enough*

- *Can't go to bed if I'm not tired*

- *Can't possibly stand in front of all those people and make that speech...*

And guess what? All those statements are true, if you tell yourself they are and you don't give yourself a big enough reason or have the courage to make the change.

To get answers that will transform your life, you must ask the right questions. So, whether you think you can or can't, you are probably right!

The likelihood is that you have been consistent over time with the neg-talk, repeating the same phrases in your head time and again until you have reached the point of believing them to be true. Flex the neg muscle, the more the reps, the stronger it will become.

Fortunately, there's more good news here – just because you're clogging up your self-belief with contrary self-talk, it doesn't mean what you're saying is true. Challenge yourself, argue the case for yourself, tell yourself that this self-beating isn't justified (get that RAS to kick in) and don't be afraid to verbalise more empowering thoughts out loud to drown out the neg head inside of you.

Here is an example of a well-known self-talk mantra: *"Every day in every way I'm getting stronger and stronger. I will survive, and never be defeated!"* This is a highly effective way of dispersing negativity – you hear high-performing sportspeople doing it all the time in order to get themselves into a peak state. Don't be afraid to pump you up! Flex the pos muscle, the more the reps, the stronger it becomes. Whenever you find yourself feeding on a neg-phrase, replace it with a pos-phrase and repeat it over and over – it will eventually stick.

I have a certain male friend whose best friend used to start many of her sentences, through sheer habit, with the words *"The trouble is..."*. The trouble is that by framing a sentence in such a way, the rest of the sentence is bound to be critical, or moany, or subversive. You're hardly likely to say *"the trouble is"* and continue with something like *"I love your handsome face, darling"* are you?!

When this was pointed out to her, it took a while for her to realise just how many times she said it, but he remained persistent so that, whenever she said it, he would then butt in and say *"there's no trouble, what trouble, where's the trouble?"* This is also known as a 'pattern interrupt' i.e. interrupting the person's thought pattern at that moment in time by asking a question or by acting outrageously such as jumping up and down or acting like a clown. Now, on the surface, how annoying is that?

However, she also realised that he was doing her a constructive favour by insisting that this phrase could be the tip of a larger problem. *'The trouble is'* was a verbal reflection of much of her inner talk. She admitted that a lot of her self-talk was negatively geared and posed her more questions than she had answers for.

She had always been frustrated at her procrastination and her inability to make decisions quickly and concisely – and to this end her self-talk led to self-doubt, which was holding her back.

Once she banned herself from saying the dreaded phrase inside and out, this was the start of a genuine and acknowledged change in her decision-making capabilities. She's even decided to stay best mates with him!

An evaluation of your self-talk will enable you to see how it fits in with the reality of your situation. I'm not expecting you to instantly view the world through sparkly new rose-tinted glasses BUT I do expect you to at least raise your thinking to a positive view of your life, rather than a downtrodden one.

How would you talk to a friend who you are supporting or giving a pep talk to? Then why not talk to yourself in the same way? Be your own best friend, because *your* life matters to you!

You Can Raise Your Game! is about equipping you to be your own life-coach and then passing your insight forward to other people that you care about in your life.

Achieving Motivational Self-Talk

The strategy here is to find the messages and form of words that are natural and original to you, and resonate with you, rather than borrowing words that seem suitable for the job but might not describe how you actually *feel*.

The process therefore needs a bit of experimenting on your part. Have fun with it and choose words that stimulate and enliven you, to bring out the hero in you. As much as we may recognise the brilliance of famous motivational speeches such as Winston Churchill's

"We'll fight them on the beaches..."

or Martin Luther King Jr.'s

"I have a dream...",

your self-dialogue is personal to you and should create your own reality.

My simple, time-tested tips are to:

- Use easy, short phrases or single words that are unquestionable and beyond doubt in your mind

- Use the present tense (to tell your mind that you are already in the 'happening mode'), such as *"I am an early riser"*, *"I love getting up early"*

- Use a positive feeling or emotion, such as *"Getting up early makes me feel amazing/great/healthy/at my very best"*

- Say these over and over again using positive body language at the same time (remember the Triangle of Communication)

- Write your self-talk statements on a piece of card, on your mobile, on your screen, on a tattoo – wherever they can be used as a constant reminder. (I've just been watching the Wimbledon tennis tournament and have happily spotted some of the top players looking at their own motivational statements when they are resting between games.)

APP ALERT!!

Stalkie's 'SELF-TALK' WORKOUT

The purpose of this exercise is to channel your thoughts towards creating your first qualified, beneficially worded self-talk statements or speeches.

Think of a goal, project or task that you absolutely want to nail. With this goal in mind, break the goal down into baby steps towards starting the goal-getting process and complete the following self-talk phrases, using the tips that you have just read:

"I am.."
(e.g. 'an early riser')

"I love.."
(e.g. 'getting up early')

"I feel at my very best when I...............

..."
(e.g. 'am up at 6.30 every day')

Now say these statements out loud, standing tall, legs slightly apart, shoulders back, head up, with a big smile. Repeat this exercise three times.

A great time to start your new regime of self-talk is when you embark on a new venture. This is when you can use it from day one as a positive instruction manual to achieve the outcome that you want to deliver from the task, without the influence of any negative thoughts that you may have already associated with the task to date. Start with a clean sheet and keep faith in positive interactions only, until these become habitual and pop into your mind without you needing to engineer them.

If you break your new task into small steps, you can then direct your messages precisely to achieving those steps. Let's say, for example, you are starting on a new health regime which entails more exercise and a better diet. This process involves a whole load of mini steps to achieve your big leap; from educating yourself to alter your current eating habits, maybe cutting down on the booze, the snacks and the restaurants or fast food, to perhaps going to bed earlier, getting up earlier, going to the gym or taking up running, cycling, swimming and so on.

APP ALERT!!

This is a lifestyle change, it involves planning and determining a whole new time cycle into your day. It will test your resolve and also test your resistance to temptation (and the temptation of others who may wish to persuade you to break some of your new rules). The size and duration of the task is big, but it's made far smaller by achieving success in each of its steps.

Let's say one of your key baby steps is to get up earlier in the morning, which will then open the door for you to achieve other vital steps in your bigger goal, such as creating the time for some simple exercise and to eat a healthy breakfast before you go to work. You are best to start off focusing on getting up earlier until it becomes a habit, and this is where your self-talk statements should initially be directed.

And here's something to bear in mind – your statements don't always have to be true when you start using them, you just want to programme your mind to believe that they are on the way to becoming true. Your internal speech is there to serve specific purposes. You can use different speeches for different tasks, review them and replace them with new ones as soon as they do the job for you.

In getting up earlier, you need to accept your emotions and the way your body feels. Don't suppress the fact you might feel tired and achy to begin with, but reassure yourself that you knew this is what it would be like, that it's okay to feel like it and remind yourself that you have the determination, the skill and the character to deal with it – it's all part and parcel of being the new hero you desire to be.

Combine your self-talk with positive visual imagery, too. When you go to bed, picturing yourself getting up early, slipping into your t-shirt, trackie bottoms and trainers ready for a power-walk, jog, gym session – whatever you have chosen to do – will all serve to programme your subconscious mind and build your self-belief.

SHORING UP YOUR BELIEF THROUGH VISUALISATION

Your sub-conscious mind is a great ally when it comes to visualisation, because it does not make any distinction between reality and fiction. It will actually pick up on your strongest desire, and then organise the facts about this to form them into a plan.

So, whatever the material you feed your mind, it will always produce a programme designed to achieve this desire. If you visualise often enough and make the visualisation as real, intense and colourful as possible and give your sub-conscious time to work, you will be amazed at the results.

APP ALERT!!

169

These are my five favourite tips to making visualisation a mighty component of self-belief:

1) Find Some Peace and Quiet

No distractions. No interruptions. Mobile off. Better still if you can do it outside, breathe in plenty of clean air and be amongst nature.

2) Clear Your Mind

This is a very difficult thing to do, and yet it's very effective. Just try to sit without thinking of anything; as thoughts come into your head (as they will do at the start of this process), imagine them flowing on a river through your mind and out the other side.

3) Focus

Once your mind is clear, focus on an object in the room or your surroundings – it is quite effective to focus on a stone, charm or candle flame. Once you feel focused, begin visualising.

4) Appeal to All of Your Senses

It is important to use all of your senses when visualising. What will you see when you glimpse into your desired future? What will you hear, smell and feel? What will success taste like?

5) Relax

The most important part of this process is to relax. Let your mind be your guide through your innermost desires. Relax, and enjoy it.

Hannah's visualisation routine was a wonderful success and source of comfort to her, during which she let her imagination paint the most graphic and memorable images in her mind. She explains:

"I thought about all the positives that would come from losing the right amount of weight. I imagined my family's reaction as I walked into a family party looking slim and elegant in my new dress and heels – I've seen the pair I want already and am saving some money to buy them as a reward to myself when I hit the magic weight!

"I visualised being fit and healthy, and able to last a full hockey tournament, reaching the final without cramping up or struggling for breath. I heard the crowd encouraging us and the sound of the girls screaming when the final whistle went and we'd won. I even punched the air in celebration!

"And I imagined some more personal stuff about meeting a boy, but I'm not sharing that with anyone other than my best friend!"

How spot on is all that! It will be a lucky boy who has the privilege of stepping out with our Hannah, I promise you.

Just like programming a computer, you must feed your brain enough information for it to work properly. When Hannah put a lot of effort into her self-talk and visualisation, she was always more likely to be successful; repetition is key and will trigger your Reticular Activating System into action finding evidence to support and prove your thoughts right.

APP ALERT!!

I think you'll gather now the case that I'm putting forward for positive self-belief. Negative self-belief tends to attract negative life consequences. You only have to go on past experience and look around at the people in your everyday life to judge for yourself whether life is better enhanced by positive self-belief, attitude and behaviour...or not.

In the summary that follows we will concentrate on reinforcing the knowledge you've gained from this chapter with the tips and techniques you can apply to develop your own positive self-belief.

"Your beliefs become your thoughts. Your thoughts become your words. Your words become your actions. Your actions become your habits. Your habits become your values. Your values become your destiny."

– Mahatma Gandhi

TOP 10 TIPS TOWARDS UNLOCKING YOUR SELF-BELIEF

1. Self-belief isn't about becoming blind to your weaknesses or believing you are perfect in every way. It is about breaking through self-imposed limitations and focusing on what you will become to serve you best. *Self-belief is learnable.*

2. Self-belief creates the freedom for you to express yourself, make mistakes and see setbacks as learning opportunities rather than confidence-bashers. When your self-belief builds, it builds people's belief in you too.

3. Self-belief is not about dwelling on if's, but's, maybe's and can't's OR saying you'll do one thing, then ending up doing another. Nope. Not allowed.

4. Henry Ford (of Ford Motor Company fame) rightly said, *"Whether you believe you can do a thing or not, you're right"*. Whether your thoughts are positive or negative, your brain's control centre, the Reticular Activating System, will seek out more of the things that you are focusing on and reduce the number of things you are not focusing on. It's there to justify your thoughts and prove you right. Use it positively to fuel self-belief.

5. The power for change and the quality of your life is massively dependent upon the quality of your internal thoughts and self-talk. Positive self-talk consists of authentic and affirming statements about your knowledge, skills and attributes.

APP ALERT!!

6. Always visualise yourself behaving in ways which optimise your probability of success in any given situation. Start by visualising yourself as if you are in a film, acting with confidence, clarity and self-belief. The sequels will soon come more naturally to you.

7. Become your own best coach. What are the supportive things you would say to a friend or family member who needed a boost of confidence or reassurance? Be that coach to yourself when you need it. Talk to yourself as if you were another person. Take a moment, relax, close your eyes and coach yourself in the same friendly, authoritative and confident way that you would expect from your coach.

APP ALERT!!

8. There is often a need for short-term pain to achieve long-term, sustainable gain. Associating bad and painful feelings with your current unwanted belief, *and* understanding the negative consequences that your current belief and behaviour will have upon your life (and the life of those around you) in the future will jump-start you into creating positive leverage for change.

9. Goals without routines are merely cravings; routines without goals are purposeless. Set yourself SMART goals (Specific, Measurable, Achievable, Relevant, Timescales) and break them down into manageable mini-goals with habits and routines to bring them alive.

10. No matter what you decide to do in life, action is everything – having the knowledge and understanding the theoretical tools to gain self-belief is one thing; doing it is another, far greater thing. Never justify why tomorrow is a better day than today to start something new.

07

WHY DO YOU DO THAT?

*Understanding why you
do what you do*

On the surface, many of our everyday decisions and deeds seem to be governed by how we communicate with each other through our words, tone and body language. But I want you to be able to peel back the layers beyond what you can see and hear, and achieve an understanding of the personal drivers that will make your decision-making quick, easy and of the highest quality.

By the 'highest quality', I mean decisions that consistently serve your purposes and needs best, and those whom you care for, and love and depend upon you.

If you search online for, 'How many decisions do I make a day', you'll find a raft of respected sources that will tell you an average adult makes about 35,000 remotely conscious decisions every day. How amazing!

Obviously the mass of our daily decisions seem to be made on automatic pilot, perhaps by routine or habit, starting with what time we decide to get up, wash and preen ourselves, what to wear and have for breakfast, how to get the kids up and ready, and so on. Then there's the seemingly bigger decisions about our jobs and careers, who we'll spend our time with and how, who to date and settle down with, whether to have kids, how to bring them up, where to live, what to believe, what to say?!

Taking on board the frequency, magnitude and consequences of our decisions, is it any wonder that we sometimes get fazed and decision-fatigued? And that we need time-out or a holiday if we're fortunate enough to afford one? But then again, where shall we go? How long shall we go for? Hotel, self-catering, camping? How much will it cost? Yup, more decisions.

One thing I'd like you to do right now, just for a few seconds before we delve deeper, is to marvel at yourself and to be grateful. Firstly, for making so many decisions every day. Secondly, whether you make 35 or 35,000 decisions a day, good or bad, just think that by existing on this earth the majority of us have been granted the amazing ability, free-will and power to make decisions and choices in the first place.

Each and every one of your decisions is based upon your motivation and needs, and the motivation and needs of those around you.

APP ALERT!!

UNDERSTANDING MOTIVATION

Motivation is goal-directed behaviour – a desire to achieve an objective, combined with the energy to work towards that goal. It can also be described as:

- That which arouses, directs and causes persistence of behaviour.

- That which moves one into action (Deckers, L. (2005). *Motivation: Biological, Psychological, and Environmental.* (2nd ed.). Boston: Pearson Education.

- The force within individuals that energises, maintains and controls their behaviour (Westen, D., Burton, L. & Kowalski, R. (2006). *Psychology* (Australian and New Zealand Edition). Milton, Queensland: John Wiley & Sons, p.370.

- The driving force behind behaviour that leads us to pursue some things and avoid others (also Westen et al. as referenced above).

Before we move on, I think it would be helpful to emphasise here a fundamental point already touched on in the *'Ignite Your Self-Belief'* chapter of this book: if you look to other people to provide your motivation and fulfilment in life then you will be disappointed. In short, the only person who can motivate you is you. It's your responsibility.

Motivation is not a reactive thing, it is proactive. In my role as a coach I can guide you towards achieving your goals, but it will be your input and your desire to achieve them that provides the impetus to make this happen.

The next few pages are specifically designed to give you an understanding of what motivation is, the various forms it takes and the tools you can employ to start motivating yourself to get to where you want to be in life.

"People often say that motivation doesn't last. Well, neither does bathing – that's why we recommend it daily."

– Zig Ziglar*

*****Zig Ziglar** was one of America's most influential and beloved encouragers and believers in the maxim that 'everyone could be, do and have more'. I have always loved his ability to condense a concept into a soundbite, such as:

- *"Your attitude, not your aptitude, will determine your altitude"*

- *"Positive thinking will let you do everything better than negative thinking will"*

Zig founded the Zig Ziglar Corporation, which is now run by his son Tom, in 1977. (www.ziglar.com)

Motivation comes in two forms:
Intrinsic and **Extrinsic**.

Intrinsically motivated behaviours
are performed because of the
sense of personal satisfaction that
they bring.

Intrinsic motivation does not
involve working on activities for
the sake of an external reward
– it involves the feeling of inner
pleasure in the activity itself. The
renowned American organisational
theorist Thomas Malone and
social psychologist Mark Lepper
provided a definition of intrinsic
motivation in 1987. They view this
type of motivation as a force that
involves doing activities without
external inducement. Without any
reward, a person is willing to act
as long as they are interested or
personally enjoy the task. (www.
learning-theories.com/intrinsically-
motivating-instruction-malone.html)

Mother Teresa is a great example
of this as she only wanted to help
others because she cared deeply.
There was no pay cheque or special
bonus for her to save lives. She
wanted to do it because it was in
her soul.

During studies conducted in the
early 1970s, researchers found that
intrinsically motivated students
willingly engaged in activities for
the sake of skills improvement
and/or knowledge enhancement.
Intrinsic motivation in these
students was caused by their
interest in mastering a topic rather
than learning the subject to get
good grades. It also emerged
from their belief of having the
skill that made them effective in
achieving their goals as well as their
sense of autonomy towards their
educational results and factors
influencing them.

Extrinsically motivated behaviours, on the other hand, are performed in order to receive something from others or to avoid certain negative outcomes.

As opposed to intrinsic motivation, extrinsic motivation involves executing an action to achieve external rewards or reinforcements. Simply put, the source of extrinsic motivation is from an individual's physical environment.

For instance, bigger salary, more job benefits and high grades are rewards that lead to extrinsic motivation. Crowd-cheering a person and competition are abstract sources of extrinsic motivation. This type of motivation also involves negative reinforcement, as in the threat of punishment, potential job loss or risk of failing grades.

Extrinsic motivation can be explained by looking at the example of the City trader. A City trader will not usually absorb the 24/7 pressure of working in a dealing room because they love it, or because it's good for their health: remember what happened to Nick Leeson, the 'rogue trader' whose misguided dealings in the financial markets led to the collapse of his employer Barings Bank? Apart from a spell in jail, he also contracted cancer from which, thankfully, he has recovered. I can't help but think that the extrinsically motivated 'greed is good' mentality which I pursued so intently many years ago also contributed to my cancer.

No, most City traders will only stand the heat for the very high financial reward it brings. This is extrinsic motivation – if the reward is not high enough, the job won't be done.

Let's look at the different types of motivation in a little more detail.

THE SIX TYPES OF MOTIVATION

There are six types of motivation, each of which can be placed under the banner of either intrinsic or extrinsic:

1. Achievement by your own efforts. This is typically where you decide to work towards a chosen professional qualification, for example, or where you self-teach for whatever trade you wish to take up, or whatever pastime or competency you wish to pursue. The bottom line is that, through your own effort, skill and attitude, you succeed intrinsically.

2. The desire to be outstanding at what you do. Maybe you intrinsically desire to be the best parent you can possibly be or get the very best out of your relationships? In which case you're the sort of person who will make the effort to seek knowledge on the subject from your friends and elders.

    Perhaps you'll study *'Men are from Mars, Women are from Venus'* – the book by American author and relationship counsellor John Gray which has sold more than 15 million copies and states that most common relationship problems between men and women are a result of fundamental psychological differences between the sexes, which can be understood in terms of the distinct ways they respond to stress and stressful situations (www.marsvenus.com)

    Or perhaps you'll just take time to listen and talk as much as you can with your loved ones, and find out what really motivates them.

By contrast, the remaining four types of motivation are fuelled by extrinsic factors; these are:

3. The wish to gain status with experts or with people you hold in high esteem – in other words, gaining recognition as a leader in your field.

4. The wish to gain status with colleagues, friends and family. Do you want your colleagues to respect you because you are good at your job? Or your friends and family to admire your personal qualities? Is the question of how people perceive you a motivating factor in your life?

5. 'Thing' motivation. Lots of people are highly motivated by 'things' – material possessions, assets or status symbols such as cars, items of clothing, bling or toys. Those motivated by material things are also more likely to want to keep the things they have, as well as to work harder on acquiring new things.

6. The quest to win and to be number one: 'the big cheese'.

How important is this to you? Do you have to be number one? Will you do anything to win? Sometimes, people cross the line to win at all costs and don't play fair. Others play within the rules and use this as the springboard to excellence.

APP ALERT!!

WHERE DO YOU WANT TO BE?

Many of my business clients occupy leadership positions and already recognise how crucial motivation is. The most outstanding leaders that I have ever worked with, without fail, also realise that their colleagues do a job to the optimum ability when they are fully engaged and want to do it. Here, intrinsic motivation is key.

Self-Determination Theory (SDT) was first developed over 40 years ago by Edward L. Deci and Richard M. Ryan. This theory is concerned with human motivation, personality and optimal functioning. Rather than just the amount of motivation, Self-Determination Theory focuses on different types of motivation.

Self-Determination Theory supports the notion that intrinsic motivation helps people perform work-related tasks efficiently and effectively.

Leaders who put Self-Determination Theory into practice create conditions in the work environment that aim to optimise employee motivation via two ways: self motivation – doing a job because it's intrinsically consistent with the employee's values; and controlled motivation – doing a job because the employee feels pressured by other forces to do it.

For a straightforward, snapshot overview of Self-Determination Theory, I would recommend a browse at the following website: www.positivepsychologyprogram.com/self-determination-theory

From personal experience, the qualities to look for when hiring your team are a person's desire to be outstanding, their drive for sheer exhilaration, and a hunger to test their limits. In a team member, you need to look for someone who wants to succeed. Their individual standards must be geared towards excellence.

If a team member is more worried about the incentives they will receive for their services than their contribution to the firm, there is cause for concern. In essence, if your candidate is 'thing' motivated you should be wary. If they are not doing the job for the good of just doing it, when someone else comes along and offers bigger rewards, they will move on. If another company offered a car and a higher salary, they would take it. They would probably move again as soon as someone could offer them a better deal than that. If the candidate has a desire to be number one, be wary; there can only be one person at the top. If they got second place, would they stop trying?

Motivation is just as essential in your personal life. If you want to improve any areas of your life – perhaps you want to be a more caring friend, or to find a lasting relationship – then you must be motivated to put in the effort required. You are intrinsically motivated when you have a desire to improve, and to be the best. You Can Raise Your Game by continually learning, which is why I would urge you to follow up on the references that I make throughout this book.

Bill Gates. the legendary Microsoft founder, for example, was famous for sticking to his annual 'Think Week' in which he consumed as many books, articles and research papers as he possibly could (apparently 112 during one session). In 2015, Mark Zuckerberg, Facebook co-founder and CEO, had a personal development priority of reading a book every two weeks. These guys are a great example of 'you need to read to lead'.

If you're not a keen reader, then there is a wealth of open source material available in audio and visual formats across the internet – I know that the videos and short films I post on my own site and share via my social media platforms are just as popular as my written materials.

Intrinsic motivation is the most fulfilling, both in business and our day-to-day lives. If you rely on extrinsic forms of motivation, and one day that external influence is not there, you won't be motivated. However, if you are motivated from the inside, then wherever you are, whatever you are doing, you will always be capable of rising to the occasion.

NEEDS AND DEEDS

The decisions you make and the actions or deeds that they lead to are all related to the personal needs you have to fulfil in your daily life to achieve balance and happiness.

In order to appreciate how this works, let's start with the 'basic human needs' as expressed by prominent psychologists, particularly the ones who have made a difference to my way of thinking and will, I hope, make a difference to your way of thinking too.

One of the most famous of these is Abraham Maslow*. His *'hierarchy of needs'* (1943 & 1954) is a motivational theory in psychology comprising five tiers of human needs, as you can see from this pyramid depiction.

Maslow stated that people are motivated to achieve certain needs and that some needs take precedence over others. Our most basic need is for physical survival, and this will be the first thing that motivates our behaviour. Once that level is fulfilled, the next level up is what motivates us, and so on.

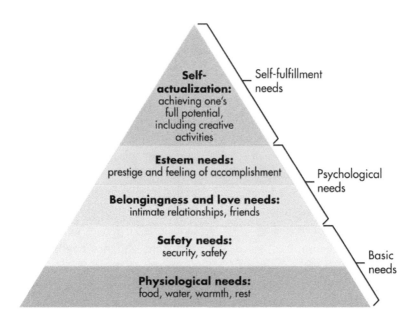

Self-fulfillment needs

Self-actualization: achieving one's full potential, including creative activities

Psychological needs

Esteem needs: prestige and feeling of accomplishment

Belongingness and love needs: intimate relationships, friends

Basic needs

Safety needs: security, safety

Physiological needs: food, water, warmth, rest

185

This five-stage model can be divided into deficiency needs and growth needs. The first four levels are often referred to as deficiency needs (D-needs), and the top level is known as growth or being needs (B-needs).

The deficiency needs motivate people when they are unmet. Also, the need to fulfil such needs will become stronger the longer they are denied. For example, the longer a person goes without food, the hungrier they will become. The case study I shared with you about my mate Ade (in the *'Fear into Power'* and *'Take the Power Back'* chapters) is a good example of this.

You have to satisfy the lower level 'deficit' needs before progressing on to meet higher level 'growth' needs.

*Abraham Harold Maslow
(1908–1970) was an American psychologist who was a professor at Alliant International University, Brandeis University, Brooklyn College, New School for Social Research, and Columbia University. He stressed the importance of focusing on the positive qualities in people, as opposed to treating them as a "bag of symptoms". A *Review of General Psychology* survey, published in 2002, ranked Maslow as the tenth most cited psychologist of the 20th century.

When a deficit need has been satisfied it will go away, and we become habitually directed towards meeting the next set of needs.

Growth needs continue to be felt and may become stronger once they have been engaged. Once these growth needs have been reasonably satisfied, we may be able to reach the highest level called 'self-actualization'.

We are all capable and have the desire to move up the hierarchy to meet self-actualization but our progress is often disrupted by a failure to meet lower level needs. This is where our life-jolting experiences – such as I encountered through becoming ill, losing my job and being separated from my wife and children – can cause us to waver between the levels of the hierarchy. It's rare that anyone moves in one arrow-like direction!

Maslow noted that only up to 2% of people become fully self-actualized because our society and lifestyle rewards motivation primarily based on esteem, love and other social needs.

In the 1960s and 1970s Maslow expanded his hierarchy of needs to include 'cognitive', 'aesthetic' and 'transcendence' needs (as you can see from the next pyramid depiction).

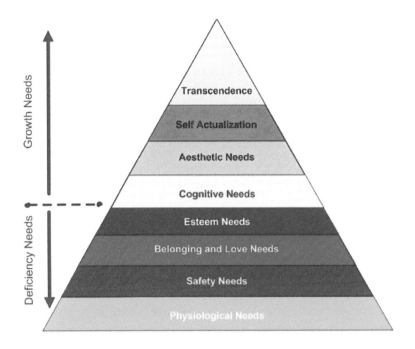

From the bottom up, the needs are:

1. Biological and Physiological needs – air, food, drink, shelter, warmth, sex, sleep etc.

2. Safety needs – protection from elements, security, order, law, stability etc.

3. Love and Belonging needs – friendship, intimacy, trust and acceptance, receiving and giving affection and love. Affiliating, being part of a group (family, friends, work).

4. Esteem needs – self-esteem, achievement, mastery, independence, status, dominance, prestige, managerial responsibility, etc.

5. Cognitive needs – knowledge and understanding, curiosity, exploration, need for meaning and predictability.

6. Aesthetic needs – appreciation and search for beauty, balance, form etc.

7. Self-Actualization needs – realising personal potential, self-fulfilment, seeking personal growth and peak experiences.

8. Transcendence needs – helping others to achieve self-actualization.

SELF-ACTUALIZATION

My desire to spend time sharing Maslow's work with you is that his interest and his studies were directed towards human potential and how to personally grow in order to fulfil it, which is what **You Can Raise Your Game!** is all about.

'Self-actualized' people are those who find a purpose, are fulfilled and doing pretty much all they are capable of. As we are all unique the motivation for self-actualization takes us down different paths, from creative arts to commerce, from teaching to sport, from being an ideal parent or caring for others to mastering technology.

Self-actualization is a continual process, but by studying people he thought were self-actualized, such as Abraham Lincoln, Albert Einstein, Gandhi and Mother Teresa (all feature in our top 50 'most inspiring people' poll in the *'Inspiration and Fulfilment'* chapter of this book), Maslow explored and captured a list of 15 characteristics that they shared to a strong degree:

- They perceive reality efficiently and can tolerate uncertainty

- Accept themselves and others for what they are

- Spontaneous in thought and action

- Problem-centred (not self-centred)

- Unusual sense of humour

- Able to look at life objectively

- Highly creative

- Resistant to enculturation (the behaviour of the surrounding culture), but not purposely unconventional

- Concerned for the welfare of humanity

- Capable of deep appreciation of basic life experience

- Establish deep interpersonal relationships with a few people

- Peak experiences

- Need for privacy

- Democratic attitudes

- Strong moral/ethical standards

Now, we can't pretend this list of characteristics is a blueprint for the perfect human being. It's well known that Einstein, for example, could also be rude, unsociable, wacky and vain, but he came as close as anyone to achieving his potential, living life to the full and creating an indelible legacy. And if we look at behaviours that Maslow concluded lead to self-actualization, there are many I would be proud to have carved on my tombstone:

- Experiencing life like a child, with full absorption and concentration

- Trying new things instead of sticking to safe paths

- Listening to your own feelings in evaluating experiences instead of the voice of tradition, authority or the majority

- Avoiding pretence ('game playing') and being honest

- Being prepared to be unpopular if your views do not coincide with those of the majority

- Taking responsibility, working hard

- Trying to identify your defences and having the courage to give them up

APP ALERT!!

THE SIX BASIC HUMAN NEEDS

American coach and psychologist Anthony Robbins* has been a constant source of enlightenment for me throughout my life. Tony introduced his model for the six human needs in 2006, at the famous TED conference in Monterey, California. That talk, which was called *"Why We Do The Things We Do,"* was one of the first six TED talks ever, and is now the No. 8 most viewed TED talk of all time.

According to Tony, whatever emotion you're after, whatever goal you pursue – whether it's building a business, getting married, raising a family or travelling the world – there are six basic, universal needs that make us tick and drive all human behaviour.

Every single person in the world has these same six needs, but each of us values them in different ways, and each of us has varied beliefs about what it means to satisfy those needs. This is what becomes the driving force behind everything we do, and determines the direction of our lives.

This model is one that I closely buy into and frequently use with my own coaching clients. I first saw Tony apply his needs-learning principles when he used them to undertake live, 'on-stage' interventions in matters of conflict between couples. When I witnessed first-hand some of the fantastic transformations and breakthroughs that his clients experienced, I was sold!

The first four of the basic needs are defined as the needs of the personality or achievement. They are:

• *Security (or Certainty)*

First of all, we need certainty, safety, security, comfort, order, stability, control and consistency in our lives. When we are certain about how things work and how others behave we can predict what will happen in the future and so feel safe.

When we are certain about others, we can trust them. When we feel safe, we can relax and reduce our constant scanning for threats.

• *Variety (or Uncertainty)*

While certainty is important, too much ain't fun... we also want surprise, challenges, excitement, stimulation and novelty to add interest and fun to our lives. This is why we try new things, take risks and gamble, even when we don't need to do so.

These first two are a paradox, but work with each other. If there is an imbalance in one, you could seek the other.

• *Significance and Importance*

We need meaning and pride in our lives and want our lives to have purpose and direction. We want to be wanted, loved, feel special, important and for others to look up to us. We may gain this in many different ways, from becoming well-qualified to being friendly and helping others. Internal significance satisfies yourself that you are doing something which makes you feel important. External significance involves the image that you project to the outside world such as looking good or driving the right car so that people notice you.

Significance is related in Maslow's needs model to esteem and self-actualization.

• *Love and Connection*

This is the need for communication, approval and attachment, to feel connected with, intimate and loved by other human beings. Without company, we easily get lonely. We are social animals and connecting with other people extends our sense of who we are.

Just as variety balances certainty, so outer connection with others balances the inner need for significance of the self. But these can also be paradoxical; too much time hunting significance might put at risk finding deep and intimate relationships that rely upon love and connection.

The remaining two needs are 'needs of the spirit' and provide the structure for fulfilment and happiness:

• *Growth*

Beyond satisfying the previous needs, we want to learn and experience different things to become more than we are. For this purpose we study and want to develop our careers. As a higher need, we can live without it and some people seek little in the way of growth, while others are highly motivated to make something more of themselves Growth is related in Maslow's needs model to self-actualization.

SATISFYING OUR NEEDS

Everyone finds different ways of satisfying these needs, positively or negatively. Some ways of satisfying them are good for us, good for others and good for society, while some are bad for us, bad for others and bad for society. Just to clarify with a few examples:

A positive way of meeting *security/ certainty* might be to pursue the recognised education path of going to school, gaining further qualifications with an eye on getting a good job and making a good living. Or maybe following a faith or doctrine.

A negative way might be through avoiding challenges, keeping a low and lazy profile, holding on to an abusive relationship or cultivating a drug habit.

A positive way of meeting *variety/ uncertainty* might be by exploring new hobbies or topics of interest, trying new things such as new foods or travelling to new places.

- *Contribution*

Contribution takes into account other people and the world at large. If we are active in contributing to other individuals and groups, rather than just 'belonging', we increase our connection with them and it feels good as our sense of identity is expanded. This could be helping out your family, doing charitable work, organising events for your local school, church or social community.

Contribution is also related in Maslow's needs model to belonging and self-actualization.

APP ALERT!!

A negative way might be by having an affair, or a similar relationship drama, under- or overeating, binge drinking, driving too fast and so on.

A positive way of meeting *significance* is by being recognised as an expert in a pursuit, subject or a sport or by providing for your family or doing meaningful work for your community. Some will need to make a major contribution to humanity to feel significant. A negative way might be by being the worst at something or by having low self-esteem, by being a bully, destroying things or tearing others down.

Some will meet their need for *love and connection* by being the best partner they can be for their loved ones, or being socially helpful, supportive, caring and kind.

Negatively, we might meet our need for connection by dominating others or attention seeking through creating and broadcasting problems in our lives to others.

Positive *growth* can be emotional, physical or intellectual – through educating ourselves, exposing ourselves to new situations, working out, or taking classes.

It is possible to fulfil a growth need negatively by becoming a tyrant in your own family, your workplace, or wider community, at worst through inhumane acts.

Parents *contribute* positively to their children by nurturing and educating them. Or we can partake in good charitable, sociable and community acts. The converse of this is destroying others and marginalising their efforts.

Now let's get down to business. In order to understand why you make the decisions that you do, and to give you the power to re-calibrate them from now on, it helps to look at the order of priority you put on your needs.

PRIORITISING YOUR NEEDS

Stalkie's
'NEEDS PRIORITISATION' WORKOUT

Take the list of six basic human needs. Beginning with just two of them, ask yourself which is more important. For example:

Question: What is more important to me, 'love and connection' or 'growth'?

Answer (for example): 'Love and connection'.

APP ALERT!!

Now, ask yourself the next question by adding a further basic need to the one you chose as your first answer. To continue with our example:

Question: What is more important to me, 'love and connection' or 'variety'?

Continue like this until you have gone through the whole list, using each need in turn.

This is quite a complex process, so I have included a table here similar to the one that Tony Robbins devised and uses throughout his seminars. By using this table and putting in your own answers, you will discover your number one need. If you continue this exercise with the remaining needs, again and again, you will have a final list of personal priorities. This list will make you aware of the motivators behind your own decision-making process.

WHICH IS MORE IMPORTANT OF THE TWO?

WRITE ANSWER HERE:

Love and Connection OR
Growth

\>

_____

Love and Connection OR
Variety

\>

_____

Love and Connection OR
Significance

\>

_____

Love and Connection OR
Security

\>

_____

Love and Connection OR
Contribution

\>

_____

Growth OR
Variety

\>

_____

Growth OR
Significance

\>

_____

Growth OR
Security

\>

_____

Growth OR
Contribution

\>

_____

Variety OR
Significance

\>

_____

Variety OR
Security

\>

_____

Variety OR
Contribution

\>

_____

Significance OR
Security

\>

_____

Significance OR
Contribution

\>

_____

Security OR
Contribution

\>

_____

Your next step is to establish your personal priority of needs. Each answer scores one point, so total up the score for each need from the answers you wrote down and enter the scores in the table below.

NEED	POINTS	RANK
Love and Connection	>	>
Growth	>	>
Variety	>	>
Significance	>	>
Security	>	>
Contribution	>	>

If any of the scores for the needs are the same – eg 'Growth' scores a total of 2 and 'Variety' also scores a total of 2, then take a look at your table and see which need you voted for when you had to choose between the two of them. Give the greater rank to the one you originally voted for. Repeat this process between each of the needs that have the same score, to complete your ranking accurately.

The example below is actually a real exercise that I did with Fergus, a client of mine, and you can see what we ascertained together as the exercise progressed.

He works in sales where he manages a team, he has a wife who is a school teaching assistant, they have two young children, he plays rugby and is in a quiz team with some of his rugby pals.

NEED		POINTS		RANK
Love and Connection	>	5	>	1
Growth	>	1	>	5
Variety	>	0	>	6
Significance	>	4	>	2
Security	>	3	>	3
Contribution	>	2	>	4

In ranking terms, his needs were:

- Love and connection
- Significance
- Security
- Contribution
- Growth
- Variety

How does this list compare with yours? And what can we deduce from it?

NEEDS AND THEIR VEHICLES

As we move on to explore your needs in more depth, we need to distinguish between a 'need' and a 'vehicle'. People often believe the vehicle is what they want but, in reality, it's the underlying need that the vehicle is supporting. A vehicle will supply you with a host of feelings, all of which directly feed your needs.

What's a prime example of a vehicle? Money, that's what. Money is not a need, it is not a value, it is a vehicle that you pay for things with – those things can then supply you with feelings that directly feed your needs.

To illustrate, if you buy a car, it gives you the feeling of freedom, and freedom feeds the basic needs of security, significance and variety.

Likewise, I had a friend who was desperate to become a police officer, citing his need for 'job satisfaction'. In reality, the job proved to be the perfect vehicle to deliver his basic need for both external importance and for contribution. Perfect for him.

Looking at Fergus's list, the love and connection he gets from his family, friends and work colleagues should be more critical to him than anything else – so that his vehicles for love and connection are the people around him.

However, when I conducted a 'needs and vehicles chart' with Fergus, the information he supplied gave some conflicting data to interpret:

Fergus's 'Needs and Vehicles' Chart

VEHICLES: NEEDS SCORE:	WORK	WIFE	KIDS	RUGBY	QUIZZING
Security	8/10	7/10	9/10	9/10	9/10
Variety	8/10	4/10	8/10	9/10	9/10
Significance	10/10	4/10	10/10	10/10	8/10
Love and Connection	9/10	3/10	9/10	9/10	7/10
Growth	10/10	2/10	8/10	8/10	9/10
Contribution	10/10	4/10	6/10	10/10	10/10
TOTAL	55/60	24/60	50/60	55/60	52/60

Warning signs, Fergus! On observing his chart, there were some eerie echoes of what my chart would have looked like in my earlier life when I went through years of being extrinsically motivated and meeting virtually all of my needs through work and through socialising with my mates rather than spending quality time with my wife and daughter.

As you know, I became emotionally and physically ill – not something that I would like Fergus to go through.

It transpires that his job and rugby are the most important vehicles in his life; they provide him with a feeling of empowerment and importance, and it is this that feeds his need for significance.

Fergus places more emphasis on this than security because he says he wouldn't mind changing his job, as long as he was moving to another significant position heading up a sales team within a bigger company.

That sort of move would give him more of a challenge, and his need for significance would be intensified – plus, he would presumably earn more money. This would again give him more significance and then, once he has overcome the initial challenge of variety (which he is not too keen on), he would feel much more secure. He would find this increases the feeling of security that his job could give him.

Because Fergus gives significance quite a high priority, he likes to come home and let his wife Beth know all about what he has achieved during the day. Beth, a gem of a lady who understands her hubby really well, doesn't always give him all the praise that he craves for, because she is usually pretty tired from being at work and looking after the kids by the time he comes home from his rugby and quiz exploits. Pre-children, Beth used to make her choices in line with Fergus's needs, but when he showed her the results of the needs exercise that we did, she really understood how and why Fergus says and does certain things.

Beth often used to make decisions based on Fergus's need for importance and significance – she wouldn't decide where to eat, what clothes to buy, or where to go on holiday without consulting him. This made him feel important and significant, which she willingly complied with; however, what we discovered is that neither of them are quite so accommodating now they have a family to look after. In fact, Beth feels pretty down-trodden and undervalued.

Although his need for significance is greater than for security, Fergus does want to feel secure over and above his desire to contribute. His needs for growth and variety are not that high and he's not that bothered about learning new skills; he likes his routine which, sadly, involves him not being with his family as often as Beth would like.

Like so many of us, Fergus wants to achieve balance in his life but required a reality check. Doing the chart flushed out the need for Fergus to re-evaluate his priorities, which resulted in us moving on to discuss some of the communication techniques that would help him to have the honest conversations he clearly had to have with Beth about both their feelings.

Bringing Fergus and Beth together for a joint needs exercise enabled him to better see the benefits of growth and learning; he's now enjoying a better relationship with Beth and his kids as a result. When Beth did the test she found that security, rather than significance, was high on her list of priorities. She actually likes Fergus to make the decisions for her as it makes her feel more secure, but he was falling way too short in meeting her love and connection needs.

Fortunately, these things are not fixed in our lives. This is where coaching and learning about human psychology gives us the opportunity to adapt and grow.

HOW TO IDENTIFY AND MEET YOUR PERSONAL NEEDS

Fergus's chart is just like a business balance sheet giving him a snapshot of where his personal 'business' was at; it shows the assets and liabilities, and whether his business is in profit or loss.

Stalkie's 'PERSONAL NEEDS' WORKOUT

Now fill in one of these charts for yourself. Remember all your scoring must be true and honest – don't kid yourself! You will see that the blank chart lists all of the basic human needs in the first column and some examples of vehicles in the top column across – I'd like you to choose your own vehicles here, to suit your life and interests.

201

Work through each human need, giving each primary vehicle in your life a score out of ten – ten means that the vehicle fulfils the need and one means that it doesn't. For example, if your children give you quite a lot of security then perhaps put a score of eight, and if they provide lots of variety in your life then maybe give that a nine and so on.

APP ALERT!!

Once you have a score for all your vehicles, total the scores for each vehicle to discover just how effective they are being for you.

VEHICLES (e.g.): NEEDS SCORE (OUT OF 10):	WORK	RELATION- SHIPS	SOCIAL	HEALTH	MONEY
Love and Connection					
Growth					
Variety					
Significance					
Security					
Contribution					
TOTAL (OUT OF 60)					

BALANCING YOUR NEEDS

I now want you to focus upon the benefits of balancing your needs, which can be done by interpreting your personal chart. Again, I am going to use some case studies to illustrate how reading other people's charts can help you read your own.

I coached three women who are all in business. They don't know each other and were coached separately. They have similar traits in common; all are considered successful within a business sense.

One runs her own chain of hair and beauty salons, one is a Managing Director of a recruitment business and one is an HR Director for a multinational company. Between them, they control millions of pounds worth of budgets and look after hundreds, if not thousands, of colleagues and customers. They are all very well paid and respected within their professions, but none of them is in a successful relationship. Two of them have children, but all are currently single.

As you see from their charts, all have major needs met at work and this has many repercussions for them – it particularly affects the balance of their lives and their significant relationships.

This is how their charts look:

Business Owner

VEHICLES: NEEDS	WORK	FRIENDS	SON	FAMILY	PARTNER
Security	10/10	10/10	9/10	5/10	5/10
Variety	10/10	10/10	10/10	5/10	5/10
Significance	10/10	5/10	9/10	4/10	5/10
Love and Connection	10/10	10/10	10/10	3/10	5/10
Growth	10/10	7/10	10/10	3/10	4/10
Contribution	10/10	9/10	10/10	6/10	3/10
TOTAL	60/60	51/60	58/60	26/60	27/60

Managing Director

VEHICLES: NEEDS	WORK	FRIENDS	HOME
Security	10/10	6/10	9/10
Variety	9/10	7/10	8/10
Significance	9/10	6/10	9/10
Love and Connection	10/10	5/10	6/10
Growth	10/10	4/10	6/10
Contribution	10/10	4/10	8/10
TOTAL	58/60	32/60	46/60

HR Director

VEHICLES:
NEEDS

NEEDS	WORK	DAUGHTER	FAMILY	DANCING
Security	8/10	8/10	8/10	5/10
Variety	10/10	10/10	7/10	9/10
Significance	10/10	10/10	6/10	5/10
Love and Connection	10/10	10/10	8/10	9/10
Growth	10/10	10/10	6/10	9/10
Contribution	10/10	10/10	6/10	5/10
TOTAL	**58/60**	**58/60**	**41/60**	**42/60**

The two women who have children have ended up relying on them to meet their needs. This isn't a bad thing – children can supply many of their parents' needs and will, of course, have many needs met by their parents in return. But this should be seen in conjunction with all the other information in the chart. When needs are being met mainly or wholly by the children, most children will find this a burden.

This type of scenario is echoed in the movie, *'About a Boy'* where a child lives alone with his mother. He is the centre of her life and vice versa, so he ends up doing anything to show his love for his mother. Scared to face reality, to look in the mirror and to appreciate that she does need to let go, the mother finds it difficult to accept that she has challenges and faults that need to be fixed – and quickly.

She has focused her needs around the boy. Her attitude is *'all men are useless and I can cope without them, thank you very much'*, but the truth of the matter is that she is not coping alone. The relationship she has with her child is a substitute for the relationship she desires with a partner.

Rather than find the time and courage to develop a worthwhile relationship with a partner, she finds it easier to satisfy her needs by putting pressure on her son because there is no risk taking the short-term pleasure and living in long-term pain.

These charts should help you come to terms with the fact that creating the correct balance in your life can impact positively upon others, but getting to this position requires an honest analysis of yourself if you are to face your fear.

If you ever drift from relationship to relationship or job to job, there is no excuse for wondering why. If you tend to blame the other person, your employers, your upbringing, even your astrological chart, then you need to face up to your own weaknesses. Who's always the one person at the scene of your various crimes?!

One of my ambitions in writing this book was to give you the power to look at yourself in an objective way, to discover the real person inside and to be able to coach yourself. This involves careful use of the techniques that I have been showing you and if it sometimes proves difficult or confusing, amazingly this is because you are about to have a breakthrough. So please do persist through the pain barrier of difficulty as you create new pathways of thinking in your brain. If you need any help call our office and we can put you in touch with one of our coaches.

If you do it honestly and conscientiously, you will improve and increase your talents. You will identify both your weak and positive areas. You will become a better person and will be able to live and care as an individual.

By understanding how you are motivated, what your predominant needs are and how they affect your behaviour, you will realise what you should keep and what you should change about your behaviour to ensure you get the very best possible outcome from every situation.

Your decisions and actions will externalise consistently with your purpose and values, giving you balance and peace of mind.

Understanding the motivation and needs of the many significant people in your life will also allow you to play to their needs and achieve the highest quality outcomes. You will be able to use your authority and become a positive force for good within your circle of influence.

Stalkie's Summary
TOP 10 TIPS FOR MAKING 35,000 GREAT DECISIONS A DAY

1. Poor decisions are often a result of focusing on short-term needs rather than the long-term consequences of our actions. Choose actions that best serve your long-term purpose and goals.

2. We tend to make better decisions when the problems are perceived as belonging to someone else. When facing a tricky decision, distance yourself from the problem you face. Ask yourself what your role models would do, or what advice you would give to someone else facing the same decision.

3. Don't let emotions hold you back. According to Dr. Daeyeol Lee, from the Solomon H. Snyder Department of Neuroscience at Johns Hopkins University School of Medicine, effective decision-making is not only based on facts and logic but on stored emotional memories that remain covert and help guide us unconsciously – it would not be possible without emotional input to provide motivation, meaning and needs-meeting.

4. Don't follow the crowd. Trust your instinct. When we rely too heavily on social information, provided by our friends and colleagues, for example, we begin to ignore our instincts and become less responsive to changes in our natural environment.

5. Don't dally. The more time it takes to make a decision, the less confident we feel. NYU's Center for Neuroscience discovered that our brains interpret decisions that take a longer amount of time as less confident ones.

6. Avoid making lots of important decisions in a short period of time. Decision fatigue – when the brain gets tired – leads us to give less thought to our decisions or to choose 'safe' options. Take a rest period in a well ventilated, oxygen-rich environment.

APP ALERT!!

7. We make better decisions in the morning. Organisational psychologist Dr Amantha Imber recommends scheduling major decisions before 11am – this is when serotonin is at its natural high which helps to calm our brains and makes us feel less risk averse.

8. A University of Twente research project discovered that if we are hungry, thirsty or sexually aroused, these physical desires can invade the decision-making areas of our brain, making us feel more desire for big rewards when we make choices – in other words, we'll make higher risk choices and want for more. You have been warned!

9. Weigh the options. What's the best and worst-case scenario? Take a solid look at the pros and cons and go with the longer list. Ask yourself would you be better off with or without this thing, person or situation? What can it bring to your life that will help you be happier, healthier, more fulfilled? Is it something you truly want or just wishful thinking?

10. Just do it! Try it now. Pick a decision you've been putting off, give yourself three minutes and make it. See how good it feels when you decide to Raise Your Game!

APP ALERT!!

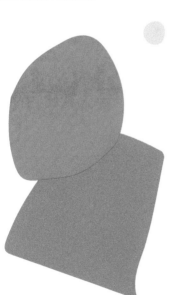

08

YOU CAN BE AN INFLUENCER

Improve your ability to communicate effectively

With a basic grounding in some of the factors that lie behind decision-making, we'll move on to understanding the art of communication and how to make it work for you. My outcome is for you to have absolute faith in your ability to make the decisions that serve your life best... and then to deliver those decisions using your powerful communication skills.

Decision-making is very closely linked with communication in two ways. Firstly, when you make a decision, you have to communicate it effectively in order to achieve the outcome you desire. The quality of your communication is essential in order to get your message across effectively. Secondly, you must be able to fully understand the message of someone who is communicating to you.

Talking is not just about using a plain and simple bunch of words (i.e. 'what you say is what you mean') which will always be interpreted by your audience just as you intended. Communication is far more complex than that, as this simple exercise will show:

Stalkie's 'MEANING OF WORDS' WORKOUT

Write down ten words in the space opposite – they could be: love, hate, shopping, football, eating, work, friends, money, reading, exercise... anything.

Then, write down three descriptive words for each of the ten original words that you have chosen.

Ask someone you know (in your family or at work, it doesn't really matter) to do exactly the same thing with exactly the same words.

You will find that many of the descriptive words are completely different to the starter word. For example, your descriptive words for 'love' could be 'peace, intimacy, ecstasy' – or they could be 'lack of freedom, annoying, petty'. Everyone's descriptions will differ according to their values and emotions, and you'll see just how many words can be used to describe the single starter word.

If people can attribute so many, and such a big range of, meanings to just one word, see how crucial it is to communicate effectively in your everyday life?

WORDS: **DESCRIPTIONS:**

_____   _____

_____   _____

_____   _____

_____   _____

_____   _____

_____   _____

_____   _____

_____   _____

The subject of language and communication is vast and fascinating, but rather than take up too many pages on the psychology of language, I'll point those who wish to drill deeper into this subject in the direction of some superb experts in this field such as Wilhelm Wundt*, Jean Piaget* and Noam Chomsky*. This frees me up to concentrate on addressing some of the most common and thorniest issues that we all experience around verbal and non-verbal communication: they always feature at the top of the list of 'things to fix' with my business and private coaching clients.

*Wilhelm Wundt was the founder of the first experimental psychology laboratory in Leipzig, Germany in 1879. His research was around the link between the mind and the body, using language as a means of studying the mind. He wrote about language acquisition, comprehension, production, sign language and reading, and developed a theory of speech production using the sentence as the unit of analysis. A good starting point for more detail about Wundt can be found via McLeod, S. A. (2008). Wilhelm Wundt. Retrieved from www. simplypsychology.org/wundt.html

Human beings are highly complex communicators. Over the course of any given day, you may communicate in many different situations, using a variety of channels from face-to-face encounters, where you're separated by inches from somebody, to telephone and online, where you could be separated by half the world. You communicate when you can easily be seen and also when you're not visible. With these various methods at your disposal, the need for clarity of understanding and message is paramount.

Have you ever wondered why it is that you get on really well with some people, while others are hard to understand? Some people speak really slowly and choose their words precisely, but others talk so fast you haven't a clue what they are saying. Everybody is different; we're all individuals, and everyone has their own mode of communication.

Let's move forward on the basis that human language can be described as a set of channels, which we all have, that enable us to transmit and receive information.

*Jean Piaget was a French developmental psychologist who played an extremely influential role in how we understand development, including language, in children. He is most famous for introducing his four stages of cognitive development (www.piaget.org)

*The work by Noam Chomsky, and experts such as George Miller at Harvard, led to a revolution in psychology towards the cognitive perspective. This was crucial to the birth of psycholinguistics, turning attention away from behaviourism toward language and mental processes. Cognitive psychology became the study of how people perceive, organise, remember and use information. Cognitive psychology and psycholinguistics converged to study how people produce and comprehend language (www.chomsky.info)

Think of it in terms of radio station transmissions. Some people will be tuned into Radio Four, the frequency where everything is articulate and precise; others prefer Radio One, where they want the latest music and news. Now, the difference between these two stations is not the problem, but difficulties could arise if the wavelengths became mixed between transmitting and receiving information. If someone was broadcasting on Radio Four, but you were receiving their message on the Radio One frequency, neither parties would be achieving their desired goals.

Another way of spotting the differences in communicating styles and methods is to look at the way people speak. Some 'talk' with their hands, while others speak with their heads; despite these differences, effective communication is still possible. The chances of success are governed by your ability to correctly evaluate the person you are communicating with. Let's delve.

WORDS, TONE AND BODY LANGUAGE

There are three key ways in which you can get your message across:

- What you say – the words you use (*the 'verbal' system*).

- Your tone – how you say the words (*the 'prosodic' system*).

- Your body language – your bearing and gestures (the *'kinesic' channel)*

We get most of our clues about the emotional intent behind people's words from non-verbal sources. And when words and non-verbal messages are in conflict, people believe the non-verbal messages virtually every time.

For example, after you have had a disagreement with a loved one and you ask them, "Are you still angry with me?" and they reply "No," with folded arms, a grimace and an angry tone, you'd be foolish to believe their verbal reply.

215

In cases such as this:

- The words you use account for the smallest portion of your overall message – 7%

- Your tone counts for considerably more – 38%

- Body posture, gestures and facial expressions make up the biggest portion of your overall message – 55%

These often-quoted figures originated from research undertaken by Albert Mehrabian, Professor Emeritus of Psychology at the University of California Los Angeles (www.psych.ucla.edu/ faculty/page/mehrab).

So, in face-to-face communication, the non-verbal message becomes the most powerful mode of communication when conveying feelings or attitudes such as "I like this" or "I don't like this". It is much more likely to be the primary indicator.

Ironically, reading this book means you only have my words to help you absorb all this information, so that's why I like to bring my material alive by including interactive exercises for you to do and by showing you how to do the exercises, which I have filmed and put on my app for you to see.

Some of my favourite exercises are incorporated into this chapter, so please do complete them all, play full out and share them with as many people as you can – not only are they quick and fun to do with your family, friends and colleagues, but I guarantee that they have all been developed specifically to help you deliver the outcomes you desire from raising your game.

MIRRORING AND MATCHING

Building rapport is far-reaching if you wish to communicate effectively. Your words and tone go a long way towards building a rapport, but with body language contributing 55% of the influence, it's crucial to use it to maximum effect.

We use body language all the time, although we're not always conscious of it, and we tend to notice other people's changes in body language more than we notice our own.

To further understand the power of reading body language and building rapport through your physiology, try this mirroring and matching exercise:

Observe people's body gestures when you meet them, then approach them in a similar way. The same principle applies with their tone of voice, speed, pitch and volume of speech and their vocabulary. All of this will make a person feel valued and comfortable because they are communicating with a like-minded person.

Stalkie's
'GIVE PRAISE HORRIBLY' WORKOUT

These brain-scramblers are just for fun – note the uncertainty of the reactions you get from the people you target with these:

1. *Say "I love you" really aggressively to your partner, family member or a friend.*

2. *The next time you're in a restaurant or shop, praise the manager about the outstanding service you've received, but do it in an aggressive tone.*

3. *Pretend to reprimand your loved one/colleague/friend using the words that you would normally use BUT deliver the reprimand in a really friendly, charming, smiling manner.*

When you give praise horribly, or give a telling off in a nice way, invariably it's your tone and your actions that will provoke the response rather than the words you use.

In a working environment, we encourage colleagues to look at their customers' body gestures and movements as they come through the door, so they can approach them in an identical manner. For example, the colleague could stand in a similar way; if the customer leans on the desk and looks relaxed, then the colleague too should be relaxed and lean on the desk. If the customer sits down to talk, the colleague should also choose to sit to have the conversation.

These things are very simple, but they really do help to build a rapport. The customer will feel well looked after, because they're dealing with someone they like – someone who is just like themselves. Try this in any given situation, and you will find that your levels of connection and empathy are reciprocated within moments.

Body language is an outward reflection of a person's emotional condition – every gesture or movement that you make can indicate, and co-ordinate with, an underlying emotion that you generally feel or feel particularly strongly at that time – so, the aptitude to tune in to body language and read it is a valuable tool in your communication box.

OUR FIVE SENSES

Powerful and effective communication relies on many different components, all of which make up the influencing power of the messages you are trying to convey. You know and understand that there are three main elements which make up your communication: what you say, how you say it and your body language – each of these factors can affect the message being received.

In addition to these elements, you also have another set of influences – your five senses:

- Sight *(visual)*

- Touch *(kinaesthetic)*

- Sound *(auditory)*

- Smell *(olfactory)*

- Taste *(gustatory)*

APP ALERT!!

The Visual, Auditory, Kinaesthetic (VAK) Learning Styles model was developed by psychologists in the 1920s to classify the most common ways that people learn. Although smell and taste play a part in our communication – the smell of alcohol on somebody's breath will instantly lead you to act in a certain way when communicating with them, for example – the majority of people will have a predominant visual, auditory or kinaesthetic sense that they prefer to learn through (although we 'mix and match' these three styles to varying degrees).

You'll probably already have a good sense of what your own learning preference is, as this will have been present from your earliest days at school. For example, is your default response to a problem or challenge to sketch something out on a piece of paper (visual), talk about it (auditory), or build a model or tangible representation of the problem (kinaesthetic)? If you are still unsure of your learning style, you may be able to identify it by considering these scenarios:

Think about how you make a complaint. When you complain about something, chances are your emotions are running high and you'll revert to the communication style you feel most comfortable with. Do you want to see the whites of someone's eyes (visual), rant at someone over the phone (auditory), or hammer your fists on the table (kinaesthetic)?

Imagine yourself in an uncomfortable situation. If you were lost in a strange city at night, how would you find your way to your destination? Would you use a map (visual), ask someone for directions (auditory), or just keep walking until you worked out where you were (kinaesthetic)?

What style of presentation do you prefer? Think back to the last presentation you attended. What was it that most stuck in your mind? Was it the charts or visual aids (visual), the words the presenter used (auditory), or any audience participation (kinaesthetic)? A quick look at the VAK learning styles will give you strong clues how to communicate powerfully and effectively with each of them.

VISUAL LEARNERS

For visual learners, 'a picture paints a thousand words'. They are likely to be drawn to art, design, film and theatre. They will appreciate colour and will often prefer vibrant tones.

The visual learner has two sub-channels: linguistic (relating to language) and spatial (relating to space). Learners who are visual-linguistic like to learn through written language, such as reading and writing tasks. They remember what has been written down, even if they do not read it more than once. They like to write down directions and pay better attention if they are able to watch the proceedings.

Learners who are visual-spatial often have difficulty with the written language and do better with charts, demonstrations, videos, and other visual materials. They easily visualise faces and places by using their imagination and seldom get lost in new surroundings.

For effective communication with visual learners:

- Use graphs, charts, illustrations, or other visual aids.

- Include plenty of content in handouts to re-read after the learning session and leave white space in handouts for note-taking.

- Invite questions to help them stay alert in auditory environments, have them act out the subject matter.

- Emphasise key points.

- Eliminate potential distractions.

- Pepper your speech with phrases such as *"how does that look to you"* or *"how do you see it"*?

AUDITORY LEARNERS

Auditory people who have sound as their key sense can be more difficult to spot. They are often articulate, appreciate the way things sound, enjoy music, and enjoy talking to someone with a 'musical' voice. They often talk to themselves and read and sing out loud.

They often do better talking to a colleague directly or on the phone and hearing what's said. For effective communication with auditory learners:

- Begin new material with a brief explanation of what is coming and conclude with a summary of what has been covered. This is the old adage of "tell them what they are going to learn, teach them, and tell them what they have learned".

- Use the Socratic method of teaching by questioning learners to draw as much information from them as possible and then fill in the gaps with your own expertise.

- Include auditory activities such as thought showers or buzz groups. Leave plenty of time to debrief activities, allowing them to make connections around their learning and how it applies to their situation.

- Verbalise your questions. Use phrases such as *"how does that sound to you?"*, *"does that idea click with you?"*

KINAESTHETIC LEARNERS

Kinaesthetic people rely on their feelings. They 'feel' their words out, go with their gut reactions (no matter what they can see or hear) and are often softly spoken and articulate.

Kinaesthetic learners have two sub-channels: movement and touch. They tend to lose concentration if there is little or no external stimulation or movement. They may want to take notes for the sake of moving their hands. When reading, they like to scan the material first, and then focus in on the details (get the big picture first). They typically use colour highlighters and take notes by drawing pictures, diagrams, or doodling.

For effective communication with kinaesthetic learners:

- Use activities that get the learners up and moving. Give them something to do with their hands.

- Play music during activities.

- Give frequent stretch breaks (brain breaks).

- Provide highlighters and coloured pens.

- Guide learners through a visualisation of complex tasks.

- Have them transfer information from the text to another medium such as a keyboard or a tablet.

- Talk slowly, carefully think about and plan your sentences and word choice.

If you would like to double check on which learning style is most predominant in you, there's a good self-questionnaire you can try out at www.businessballs.com

THE VALUE OF COMMUNICATION IN AWKWARD CONVERSATIONS

It's likely that you are reading this book because you have identified changes that you wish or need to make in your life. **You Can Raise Your Game!** is all about supporting you to channel your energy to uncover and realise your values, strengths, courage, love, faith, kindness and sense of fun. It is about investing in YOU, to create an existence in which you become effective, fulfilled and truly play the game of life to the full.

But I'm pretty sure these changes will involve conversing and communicating with those who are closest to you, as well as those you don't hold close to you at all, and maybe with people whom you have yet to come into contact. So, what do I mean by 'awkward conversations'?

We all face the prospect of those stomach-churning conversations in our workplace, at home and in our social lives, such as:

- Appraisals, disciplinaries, hiring and firing, or the whole leaving, finding and starting a new job process.

- Disagreements and differences of opinion with family members, loved ones, friends, colleagues, even strangers.

- Challenging and realigning anti-social or bad behaviour.

- Dealing with indiscretions and disputes.

- Complaining or standing up for yourself, or on behalf of others.

- The need to re-evaluate or move on from a relationship.

- Addressing legal, financial or health concerns.

- Reporting bad news or telling people something that's not going to go down well.

All in all, awkward!

223

What real life examples of awkward conversations are you currently facing? Chances are that you'll not be relishing the idea of approaching them, or you may feel ill-equipped to find the right words to say or use? Alternatively, you may feel gung-ho about dealing with them because you need to get something off your chest and you don't really care about what the consequences will be? Either way, as I have explained in the *'Fear into Power'* chapter of this book:

1. You won't achieve anything by procrastinating or by thinking that the problem will go away without you needing to act – it will just escalate or go in a direction further beyond your control.

2. There are always ways and means to achieve the outcome that you desire.

We have already probed the principles of how you can use words and tone, body language, mirroring and matching and tailoring our communication to the predominant senses in people, so let's now cover some of my tried and tested techniques to consider when dealing with awkward conversations.

SEPARATE THE BEHAVIOUR FROM THE PERSON

You may well have heard this concept discussed as an important part of problem solving and conflict resolution: separate the people from the problem. However, if it were easy to do, we would all do it all the time.

Divorcing the behaviour from the person means that we attempt to avoid labelling someone on the basis of their actions. When you separate the unwanted behaviour from the person and talk about it as a separate entity you are allowing that person the opportunity to change their behaviour positively without having a go at them as a person. For example, rather than saying to a work colleague, "Why are you late for work again today?", say, "We really like working with you because you're talented and a lovely person, but your behaviour of being late can't continue as it could become an issue between us".

THE PATTERN INTERRUPT

The intention of a pattern interrupt is to stop a type of behaviour that is ineffective and open up the possibility of creating a more positive direction for the conversation.

This is the ideal way to calm down somebody having a moan or a rant. Ask them an outrageous question to change their focus – say something not normally acceptable, stupid, funny or confusing.

You can also use your physical being to pattern interrupt, through body movement or facial expressions. Remember the aim is to introduce a new element to the conversation so that the person is interrupted and unable to continue with their original line of argument.

As an example, imagine that a customer is shouting at you because the product they bought does not work and they are frustrated. You could try a pattern interrupt such as this:

Customer: *"I have just about had enough of your company – this is the third time I've come to you with a faulty television set!"*

You: *"Oh, right – by the way, what is your favourite TV programme?"*

Customer: *"What has that got to do with my television not working?"*

Now, you have managed to successfully interrupt the customer's train of thought, because they have responded to your unexpected question.

You: *"You look like someone who is interested in sports, and at the moment we are offering free set-top boxes."*

APP ALERT!!

225

The customer has now thought about something completely different to the subject that was making them angry, thus lessening their emotional state – they have to stop and think of an answer, making them forget the next line of their argument! The brain finds it difficult to focus on two things at once, hence they cannot concentrate on being angry and answering a question. The question is a deliberately confusing one for them.

Subsequent mirroring and matching will put the customer further at ease and bring the conversation back under control. If the customer is now speaking softly or loudly, do the same. Choose to use similar vocabulary as them, and adopt a similar pose.

This process of interrupting someone's pattern, then mirroring and matching them, can also work when a person is sad. Firstly, you could ask a 'confusing' question or, even better, try acting sadder than they are. Their reaction may be that they want to help you – in this way, you have efficiently reversed the situation. Naturally, this will take their mind off their own problems. To do this well, try speaking in a low pitch with a monotone voice, and have your head and shoulders down, breathing in a very shallow way.

A colleague of mine has a favourite pattern-interrupting question that he uses at funerals. If he is in a line of mourners who are approaching the grieving relatives to pay their respects after the funeral, and the relatives are struggling to be consoled, he will have made a point of finding something unusual or uplifting about the deceased person (who we will call 'Keith') such as a hobby (say, 'wood-carving') or an event that gave the family much joy and laughter.

When it comes to his turn in the line of mourners, my colleague will smile positively and say to the grieving relative, "I never knew that Keith was such a dab-hand at wood-carving? How long was he doing that for? Did he sell them or exhibit them at all?!" Or "Someone reminded me the other day of the time Keith surprised everybody by getting up and doing a rendition of that Frank Sinatra song at the social club's karaoke night – do you remember? What was the song again? He was some character, eh?" This will usually break any pattern of upset, as the relative remembers the fun and fondly reminisces.

When I'm at home with my wife and children, we often find ourselves 'out-pattern-interrupting' each other! If arguments are arising and any of us wants to calm the situation down, it's hard not to laugh when someone suddenly behaves crazily, barking like a dog or pulling funny faces. The whole situation instantly defuses and we can move on to look for the sincere solution.

There are many different ways you can use pattern interrupts, but the crux is to get the conversation back under your control. Obviously, this technique improves with practice. Try it out at home first with family and friends, then use it at the pub or supermarket. Eventually, you will feel confident enough to try it at work and in more pressing circumstances until it becomes second nature to you.

MALE AND FEMALE COMMUNICATION

Aside from the fact that we both come from the same species, men and women are totally... different! Equal, but different.

As John Gray says in his famous 'Mars and Venus' series of books, it's as though we are from different planets. Of course, the degree of disparity between us varies from man to man and woman to woman, but we are still left to face the stats that around 43% of all marriages end in divorce. The UK's largest provider of relationship support, Relate (www.relate.org.uk) cites the following main reasons for divorce:

Money disputes, affairs, ex-partners interfering, children from previous relationships, differences in sexual libido, intrusive parents, inability to resolve conflict, lack of communication and privacy problems (i.e. when one person has a different view of what should be kept within the relationship). And, at the heart of most of these issues? A lack of understanding and communication.

THE WAY WE ARE WIRED

Men and women are different, nothing can change that, but what can we do to improve our understanding and communication in our inter-gender relationships at home and at work?

Men and women evolved differently, because they had to. Simply put, early men were hunters and gatherers and developed survival skills to do so; women were gatherers too, but they also had to be multi-tasking homemakers and child carers. The men protected, women nurtured. Our brains and bodies have been designed according to these various job roles and hence they are very different, simply because they've needed to function in different ways.

Roll forward 200,000 years from when *Homo sapiens* first evolved, and the line between our contrasting skills and abilities may be blurring. But...tell me you don't recognise the following peculiarities!

Men can't find things; keys, phone, glasses, wallet always missing? They will stand by the wardrobe insisting that their best shirt isn't in there, until the lady in their life comes along and picks it out without a second glance. This is because women developed wider peripheral vision for their nurturing role, plus an attention to detail that men did not need in their role as hunter.

A couple drive along for hours, with no SatNav. The man is not able to say exactly where they are, but insists he's not lost and refuses to ask for directions. However, for a woman, stopping to ask someone for guidance provides the chance to solve a difficult problem – hence, she will not hesitate to do it.

Meanwhile, seeing as we're talking about car journeys – gulp, yes I'm going to say it – women and parking! Cars in tight spaces? Inferior spatial ability? Although women are perfectly able to learn the task, changing conditions of light, distance and surrounding traffic mean that they find parking more naturally difficult than men.

This is not just a myth aimed at criticising women. Men, hardwired to those hunting skills, can often simply judge distance, speed and the size of a parking space (as they would have when judging a potential kill) better.

Unfair? Here's where women even things up in this regard. A woman's brain software allows her to see clearly 45° either side of her head, plus above and below her nose. Men are programmed to see targets at a distance. They have a sort of 'tunnel vision', meaning they tend to see clearly when looking directly in front of themselves.

This wider peripheral vision is a useful tool for women to have. They see everything! They will notice when their children are straying towards danger, and when their man is checking out another woman! But, due to superior peripheral vision, they'll rarely get caught when doing the same!

Men and women perceive the world through very different eyes. On the one hand, men take note of objects and their relationship to one another; women literally see the bigger picture – they see the fine detail. Colours are a good example: a male sees blue, where a female may see cobalt, lilac, navy, sapphire, indigo, powder blue and so on.

When a woman asks for more attention, why is there often a characteristically blank look on her male partner's face? He may think he has been tasking on her behalf and supporting her needs, but she still requires more affection?! For a man, showing emotion doesn't come quite so naturally and often equates to being out of control.

So, do women really like to communicate and talk more and, if so, what about? What really matters to them? And men, what's on your mind that might not always be given full exposure through your communication channels? How can the sexes learn to appreciate and account for their differences when communicating meaningfully with each other? My tips should help you smooth the path!

Stalkie's Summary
TOP 10 TIPS TOWARDS BECOMING A POWERFUL INFLUENCER

1. **There are three key ways to get your message across:**

   Your words (the 'verbal' system) account for the smallest portion of your communication; your tone (the 'prosodic' system) accounts for considerably more; and your body language (the 'kinesic channel') makes up the largest part of your communication. To be a powerful communicator/influencer, you need to understand how we synch our words with our body language.

2. **Seek to understand before being understood. Be a brilliant listener and observer.**

    Body language is an outward reflection of a person's emotional condition; every gesture or movement that we make indicates an emotion that we're feeling at any given time. Listen attentively to what a person is saying and acutely observe their body movements too. This will put you in the best possible position to establish rapport.

3. **Building rapport is the door to influential communication.**

    To establish rapport, observe others' body gestures when you meet them, then 'mirror and match' them with your own body language. The same principle applies with your volume, tone and speed of voice, and the choice of vocabulary you use. All of this will make the person feel valued and well looked after, because they are communicating with a like-minded person.

4. **Adapt your communication tactics to appeal to your subject's predominant sense (VAK).**

    Although smell and taste play a part in our communication, the majority of people have a predominant learning style and express themselves based on one of the following senses:

    - Sight (visual) – for these people 'a picture paints a thousand words'

    - Sound (auditory) – they enjoy 'rhythmic' listening and talking things through

    - Touch (kinaesthetic) – they rely on their feelings, movement and touch

    Understanding the VAK learning styles will give you strong clues how to communicate powerfully and effectively using each of them.

5. Do not pre-conceive people's intentions based on your own fears.

If you have a fear or a concern about the outcome of a conversation, do not assume that others will make your concerns become true – jumping to conclusions can lead you towards wrongful decisions (e.g. you think your partner is unhappy and is going to break up with you, so you break up with them first). Avoid this behaviour by acknowledging your fear and logically mapping it to the way the other person is behaving. Ask the opinion of trusted advisors. Put yourself in the shoes of the other party; is there really a reason why they would make your fears come true?

6. Divorce the behaviour from the person.

Avoid labelling a person on the basis of their behaviour. When you separate the unwanted behaviour from the person and talk about it as a separate entity, you allow that person the opportunity to positively change that behaviour and they don't take it so personally. Instead of saying "Why were you late today?", say "We really like working with you. You're great and we have a lot of respect for you, but the unwanted behaviour of your lateness cannot continue. Please don't let that behaviour let us all down".

7. Pattern interrupt

The outcome of a pattern interrupt is to stop a type of ineffective or challenging behaviour (e.g. someone who is terrorising sympathy or tearing you down) and open up the possibility of creating a more positive direction for the conversation. To calm down somebody having a moan or a rant, ask them an outrageous question to change the person's focus – say something not normally acceptable, stupid, funny or confusing.

Use your physical being also to pattern interrupt, through body movement and facial expressions. Remember the aim is to introduce a new element to the conversation so that the person is interrupted and unable to continue with their original line of argument.

8. Male communication tip

When talking to a man, keep it direct and to the point. There must be a clear agenda and outcome. Male brains are organised into compartments: it suits them to separate, file and store information away. Give a male just one thing to think about at a time. If you multi-track subjects (and on top of multi-tracking, go around the houses a bit), men get lost and stop paying attention.

9. Female communication tip

Women gain a lot of comfort and clarity through verbalising any problems or issues that arise rather than storing them up. This is fulfilling a biological need, and not just talking for the love of it, as some men might view it! Sharing thoughts helps women to feel valued and understood... men are not always expected to respond, take control or offer a solution!

It is not difficult to see how this brain-clash can lead to problems, but with a little bit of knowledge about this subject, laced with a good sprinkling of patience, sensitivity and respect, you can now agree with your partner how to serve both of your needs equitably!

10. Respect differences

When people approach a problem from different emotional, cultural, social and political perspectives, conflict is often the result; then respect for each other diminishes, and work efficiency or domestic harmony can suffer. You must understand and appreciate that differences will always exist but can be worked around – your use of communication in achieving this process is vital. There are far more than 50 shades of grey here – vive la difference! Respecting each other's approaches, building trust and efficiency can take education and patience, but always aim to work together to reap rewards.

09

PRAISE YOUR GAME NOW!

Benefits of looking for the good and celebrating

"Build your self-esteem by recalling all the ways you have succeeded, and your brain will be filled with images of you making your achievements happen again and again. Give yourself permission to toot your own horn, and don't wait for anyone to praise you."

– Jack Canfield*

*Best known as the originator of the *'Chicken Soup for the Soul'*® series (more than 123 million books sold through the franchise), **Jack Canfield** is uniquely qualified to talk about success. He is one of America's leading experts in creating peak performance. (www.jackcanfield.com)

Whenever I find a way to celebrate and praise anything good or positive that happens each day, the more there seems to be to celebrate and praise. What we praise increases – it's a kinda magic!

Praising and celebrating an individual's strengths and success levels, however small they may be, is something that falls into the arena of positive psychology which, as you may well have recognised in the pages of this book, I'm a big fan of. For me, my family, friends, colleagues and clients, it's the gift that keeps on giving.

In the years immediately following the Second World War, psychology was a science largely devoted to healing – it concentrated on repairing damage. This neglected the idea of a fulfilled individual. Now, psychological treatment is not just about fixing what is wrong; it's also about building things that are right. The aim of positive psychology is to move on from repairing the worst things in life to building the best qualities in life. Positive psychology aims to measure, understand and then build on human strengths and virtues.

According to Dr. Martin Seligman*, often called the 'father of positive psychology', the aim is to

"Catalyze a change in psychology from a preoccupation only with repairing the worst things in life to also building the best qualities in life... positive psychology takes seriously the bright hope that if you find yourself stuck in the parking lot of life, with few and only ephemeral pleasures, with minimal gratifications, and without meaning, there is a road out. This road takes you through the countryside of pleasure and gratification, up into the high country of strength and virtue, and finally to the peaks of lasting fulfilment: meaning and purpose."

APP ALERT!!

*__Martin Seligman__ was born in 1942 in Albany, New York. He was the Director of the Clinical Training Program of the University of Pennsylvania for 14 years. His work mostly regards the topics of learned helplessness, positive psychology, depression, resilience, optimism and pessimism. Today he is the Zellerbach Family Professor of Psychology as well as the Director of the Positive Psychology Center at the University of Pennsylvania. He is the author of around 20 self-help books and more than 250 articles and is an excellent speaker.

You can see him in action, talking about his work and his principles at www.ted.com/speakers/martin_seligman or follow him via the website www.pursuit-of-happiness.org

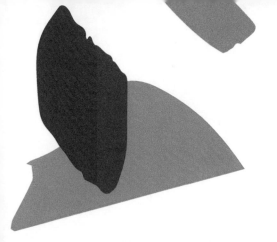

"Looking for the good in yourself, your essence and your qualities and catching yourself doing things right and well, is a potent tool for self-esteem and growth."

– Paul Stalker

What I'd like to transmit to you over the next few pages are some straightforward reasons why and how some of the positive psychology tools that I use in my life can provide you too with the foundations for a positive self-image and support you to live according to the standards and values that you aspire to.

I'm not talking about creating egotistical, self-centred monsters: there is a line between confidence and arrogance that we need to be aware of, but we all enjoy and benefit immensely from being loved and praised, don't we? Think of the gorgeously sloppy grin that a toddler gives when they've just taken their very first steps, resulting in cheers, hugs and kisses of praise and encouragement. Do they respond by refusing to get up on their feet again? No... they just want to keep doing it. And for all those present at the time, it's a win-win, everybody's happy.

It's worthy of celebration. Start with praising yourself and this will also stimulate you to do the same for others in your life, creating a virtuous circle of like-minded people. Around we go, it's a win-win again.

APP ALERT!!

WHERE'S YOUR HAPPINESS AT RIGHT NOW?

In fact, why don't we start by understanding where you are on the happiness spectrum right now?

Martin Seligman set up the Positive Psychology Center at the University of Pennsylvania as part of his quest to understand the emotional drivers behind authentic happiness, with the mission of promoting research, training, education and the dissemination of positive psychology.

If you visit www.authentichappiness. sas.upenn.edu/home you'll find resources about positive psychology including readings, videos, research, opportunities, conferences... and, when you register for free, you can access a host of insightful questionnaires with feedback.

Take the *'Authentic Happiness Inventory'* questionnaire which measures your overall happiness, or the *'General Happiness Scale'*, assess your *'Enduring Happiness'* or measure your *'Current Happiness'*.

There are also questionnaires that probe your strengths, life satisfaction, optimism, gratitude, work life balance and compassion. These exercises take a very short time to do, they will cost you nothing and you can use them as a benchmark for where you are now and where I know you could get to with my **You Can Raise Your Game!** tools and application.

BUILDING ON YOUR STRENGTHS

"A strength is a pattern of behaviour, thoughts and feelings that produces a high degree of satisfaction and pride; generates both psychic and/or financial reward: and presents measurable progress toward excellence."

– Donald O. Clifton*

Your personal strengths are the things you are good at. Whether it relies more on your hands, head or heart, a strength can be anything, including artistic talents, writing, selling, gardening, sports, cooking, interpersonal skills, teaching etc. These become strengths when you devote a significant amount of time to them and, as you do so, your feelings of pride and satisfaction grow.

*Donald O. Clifton, Ph.D. (1924-2003) was an American psychologist, World War II veteran and Chairman of Gallup, the globally famous research-based, performance management consulting company, best known for its public opinion polls. He was the chief designer of the Clifton StrengthsFinder Profile (Gallup's online psychological assessment) and cited as the "Father of Strengths-Based Psychology" by the American Psychological Association. He co-authored several books, including the bestseller *'How Full Is Your Bucket?'*.

I've drawn a lot of inspiration and use a lot of material from his books *'Now, Discover Your Strengths'* (written with Marcus Buckingham) and especially *'Soar With Your Strengths'* (which Donald co-wrote with Paula Nelson). Based on over 40 years of research with some of America's most successful companies, it reveals how to find out what you do well and states you should do more of it – and how to identify what you don't do well and that you should stop doing it. It scientifically argues how to achieve the absolute best by focusing on strengths and steering away from weaknesses. See www. gallupstrengthscenter.com/Home/en-US/About for more detail about Donald Clifton and strengths finding.

Think back to what you really enjoyed doing at school. Was it English, maths, cookery or sport, science perhaps? Whatever subject you enjoyed, you were probably good at it. Through taking part in that activity and succeeding, you would have experienced a feeling of satisfaction and the results were probably amongst your best measured.

As you know, I struggled at school with English, in particular spelling and reading. So my parents very kindly bought me extra lessons and home tuition for both. Knowing what I know now, it would have been much better for me, and my parents' money, to buy me extra cookery or football lessons, which I loved. In fact, I asked to be moved from the metalwork class to the cookery class, and 38 years on I still remember those lessons, the enjoyment and the fun. To this day, I am super passionate about cooking and growing my own vegetables to cook with.

My point here is that, even at an early point in our growth – especially at school – the system, agenda or personnel are rarely geared towards praise and the promotion of individual strengths.

League tables and results are the main currency; praise and individual accomplishment not so much.

"But if you have a strength, focus upon it with dedication and passion, and invest enough time in it – anything is possible."

– Paul Stalker

There is compelling evidence to suggest what it takes to become world class at a certain pursuit or activity. It has been calculated that it can take a minimum of ten and up to 17 years of dedicated effort from beginning an activity to mastering it – this was suggested by Dr. Benjamin Bloom in his 1982 University of Chicago and Northwestern University study.

Bloom was an educational psychologist who made several contributions to the classification of educational objectives and to the theory of mastery learning. His research showed that educational settings and home environments can foster human potential, but also showed it is not innate giftedness that allows one to succeed, but passion, hard work and practice. Your signature strengths do not necessarily have to be genetic, or to come naturally, for you to excel.

"What's really interesting about this 10,000-hour rule is that it applies virtually everywhere. You can't become a chess grand master unless you spend 10,000 hours on practice. The tennis prodigy who starts playing at six is playing in Wimbledon at 16 or 17 like Boris Becker. The classical musician who starts playing the violin at four is debuting at Carnegie Hall at 15 or so," he says.

'Outliers: The Story of Success', by best-selling author, journalist and sociologist **Malcolm Gladwell** repeatedly supports the '10,000-hour rule', claiming that the key to achieving world-class expertise in any skill is, to a large extent, a matter of practising the correct way for a total of around 10,000 hours.

Gladwell backs up his theory by citing sports stars such as Boris Becker, Jonny Wilkinson, Tiger Woods and the Williams sisters, who have all become world-beaters because of the obsessive devotion they have shown to their respective strengths since childhood. He says that if you examine the greatest athletes, entrepreneurs, musicians and scientists you will notice they only emerged after spending at least three hours a day for ten years practising their strength:

Much of Britain's Olympic success in cycling, Gladwell argues, is down to a combination of natural ability and sheer dedication. Victoria Pendleton's emphatic gold in the women's sprint cycling in Beijing 2008 came only after humiliating defeat in Athens four years earlier. After training for four hours a day, six days a week the 27-year-old finally reaped the rewards.

Rebecca Adlington, the 19-year-old British swimmer who won two gold medals at the Beijing Games, put in an estimated 8,840 hours of training since the age of 12.

IDENTIFYING YOUR STRENGTHS

Such dedication is also apparent in musicians. Maxim Vengerov, 34, is one of the world's greatest violinists. He was born in the Siberian city of Novosibirsk and, after being given a miniature fiddle at the age of four, he matched his talent with an immense work ethic. He practised seven hours a day, giving his first recital at the age of five and winning his first international prize at 15 (you can see more about Gladwell's findings on his website www. gladwell.com. He's also a very entertaining blogger and podcaster. See www.gladwellbooks.com).

Clearly, the years spent intensively focused on their area of strength and expertise place the world's most successful people above their peers.

According to Gallup, people who do focus on their strengths every day are six times as likely to be engaged with their jobs. They are more productive too, both individually and in teams. And they are more than three times as likely to say they have an excellent quality of life.

How then, do you go about identifying a strength if it isn't already staring you in the face?

"The good life is using your signature strengths every day to produce authentic happiness and abundant gratification."

– Martin Seligman

Not everyone is aware of their personal strengths, so my message is 'variety is the spice of life'. Until you've given yourself the opportunity to try as many outlets and experiences as you can, you may never know what you are capable of. Obviously this is subject to factors such as available time, resources, qualifications and location – not many of us get to find out whether we'd be the world's best astronaut, horse whisperer or catwalk model even if we'd like to have a crack at it! But remember the rocking chair test... don't regret in later life what you didn't do.

APP ALERT!!

Did you know that there is such a job as a professional cuddler (currently charging around £60-£80 an hour)? Yup – I think I'd be great at that! Cuddle Professionals International was founded by Kitty Mansfield, owner of BeSnuggled, the UK's first independent professional therapeutic cuddle service, and BeCuddled, Today, Europe's first professional cuddle agency. Kitty is a qualified holistic therapist with over a decade of experience, and she saw cuddling as a logical extension of, and vital addition to, the therapies she was already offering:

"Cuddling as a stand-alone therapy and profession is still in its infancy in the UK, but it's well established in the USA. Indeed, US cuddle professionals report that business is booming. All over the world those who are touch-deprived are seeking the reassurance and security of a simple cuddle, capturing the zeitgeist of a technologically advanced but increasingly disconnected society", Kitty says. (www.cuddle-professionals.co.uk)

In his previously mentioned book *'Now, Discover Your Strengths'*, Donald O. Clifton maintains that there is a definitive way to identify your greatest potential for strength:

"Step back and watch yourself for a while. Try an activity and see how quickly you pick it up, how quickly you skip steps in the learning and add twists and kinks you haven't been taught yet. See whether you become absorbed in the activity to such an extent that you lose track of time. If none of these has happened after a couple of months, try another activity and watch – and another. Over time your dominant talents will reveal themselves, and you can start to refine them into a powerful strength."

Do you have a yearning – something that always interested you as a child, an ambition that you had, or an experience that you had a fleeting brush with that brought you a sense of joy, well-being and satisfaction? Raising your game is all about giving yourself the permission and untapping the belief to experience the very things that will serve you the best and fulfil your ambitions.

Back to Clifton – he has identified a few simple questions which will help you initially test for your strength:

- Do you feel you always knew how to do it?

- When you practise it, do you get better at it?

- Do you know you can perform it well?

- Do others applaud you when you do it?

- Can you get paid well for it?

- Do you feel pride and pleasure when you do it?

Answering these questions will steer you towards doing more of what you love and are good at rather than burn up belief, time and energy in what you don't.

RECOGNISING YOUR WEAKNESSES

I should say here that weaknesses are not everything you don't do well – a weakness is only a weakness when it intrudes on areas that you are great at, undermining your confidence along the way.

Weakness is nothing to be ashamed of, it is part of our fabric and our uniqueness as an individual. Life is too brief to overcome all our shortcomings and we certainly don't want to become emotionless automatons. We are often attracted to those whose flaws we can relate to and when we open up and share our own flaws, insecurities and doubts with others it can bond and strengthen our friendships.

You Can Raise Your Game! is not a campaign to ban or belittle the underdog; we are focusing here on the practicalities of building personal power and managing those areas in our lives where power is absent.

APP ALERT!!

Ask someone you trust, such as a friend, a family member or established work colleague, about your weaknesses. Although most people find it difficult to give or take criticism, giving them permission to do so and telling them why you wish to understand your weaknesses should produce a candid conversation.

When you find a weakness, the objective is to manage it, and not to think that it can be turned into a strength. Clifton points to eight pretty self-explanatory behaviours that may help to indicate a weakness. These are:

- Defensive about performance

- Obsessive attempts to overcome it

- Slow learning (just don't "get it")

- Repeated experience produces no improvement

- Continue to have to think through the steps

- Confidence drops when performing the activity

- No vision of the future during it, just the struggle to get through it

- Burnout while engaged in the activity

You must realise, however, that attempting to convert weaknesses to strengths wastes time. The aim is to manage weaknesses so that strengths are free to develop without interruption. In this way, the strengths will become even stronger and the weaknesses are relegated to the status of being irrelevant.

APP ALERT!!

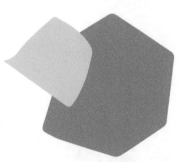

MANAGING WEAKNESSES

Weaknesses can be removed, reduced or corrected with a large amount of time, energy and in some cases money, but they cannot be transformed into strengths. Clifton suggests five strategies for managing weaknesses:

- Find out what you don't do well and stop doing it

- Enlightened leverage – delegate a weakness to someone who possesses strengths in those areas

- Complementary partnering – team up with people whose strengths are your weaknesses and vice versa

- Support systems – if you can find a way to make your life work better, use it

- Alternatives – find a different way to do the same task

To return briefly to my earlier years, I've mentioned that I was a poor reader and writer. It was only in my adulthood that I discovered that dyslexia and attention deficit hyperactivity disorder (ADHD) were contributory factors to this but, without knowing this and familiarising myself with the prescribed coping mechanisms for these conditions, I spent a lot of time in a mental 'fog'. It also meant that I was disruptive and difficult to teach.

My frustration and embarrassment at being a 'slow learner' (weaknesses), thoroughly dented my confidence, my vivacity, my desire to learn and my ambition (strengths). After leaving school early without troubling the examination boards too much, it was almost by accident that I discovered an ability to build rapport with people and to be an influencer. Thus, when I got my first telesales job, I was able to play to my strengths and, through using the telephone as my primary means of communication, manage my weaknesses at the same time. Great news!

There were others in the telesales company who could look after the administration, the contracts – the day-to-day reading and writing – which freed me up to sell and build up our client base. And in subsequent years, my successful trajectory in building companies has always been far steeper when I've concentrated on my signature strengths and trusted my weaker areas to delegation, complementary partnering and support systems.

Whenever I wavered from this proven model, usually by unleashing my control freak from within and wanting to prove that I could master everything involved in running a business myself (weakness), it was a double whammy. Not only was my valuable time and energy taken up by trying to conquer aspects of the business that I was not effective or efficient at and didn't enjoy doing (simultaneously irritating and sabotaging my better qualified colleagues), but I also spent less quality time prospecting and looking after clients, who all demanded my personal service. Not good! The consequences of this behaviour were life-changing.

It is not always possible to manage weaknesses by stopping any involvement with them – reading and writing, for example, plays a massive part in my daily life and education – but I'm a big buyer of finding different ways of doing the same task, such as reading! For example, I find audiobooks, podcasts, video recordings, videoconferencing, Skype, Facetime etc. extremely effective ways of gathering knowledge and communicating productively and fluently.

I do like a bit of an inspirational list to exemplify a point and to spur me on, so allow me to share a few of these examples who have managed similar weaknesses to myself:

- **Leonardo da Vinci** (1452-1519), Italian polymath: scientist, mathematician, engineer, inventor, anatomist, painter, sculptor, architect, botanist, musician and writer. As an engineer, Leonardo conceived ideas vastly ahead of his own time, conceptualising a helicopter, a tank, concentrated solar power, a calculator, and the double hull, and outlining a rudimentary theory of plate tectonics. He also had the gift of dyslexia. Most of the time, he wrote his notes backwards.

- **Thomas Edison** (1847-1931) was an American inventor and businessman. In school, he was terrible at maths, unable to focus, and had difficulty with words and speech, so much so that he had only three months of official schooling. He was a problem child, a mischief-maker, he spoke over his teachers, had no patience or empathy, was not well-coordinated and did poorly in sports. It's said now that he probably had a combination of dyslexia, dyspraxia, autism and ADHD. He applied himself with a passion to whatever took his interest, though, including the development of many ingenious devices that have greatly influenced the world, including the light bulb and the phonograph. It's a similar tale to that of **Alexander Graham Bell** (1847-1922) who invented the telephone.

- **Michael Phelps** is the most decorated Olympian of all time, with 23 gold medals in a total of 28 medals altogether. Of managing his ADHD he says; *"When I'm focused, there is not one single thing, person, anything that can stand in the way of my doing something. There is not. If I want something bad enough, I feel I'm gonna get there."* (taken from his book *'No Limits: The Will to Succeed'*.

APP ALERT!!

- **Salma Hayek**, director, producer and Oscar-nominated actress and dyslexic: *"I'm really a fast learner. I always was, which is maybe why in high school they didn't realise I had dyslexia. I skipped years without studying too much. [The dyslexia] doesn't bother me now. Some people read really fast, but you'll ask them questions about the script and they'll forget. I take a long time to read a script, but I read it only once."*

- **Will.i.am**, Grammy-Award-winning singer and producer: *"[With ADHD] You're always moving and thinking about a whole bunch of things. But those traits work well for me in studios and in meetings about creative ideas. If you listen to the songs I write, they are the most ADHD songs ever. They have five hooks in one and it all happens in three minutes. I figured out a way of working with it."*

249

- **Whoopi Goldberg**, award-winning actress and comedian, and dyslexic: *"They thought I was lazy so they put me in the slow class. But my mom was a Head Start teacher, and she told me, 'You're not slow, you're just different'."*

- Then there's **Steve Jobs, Bill Gates, John Lennon, Joan Rivers, Cher, Einstein, Tom Cruise, Keira Knightley, Stevie Wonder...**

Our world is abundant with inspirational individuals, role models – everyday superstars – who manage their weaknesses, big and small, and play to their strengths. When such attitudes and behaviours are recognised, praised and celebrated by yourself and by others, the recipe for improving your life is a very tasty one.

CATCH YOURSELF, AND OTHERS, DOING THINGS RIGHT

When you catch people doing things right, you must follow it up with praise and positive affirmation. But I'm keen to impress upon you that this must start with yourself! If you live in an environment where praise is slow to be given or not given at all, you may feel undervalued and unloved. Whilst being appreciated by others definitely boosts your juices, it is immensely valuable to turn your attention upon yourself and celebrate your own qualities. Patting your own back not only helps to propel you towards the summits you envisage for yourself, but it also helps you in times when those summits are in danger of obscuring your view and you're questioning whether you can conquer them.

We are all prone to self-criticism, probably more than we are prone to self-praise. How often do you praise yourself, not just for achieving the biggest goals you set yourself, but also for the seemingly minor ones too? Setting high standards, values and goals for yourself is key to achieving excellence (as we discussed in some detail in *'Let the Real You Shine Through'* chapter).

Aligning your strengths and managing your weaknesses to consistently deliver upon your personal mission statement comes close to achieving the holy grail of self-improvement. But reaching these great things involves praising and celebrating bite-size successes on the journey. To adapt a Napoleon Hill phrase, if you can't do great things immediately, do small things in a great way to lead you there.

Remember, what you focus on you feel, which means focusing on your successes and praising them will instil the feelings that you will want to replicate. Self-positive feedback pricks the subconscious to give you more things to praise. On the other hand, an absence of self-praise could signal that others' opinions are more important to you, which means you should return to my *'Take the Power Back'* chapter.

SUCCESS LOG

This brings me to the power of the log or diary. I find this massively helpful on a personal and business basis too. I also know that by insisting this tool is used by my children and my clients it has played a massive part in instilling the benefits of positive psychology into their everyday lives.

I have a gratitude log and I have a success log. I simply enter between three and five things a day that I am grateful for and that I have accomplished. The optimum time to update a log is at night, just before your head hits the pillow, which allows thoughts to be picked up and processed by your unconscious mind. It's a simple technique, but needs to be repeated with discipline and determination to make it a habit, which is truly empowering, turbo-charging your positive attitude and self-belief. And it's there for you to refer to if you ever need a sense-check.

When 'logging in', don't underestimate the power of what might seem like a small or mundane victory. My logs are not like Shakespearean sonnets or da Vinci's notebooks full of art, imagination, purple prose and genius. They're more likely to read:

Thursday February 23rd...

Well done, Stalkie, today you:

- *Didn't swear*

- *Emptied swimming kit from gym bag and put it in the wash*

- *Called mum about arranging for her to stay*

- *Cooked a lovely meal for the kids*

- *Nailed a couple of great ideas for next week's keynote speech*

- *Slept well*

- *Got the children up*

- *Stopped an argument*

- *Great chat with clients*

- *Great reading session*

- *Picked up children from school*

Woohoo! It's tough at the top. But they all had a role to play in achieving my bigger picture.

Try it for yourself (over a four-week period, please) and I promise you it will pay dividends. Use a diary or a note book that you can also put significant things in, such as mementos and photos of your successes or receipts of the treats you may have bought yourself to celebrate your accomplishments.

Whether your bigger picture is to lose weight, become fit, stop smoking, save money, start a business, keep more in touch with your family, whatever... catching yourself doing things right, using positive internal dialogue and visualising success ahead (as we described in the earlier *Fear into Power* chapter) is the stuff of self-perpetuation.

> *"When we take time to notice the things that go right, it means we're getting a lot of little rewards throughout the day."*
>
> – Martin Seligman

APP ALERT!!

THE COLLECTIVE POWER OF LOOKING FOR THE GOOD

Whilst I want you to concentrate on using positive psychology to create the 'you' that you deserve, I would also like to demonstrate what is possible when such principles percolate further and become part of a culture shared by a wider like-minded group.

Team sports are of course a great example of this. I have had the pleasure of working alongside **Humphrey Walters** who for the past 30 years has been inspiring and motivating individuals, teams and corporations in leadership and management and the concept of "The Business of Winning" (www.humphreywalters.com)

Humphrey has studied both academically and practically all aspects of human nature that motivate and inspire people to succeed and win. He is very involved in sports, spending 11 months in a force 10 gale doing the BT Global Challenge – a yacht race sailing the wrong way around the world. He has worked with Premiership football teams, the British judo team and helped the 2003 World Cup-winning England Rugby Team with their team development (they won in the dying seconds of the game with Jonny Wilkinson's iconic drop goal).

Humphrey helped to engender a team spirit in the England team which was underpinned by positive principles such as *"Perpetual optimism is a multiplier: Am I excited? Am I a possibility thinker?"* which he says that the team, led by manager Sir Clive Woodward, was *"bloody good at. He (Clive) always knew England could win the World Cup. Everyone has seen videos of everyone else playing so you have to think the unthinkable. That's one of the reasons why he is such a delight to work with. If you come up with a new idea he'll say "Wow, that's interesting" rather than "That will never work".*

It's this positive mindset, the kind that Sir Clive has, that we look for when we work with corporate clients. We accredit them in the **Raise Your Game** methodology so they can then practise this in their business.

The methodology they learn is largely based upon the principles contained in this book, such as how to use positive psychology in their everyday lives and then apply it to the workplace and coach their colleagues accordingly.

Much of the communication and procedures I teach have the intent of looking for the good and empowering colleagues to meet their needs positively. Showing appreciation is invaluable, and employee reward and recognition systems are put into place that reward attitude and behaviour over and above 'amount of sales made or productivity achieved'.

One of my favourite companies I've worked with, which operates in the demanding, high-stress care sector, is a superb example of how a fear-based, carrot-and-stick management culture can be transformed when members of the leadership team finally say "no more" and take the brave step of creating a new culture in which their colleagues are encouraged, often against the odds, to look for the good.

Under the previous management culture, this company exhibited many of the classic traits of a "'we don't do praise, sympathy or empathy" regime. Emanating from the top of the organisation, and spreading right through to the social workers and carers at the most needy end of the care-giving process, internal communication and methodology was abrupt, prescriptive and of the "just do it and do it now" variety.

There were clearly those in the team who were considered 'favourites' and those who needed to suck up to their superiors in order to avoid the bullets and preserve their jobs. This type of environment resulted in a back-stabbing, moaning and blame mentality, in which insecurity was rife and certain members of the management team felt obliged to protect others. One senior manager estimated that he spent over two days per month placating concerned and upset colleagues.

In an organisation where colleagues are just concentrating on 'getting through the day' rather than flourishing in their work, and disengagement levels are high, there is always, always a large turnover of staff, which in turn costs the organisation a significant slice of their turnover in the recruitment and training of new colleagues. Standards then slip, customer satisfaction reduces and the organisation starts suffering financially. This then puts the senior management team under more pressure to perform and the whole vicious circle begins again.

The catalyst for change within this company was the owner himself who, firstly, had the courage to face the difficult conversations he needed to have with the main people promoting a negative culture within his business. By taking the power back from them and putting like-minded individuals in some of the key leadership roles, he then proved wholly amenable to undertaking a complete review of the business' core values and focused on the behaviours required throughout the team to bring those values alive and cascade them through the layers of management to the 'shop floor'.

This was very much the process that I discuss in detail in *'Let the Real You Shine Through'* chapter of **You Can Raise Your Game!** Whether it is on a personal or business level, similar principles apply – understand and establish the values that will serve you the best, then follow them through authentically with your behaviour through all your relationships.

Under their new set of behavioural rules, the management team are encouraged to stop sending the "just do it" emails and communications, and replace these with positive messages which focus on the good. Managers were also upskilled to take more responsibility for their teams and become more visible to them, with an open-door policy. There is now a rhythm and structure to all meetings so that responsibilities, goals and commitments are open and shared, rather than prescribed and the consequences of failure feared.

The management team will now pick up the telephone or visit colleagues personally to tell them that they are doing a great job; colleagues may well receive a handwritten note of thanks; receive a day off on their birthday; be bought lunch by the boss. Such acts of kindness mean so much to the recipients and create an environment where positive employee engagement and teamwork are the kings.

There is a log of success stories and anecdotes which are collected throughout all areas of the business, and stories which successfully reflect the core values of the business are publicised and celebrated.

Peer feedback and suggestions are encouraged from all levels of colleagues. Mistakes may happen in the course of the day, but instead of being blamed, those who make mistakes are supported and solutions are sought. Challenges are no longer brushed under the carpet or left for others to solve: teams work together to rally round and solve them.

As the change in culture embeds, the payback for the company is colossal, as measured by its improvement in staff retention.

An engaged workforce will know exactly what best practice looks like and they'll want to contribute to it. If it's in a retail shop, for example, colleagues will know the exact words to say to greet a customer, to build rapport and to identify their needs before selling to them. They'll give real-time feedback to their co-workers, congratulating them if they catch each other doing something well, whereas inappropriate behaviour will be realigned through training and mentoring.

The result of this is that customers benefit from outstanding customer service and satisfaction and they'll vote with their feet (by returning again and recommending the service to their friends and family) and vote with their wallets (spending more, more often).

I have unprecedented proof of how this methodology, based upon my principles, transforms individuals and teams and creates a corporate culture where sales, profits and customer care increase sustainably. (You can read about a number of my business case studies and their respective results at www.paulstalker.com/case-studies)

APP ALERT!!

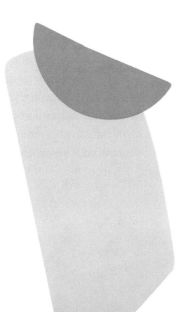

CELEBRATE!

Maureen has always smoked. No one else in her family has ever smoked and they always tried to discourage her from the habit. When she could endure her family's constant nagging no longer, She made the decision to quit. She smoked 40 a day, so it was always going to be a tough journey; but after many false starts, Maureen had her daily quota down to only five or six. Despite her obvious success, she felt disappointed that she was still a smoker. Her family, on the other hand, were very proud of her, husband Ernie in particular.

Maureen felt disappointed with herself; she only recognised her weakness, i.e. the fact that she could not give up completely. On the other hand, Ernie could see her powers of persistence, willingness and determination. By looking positively at the situation, Ernie felt Maureen's success was worth celebrating.

Giving up 35 cigarettes a day, with only five more to go – why, that was going to save lots of money, perhaps enough for Maureen to take them on a few nice weekend breaks or theatre trips! There are often many things to celebrate that will encourage further success.

Ernie has it right. Celebrate each and every achievement with yourself, your loved ones, friends, team mates and work colleagues. They all have their strengths and victories, whether minor or major, worthy of being recognised and celebrated.

As **Tom Peters**, the brilliant American business management guru (best known for his seminal book *'In Search of Excellence'* (www.tompeters.com) wrote:

"Celebrate what you want to see more of."

APP ALERT!!

Stalkie's Summary
TOP 10 TIPS TO HELP YOU PRAISE YOUR GAME NOW!

1. Using positive psychology tools will build the foundations for a positive self-image and support you to live according to the standards and values that you aspire to.

2. Loved ones, family, friends, team mates and colleagues all benefit from your praise and love, but start with yourself and catch yourself doing things right!

3. When you do something you enjoy, reinforce the joyous feelings associated with it; video it, record it, write it down. Create a memory bank of good feelings and learning experiences that you can always call upon.

4. Identify your strengths, and your weaknesses. Align your strengths to the standards to which you aspire, to your values and to your personal mission statement and assess how your weaknesses diminish from this.

5. Play to your strengths, manage your weaknesses. Do more of what you love and what you're good at, rather than burn up belief, time and energy in what you're not good at. The aim is to relegate your weaknesses to the status of irrelevance, so your strengths are free to develop without interruption.

6. Grow your strengths through positive internal dialogue and visualising the outcome you want – what you focus on you feel.

7. Setting sky-high standards for yourself is key to achieving excellence, but reaching them involves celebrating bite-size successes on the journey.

8. Looking for the good and focusing on your successes is truly empowering. Make it a habit by writing a daily success log and noting all the things you are grateful for.

9. When you experience the power of focusing on your achievements, share your knowledge. Make sure your family, your friends and colleagues do the same. Be the catalyst and radiator of what you want to see more of.

10. Don't wait to celebrate your successes or that of others. Celebrate the simple things. The more you do, the more addictive it becomes and the better you feel. Start now. Remember: action supersedes everything!

APP
ALERT!!

10

RAISING YOUR HEALTH AND VITALITY

Take control and manage your energy

WHAT PRIORITY ARE YOU GIVING TO HEALTH IN THE BALANCE OF YOUR LIFE?

Before the age of 35, I'd nearly worked myself into an early grave. What on earth is the point of being one of the richest people buried in the graveyard? I've known a number of highly successful business people who have achieved that mantle well before the age of 50 and have left devastated families to cope without them, and I know plenty of others who are in danger of following suit unless they re-calibrate their priorities speedily. What cost health and happiness?

I learned the value of treating my body with respect just in time and I was lucky to be educated in the rudiments of optimum health and nutrition under the wing of a fantastic team at the Bristol Cancer Help Centre. These principles have formed a part of my life's routine and habits ever since.

"A healthy body is a guest-chamber for the soul; a sick body is a prison"

– Francis Bacon*

Sometimes I've pushed myself to my physical limits just to see where the boundaries of my endurance lie. I've also competed in some sporting events that were ambitiously on my bucket list and seemed highly unlikely that I would ever manage.

Mostly I just keep my engine serviced regularly, intake the right fuel and tick along nicely, setting what I hope is a good example to my kids. What I've learned is that there is no point in honing a six-pack or being the epitome of a gym bunny if it stresses you out or harms you. It's all about achieving balance.

*Francis Bacon (1561-1626) was a philosopher, statesman, scientist, lawyer and author.

I want to be clear that I'm not a puritanical health freak or a goody-goody non-drinker: there's nothing I like more than a few pints down the club with my mates watching the sport on TV. I adore cooking at home with my family or eating out, accompanied by some decent wine, and I like treats of the chocolate variety. But I also seriously, seriously value my health.

APP ALERT!!

So please don't be an accident waiting to happen like I was and countless others like me are destined to become. Rather than avoid or worry about the signs of fatigue or ill health, rather than sit and procrastinate, rather than fly in the face of reasonable personal health management – be bright, be proactive and watch your energy and effectiveness flourish when you work with, and not against, your brilliant body.

It's more than likely that you have at least an understanding of what a basic level of physical activity looks like, and what you should and shouldn't eat and drink. The messages are out there, such as The Eatwell Guide (www.gov.uk/government/publications/the-eatwell-guide) which is a policy tool used to define government recommendations on eating healthily and achieving a balanced diet, summarised in picture form on the next page.

Eatwell Guide

Use the Eatwell Guide to help you get a balance of healthier and more sustainable food.
It shows how much of what you eat overall should come from each food group.

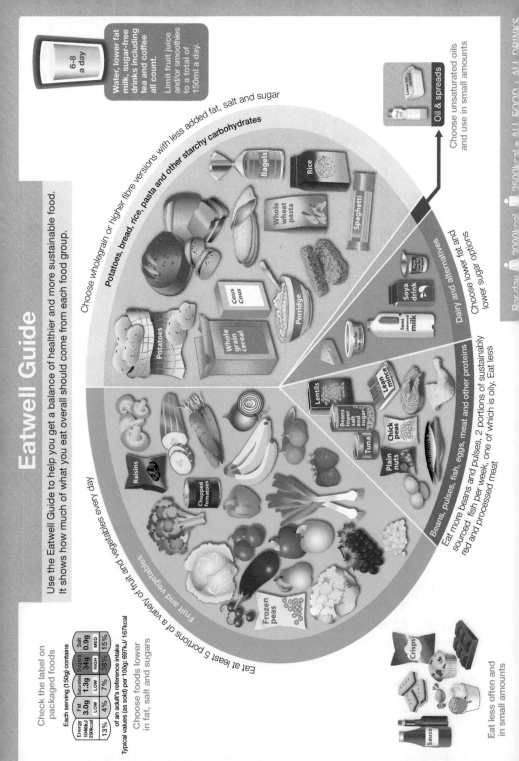

6-8 a day

Water, lower fat milk, sugar-free drinks including tea and coffee all count.

Limit fruit juice and/or smoothies to a total of 150ml a day.

Choose wholegrain or higher fibre versions with less added fat, salt and sugar

Potatoes, bread, rice, pasta and other starchy carbohydrates

Bagels

Rice

Whole wheat pasta

Spaghetti

Cous Cous

Porridge

Potatoes

Whole grain cereal

Oil & spreads

Choose unsaturated oils and use in small amounts

Dairy and alternatives

Choose lower fat and lower sugar options

Soya drink

Semi skimmed milk

Lower fat

Beans, pulses, fish, eggs, meat and other proteins

Eat more beans and pulses, 2 portions of sustainably sourced fish per week, one of which is oily. Eat less red and processed meat

Lentils

Lean mince

Beans lower salt and sugar

Chick peas

Tuna

Plain nuts

Raisins

Chopped tomatoes

Frozen peas

Eat at least 5 portions of a variety of fruit and vegetables every day

Fruit and vegetables

Crisps

Sauce

Eat less often and in small amounts

Check the label on packaged foods

Each serving (150g) contains

Energy	Fat	Saturates	Sugars	Salt
1046kJ 250kcal	3.0g	1.3g	34g	0.9g
13%	4%	7%	38%	15%
	LOW	LOW	HIGH	MED

of an adult's reference intake
Typical values (as sold) per 100g: 697kJ/ 167kcal

Choose foods lower in fat, salt and sugars

Source: Public Health England in association with the Welsh government, Food Standards Scotland and the Food Standards Agency in Northern Ireland

Your body, just like your mind, needs stimulating and nurturing in order that it can grow and perform successfully. Health is defined by the World Health Organisation as being *'soundness of body'*, but it is also energy, zest for life, enthusiasm, keenness and 'get up and go'. Without good health, the rest of your life could suffer – the state of your body affects everything you do, including how long you are able to concentrate, your behavioural patterns, your ability to cope with pressure and the amount of energy levels you have for the day.

My aim in the first part of this chapter is to lay out some factual health-based information about the value and benefits of treating your body – and hence your well-being – with the respect it deserves so it will continuously serve you with vitality and energy.

I'll then move on to the essential elements of constructing a strategy that you can implement to raise your health and energy levels above and beyond your expectations, allowing you to thrive not just physically but socially, mentally, emotionally and spiritually.

OUR VITAL ELEMENTS

In order to achieve optimum health, we all need to understand our relationship with the basic elements of our personal ecosystem:

Cells

Every living thing displays an organised structure which is made up of a cell or cells; it requires energy to survive or sustain existence and the ability to reproduce and grow. The average human body has approximately 75 to 100 trillion cells, and they all need to be kept healthy.

What makes some people more enthusiastic and energetic than others?

The answer is in our cells. Take a look at the photos of some blood cells shown on the next page:

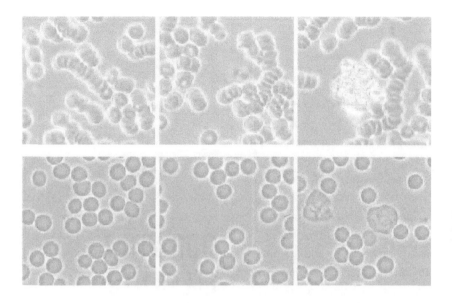

The top row of photos reveals what unhealthy blood cells look like under a microscope. These were shown to me at the health clinic where I go every year for a health screen. The practitioners evaluate my level of health and fitness and prescribe supplements and exercise for any areas that they feel are in need of improvement.

Unhealthy blood cells may show up as irregular in shape or 'spikey' looking, or can be seen stuck together in long chains. The spikey cells are called acanthocytes and the presence of these in the blood indicates possible free radical damage and nutritional deficiency states. Blood cells that are stuck together in long chains are generally indicative of dehydration or free radical activity.

Free radicals are mostly negatively charged particles that can damage arterial vessels and cause cellular changes. The principal causes of free radicals are toxins, pollutants, fried foods, lack of exercise and stress.

I will be explaining as we go along some of the simple things that can be incorporated into anyone's lifestyle, the results of which can change unhealthy looking blood cells into the healthy looking ones you can see in the bottom row of photos. Remarkable, isn't it, to look inside the body and see how good nutrition and exercise affects the very cells themselves? Let's take a look at what's needed to keep cells healthy.

But don't just take my word for it. Other than helping to replenish your body's engine, there's much scientific evidence to suggest that being one with nature encourages relaxed, harmonious feelings and well-being in us all.

Oxygen – Take Time for a Natural High

As a nature loving Dorset person, I spend as much time as I can communing with nature and marvelling at the ecosystem which we can easily fail to appreciate in our ready-meal, everything-always-in-season lifestyles.

Breathing in the clean air of the New Forest is something I do most days, and swimming or surfing amongst the more bracing elements of the 100 miles of Dorset coast is an essential ingredient of my quality of life – particularly after cancer specialists told me of the vital need to fill my body with plenty of clean oxygen.

You breathe in oxygen, and its energy is then coupled with a complex molecule called Adenosine Triphosphate (ATP). ATP is the nucleotide known in biochemistry as the "molecular currency" of intracellular energy transfer; like a battery for the human body, it stores and transports chemical energy within cells.

According to researchers from the University of Essex, just five minutes of fresh air and 'green exercise' makes a huge difference to mood and self-esteem, and this is even greater by open water. The researchers analysed data from ten separate studies and looked at nature activities such as walking, gardening, cycling, fishing, boating, horse-riding and farming. The study found that the largest positive effect on self-esteem came from a five-minute spell:

"For the first time in the scientific literature, we have been able to show dose-response relationships for the positive effects of nature on human mental health".

Researchers from the University of Edinburgh and Heriot-Watt University used portable EEGs to monitor the brain activity of study participants who strolled through different urban environments in Edinburgh. When they walked through the busy urban areas, their brain-wave patterns consistently showed that they were more aroused and frustrated than when they walked through the parkland, where brain-wave readings became more meditative.

A long-term study by the University of Exeter revealed that people living in urban areas with greater amounts of green space were happier than those who didn't. The researchers analysed data from 5,000 UK households (around 12,000 individuals) and followed people who moved closer to and away from green spaces and noted the changes. When compared to living in areas with less green space, the study participants showed significantly lower mental distress and significantly higher well-being and life satisfaction. The effect of urban green spaces on well-being appears to be comparable to the effects of positive job satisfaction and a flourishing marriage.

'Shinrin-yoku' is a Japanese term which means 'forest-bathing' – taking time to walk in the woods. Japanese scientists have established that forest environments promote lower concentrations of cortisol, lower pulse rate, lower blood pressure, greater nerve activity, and lower sympathetic nerve activity than urban environments.

In one study a group of middle-aged Tokyo businessmen were taken to hike in the woods for three days. By the end of the trip, blood tests showed that their Natural Killer or NK cells (a type of white blood cell and a component of the innate immune system which plays a major role in the host-rejection of both tumours and virally infected cells) had increased 40%. A month later, their NK count was still 15% higher than when they started. Even a one day walk in a suburban park boosted the levels of both NK cells and anticancer proteins for at least seven days afterwards. During urban walking trips, NK levels didn't alter at all.

So convinced are they of the benefits that Japan has upwards of 50 official Forest Therapy trails, designated for shinrin-yoku by Japan's Forestry Agency.

So please remember to take time out of your schedule to always smell the roses (and I don't mean in the supermarket).

APP ALERT!!

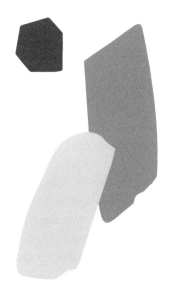

Stalkie's
'FILLING YOUR BODY WITH GOOD CLEAN OXYGEN' WORKOUT

Make sure that you are in a high oxygen environment – ideally outdoors or by an open window – and that the air is clean and not polluted with smoke, chemicals or exhaust fumes.

Standing with your feet slightly apart, check that you are not holding tension in the chest wall, diaphragm or shoulders, by massaging or shaking it loose. Start by breathing out, then take a really good full breath in that starts low down in the belly. When you do this it means that you are breathing from the diaphragm at the bottom of the lungs, so first let go of the stomach muscles and allow the belly to expand, then the mid part of the chest, going right on up to the tip of the lungs under the shoulders. As you do this, count to six so that the in-breath is long, slow and smooth.

At the top of the breath hold it in for a count of three, and then equally smoothly breathe out for a count of six, until the lungs are completely empty and the stomach muscles pulled in. Hold the breath out for a count of three. Repeat the process a further five times, until you have taken six completely full, deep breaths.

269

When you hold your breath in at the top, oxygen in the air you have breathed in is moving into the blood stream. When you hold the breath out at the bottom, carbon dioxide is leaving the blood to go back into the lungs, ready to be breathed out again.

By practising this full breath you will achieve higher oxygen levels and lower carbon dioxide levels than you have experienced in a very long time! At first you may be a little dizzy, because our bodies get used to working without the proper level of oxygen, and with far too much carbon dioxide in our system. So, start gently, and stop to rest if you feel dizzy. You will recover quickly.

If you practise once a day, you will gradually retrain your breathing mechanism in such a way that you will feel calm and refreshed; you'll soon find that you naturally go into a much deeper breathing pattern: the count should be roughly one per second.

APP ALERT!!

Stalkie's
'CREATE INSTANT HIGH ENERGY THROUGH BREATHING' WORKOUT

If you wish to create instant high energy through breathing, a great way is to use the 'bellows breath'. This involves bending over slightly, resting your hands on your knees, and then pumping the breath in and out with your diaphragm, just like a bellows. This is a noisy, chaotic breath, and you are using the considerable force of your diaphragm to pump all of the stale air out of your lungs.

The action is to contract the stomach wall and diaphragm sharply, so that air is literally forced out. Then, let go of the muscles quickly, so the air comes back in quickly too. Once you have got the movement, pump the breath at the rate of one or two per second. As you release the diaphragm, clean air comes flooding in. Again, slow down if you start to feel dizzy at first.

Start by executing ten breaths in rapid succession, then take a long, slow full breath as in Workout 1. Repeat the cycle twice.

This is a great way to energise yourself quickly if you ever feel run down, tired and in need of a quick burst of energy – but don't do this exercise if you suffer from acute asthma, heart problems or high blood pressure, and check first with your gp if you have any other health concerns.

When you've had some practice, you can build up to as many as 50 bellows breaths per cycle, and three full cycles. If you do this every morning, it will only take five minutes, and you'll feel fantastic!

EFFECTIVE NUTRITION

As well as oxygen, your body also requires healthy food; it is absolutely worth knowing how good nutrition plays its part in keeping you healthy by providing the vital energy and all the vitamins, minerals and nutrients you need.

My mentor and health expert, Dr. Rosy Daniel*, has worked for 30 years to help people with serious cancer fight back from the brink.

APP ALERT!!

Dr. Daniel is committed to helping people become more involved in the creation of their optimum health and happiness, whether they are currently suffering from illness or seeking to prevent it. Her Regenerative Health Programme is at the forefront of preventive healthcare and offers specialised, individualised care and support from Dr. Rosy and her select team of mentors, therapists and trainers to achieve measurable health gain.

*Dr. Rosy Daniel joined the Bristol Cancer Help Centre in 1985, later becoming the Medical Director and CEO. As an Integrative Medicine Consultant she provides expert medical help, combined with her knowledge of nutrition, complementary therapy and the mind-body connection, to design individualised programmes which have helped thousands of people to engage in proactive self-help and achieve levels of health and well-being never envisaged by their conventional medical teams. Dr. Daniel's services are integrated alongside those of a client's GP or consultant throughout the programme. Regular assessments and good communication between the multi-disciplinary team provide vital feedback on progress to enable sensitive tailoring of ongoing care. www.drrosydaniel.org

EATING YOURSELF HEALTHY

A study published last year attributed Japan's impressive average life expectancy of 85 years to its healthy diet. Researchers found that people who closely followed the Japanese government's official food guide, created in 2005, had a 15% lower mortality rate. This involved a diet low in saturated fats and processed foods, and high amounts of vegetables and carbohydrates from eating rice.

In essence, to be healthy you need to eat meals that are rich in fruit, vegetables, pulses and grains; they should be low in animal fats, animal protein, sugar, additives and refined foods.

The mainstay of the cancer recovery plan that Dr. Rosy put into place for me was based around healthy eating. I'd like to pass on to you some of the simple guidelines I was given to create and sustain a top-class, healthy body. It's something that I believe in, treasure and adhere to.

Include a high proportion of raw fruit and vegetables every day, either on their own, in salads or via homemade vegetable juices – these represent an excellent source of nutrition. Get yourself a juice extractor, or better still use a juice press.

Replace refined and processed foods with the whole food, unprocessed equivalent. This means looking to replace, for example:

- White bread with wholemeal bread

- White rice with brown rice

- White pasta with wholegrain pasta

- Ordinary cheese biscuits with oatcakes

- Processed breakfast cereal with muesli or porridge

- Sweets and chocolate with nuts, dried fruits or fresh fruit

- Sweetened drinks with mineral water, or homemade juices

- Replace intensively farmed red meat, chicken and fish with vegetable protein from beans, lentils, peas and quinoa. Go the vegan route if you wish, but if this is not realistic, supplement your diet with occasional organic, wild, deep-sea fish, salmon or trout, free-range organic chicken and game, free-range organic eggs and very occasionally organic red meat. Introduce as much variety into your diet as possible, and try different pulses so that you get a full spectrum of minerals and vitamins.

- Replace animal fats with vegetarian equivalents. The exception to this rule is fish oils, which are helpful because they contain essential omega 3 fatty acids. These are found in oily fish such as mackerel, herrings and salmon (organic), and you can also take fish oil tablets.

- Replace regular milk with skimmed milk or, better still, vegetable milks such as soya, oat or rice milk. Try to cut dairy milk from your diet altogether by drinking tea weak and black, and using home-made fruit juices on muesli. Porridge can be eaten without milk – instead, flavour it with fruit concentrates, or date/maple syrup.

- Replace cheese with vegetable pâtés, such as olive, aubergine, avocado (guacamole) and mushroom. It is also better to use a fish pâté than cheese. However, you should check that pâtés or pastes are not full of 'hidden' cream cheese.

- Replace animal cooking fats with vegetable oils. Use speciality oils to flavour salad dressings, e.g. sesame oil and walnut oil.

- Replace dairy cream and ice cream, and dairy yoghurts, with soya or other plant-based alternatives. Instead of butter use vegetable equivalents such as olive oil based spreads or margarines which do not contain hydrogenated fatty acids.

APP ALERT!!

THE IMPORTANCE OF BEING ALKALINE

Here's an indispensable piece of health advice which I follow: many of our most common degenerative diseases such as cancer, heart disease and arthritis, are caused by our bodies being too acidic. Food, drink and behaviour which acidify the body are:

- Drinks such as wine, fruit juice, tea and coffee, fruit teas, fizzy drinks and fruit cordials

- Fruits such as berries (eat fruit when it's as ripe as possible because that will make it less acidic)

- Yoghurt

- Pickles

- Vinegar

- Berry jams

- Excess protein from meat, fish and shellfish

- Smoking

- Lack of exercise

- Shallow breathing or breath-holding if you are anxious

To counteract acidity in your diet, choose the following:

- All vegetables except tomatoes

- Pulses, nuts, seeds, grains and cereals

- Non-acid fruits such as melon, banana, papaya, dates, figs and sharon fruit

- Fresh filtered water, herb and green teas, and vegetable juices

- No more than 4oz (120g) of protein in any one day

Confusion can exist looking at lists of foods that are 'acid-forming' and 'alkaline-forming'. Lemons, for example, are clearly acidic, but it is an alkaline-forming food because when eaten the body buffers its acid with alkali. In order to do this, alkaline buffers are used up and so the tissues become progressively more acidic. For this reason, it is vital to eliminate food and drink types that are acidic themselves, rather than being acid-forming.

Your body is constantly trying to maintain an alkaline balance. Your cells work very hard to keep you healthy, but if you are consistently too acidic the likelihood is that you will become ill. Further information on the benefits of an alkaline diet can be found at: www.americannutritionassociation.org and www.diabetes.co.uk

KEEP THINKING OF GOOD HYDRATION

THE LITMUS TEST

The pH (acidity) of your body can be tested with litmus paper. By checking your salivary and urinary pH twice a week, you can assess your body's status. This should be done first thing in the morning before drinking, eating or brushing your teeth. It can be helpful to keep a chart, because this will enable you to notice changes as you eliminate acidic foods.

You are aiming for a salivary pH of 7.5. Results less than 7 are acid, indicating that you have work to do to get your body alkaline. Litmus paper can generally be bought from pharmacies, health food shops or from specialist heathcare companies such as www. healthcreation.co.uk/shop/low-acid-living/litmus-paper

The earth is made up of approximately 70% water and 30% mass, and your body closely mirrors these proportions too – we all consist of around 80% water.

This is why you need to have a recommended daily intake of quality, filtered water. Whenever you become ill, the first thing you're told is to make sure you drink lots of water, so that all the toxins which have built up overnight from the chemical processes of the body can be flushed out of the tissues.

Aim to drink three litres of good quality water per day. This means consuming 1 x 250ml glass of water per hour, which is not so much when you think about it. The water you drink should be filtered or spring water, as tap water can be chlorinated and open to a degree of contamination.

APP ALERT!!

KEEP IT LIVE

I encourage eating 'live food' – which has not had the life cooked, microwaved, processed, fried, irradiated, frozen or chemically taken out of it – wherever possible as this ensures all the beneficial living vitamins, minerals, enzymes and phyto-nutrients are intact.

Foods in this category include fresh vegetables, fruits, salads, nuts and seeds, plus fresh cereals and grains. In nature, these substances have been shown to reverse the formation of cancer cells – but only if food is still live. All such substances are very sensitive to heat, cold and irradiation, not to mention many of the other processes by which food is processed and chemically treated to keep it fresh and looking perfect for the supermarket shelves.

When altered too much, the good things in these foods effectively die, and therefore become useless at protecting us from disease. The aim is to ensure you include live fresh food with every single meal. A great way to supplement this is by juicing vegetables every day.

JUICING

Vegetables and non-acid fruits provide the very best way for you to protect your health, and the quickest way to get large quantities of vital plant phyto-nutrients into the body is by making your own vegetable juice daily.

Juicing large quantities of fruit and vegetables breaks the nutrient goodies out of their cellulose fibre casing, and turns them into a form that the body can easily digest. In this way, it is possible to get all the nutritious substances that your body craves without having to chew your way through many kilos of raw vegetables.

The best juicer to buy is a press, because this does the least damage to those essential plant enzymes. Next best is the cheaper juice extractor, but purists say these machines do break up some of the powerful enzymes because they operate with a very high centrifugal force.

Vegetables are very alkaline in nature, so because many fruits are acid, make sure that your juices feature mainly vegetables such as carrots, beetroot, and celery, plus the non-acid fruits I listed earlier. Drinking a glass of vegetable juice a day can quickly restore the essential alkaline balance in your body.

APP ALERT!!

Stalkie's 'LIVE FOOD' WORKOUT

Write down everything that you have consumed over the last two days (you may need a sheet of paper for this in addition to the table below). Now highlight the live foods – the fruits, raw or lightly steamed/stir-fried vegetables, salads, nuts, seeds and raw cereals in your diet.

When you have completed that, look at what percentage of live food you are eating. If you are eating 70% live food or more, then you are on the right track. If you are eating 10% live, it's a lot better than 0% and it is a starting point to improve your score.

LET'S TALK TOXINS

Awareness of what you should give your cells to keep them working properly is only half the story when committing to an optimum healthy lifestyle. You must also know how your body works with regard to toxins.

There's little to be gained by going vegetable-tastic, if you are also toxin-tastic.

The main toxins to avoid are:

- Chemical additives that extend shelf life, 'enhance' colour and flavour. In rare cases, some of these are carcinogens themselves.

- Foods which are chargrilled or smoked, which have a higher possibility of containing carcinogenic substances.

- Excess alcohol and nicotine – the two most common toxins which destroy our bodies' health.

Did you know that the foods we need become toxic to the body if we overeat them? This is because the body has to control the levels of all substances very finely in the blood such as sugar, protein, salt and fat. But if the body is regularly flooded with too much of these substances, it goes into collapse and the organs which control these levels become diseased.

The table below shows the effect of eating too much of our basic foods.

	Excess of – Diseases Caused	Key Organs Affected
Fat:	Obesity, hardening of the arteries, heart attacks, strokes, cancer, arthritis	Heart and liver
Sugar:	Obesity and diabetes	Pancreas and liver
Salt:	High blood pressure, heart disease, strokes, obesity	Kidneys
Protein:	High acid levels, cancer	Acidification of all tissues

BEWARE OF THESE BAD BOYS...

Fat

Excess animal fat from dairy products, meat and fried foods becomes deposited in the blood vessels and this, combined with high stress levels, is a profound contributor to heart disease.

Some fat is necessary for the body to function efficiently; essential fatty acids from nuts and seeds, plus oily fish, are essential for health because they help to regulate cholesterol, maintain healthy skin and provide us with energy and insulation. However, most people eat far too much fat. Fatty foods are more readily available, and they're made to look very attractive in the form of ice cream, crisps and fast food products.

Many of these fast foods give you empty calories, with the result that you are overfed and undernourished. To keep fat levels down in the blood, the liver works very hard to lay down fat into the tissues; this exhausts us, putting stress on the heart and joints. Worse than that, the fat becomes a storehouse for chemicals from the environment, and also produces excess hormones, which fuel breast and prostate cancer.

Sugar

Your body runs on sugar, after it has been broken down to glucose. All other foods can be broken down into sugar to keep you going, if your levels become low. Sugar, like fat, is highly present in a modern diet.

Natural sugar (fructose) used to come from ingesting fruits and vegetables, and this also provided many essential vitamins and minerals but consumer habits have gravitated to buying sweeter, processed foods including chocolates, biscuits and cakes, fizzy drinks, cocktails and ice creams. Sugar is even tucked away in the ingredients of products like baked beans, tomato ketchup and soups.

APP ALERT!!

279

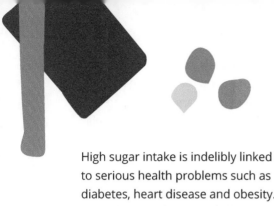

Protein

Protein repairs the wear and tear on your muscles, but you don't need more than 4oz or 120g of protein a day – so, it is easy to see that a day with bacon, sausage and eggs for breakfast, a cheese, chicken or tuna sandwich at lunchtime and fish, steak or chops for dinner will take you way over your protein requirement.

Once you exceed your needs, the protein will be broken down and converted to fat for storage and produces acid in your body. Too much protein will therefore promote fat, and we know that acid bodies lead to achy, rheumatic joints and offer an ideal environment for cancer and arterial disease to develop.

High sugar intake is indelibly linked to serious health problems such as diabetes, heart disease and obesity. Put it this way: have a naughty wee Mars bar and it will contain the sugar content of five pounds (2.5kg) of apples, and is absorbed into the bloodstream within 30 minutes. Just think how long it would take you to chew and absorb that level of sugar from all those apples!

Salt

The body needs a level of salt to maintain the correct volume of circulating blood and tissue fluids. Too much salt puts stress on the kidneys resulting in high blood pressure, which in turn can contribute towards strokes and heart disease. The main salty culprit is processed foods.

APP ALERT!!

Tobacco

Smoking lowers the availability of oxygen to our tissues, and it raises blood pressure because carbon monoxide in the tobacco smoke reduces the blood's ability to carry oxygen. Smoking can cause many other problems apart from heart disease, including respiratory tract disorders.

The main problems are caused by carcinogenic tars in cigarettes, which cause cancer directly. But, smoke also causes fat to be laid down on our artery walls, increasing the risk of heart attacks; this can also cut off the blood supply to the extremities of our body. Did you know that a significant number of smokers end up as amputees, because their limbs become too painful to bear when the blood supply is impaired? Smoking makes our skin look awful too – we age quicker when we smoke because it destroys the elastin: yes, smokers wrinkle much faster!

Alcohol

Like most people, I find the occasional drink most convivial and socially acceptable. So I'm never going to preach abstinence from alcohol for all people but I couldn't possibly turn a blind eye to the impact that reliance on alcohol or regular spates of binge drinking can have on physical health and emotional well-being.

Alcohol is extremely toxic, and it affects every area of your body; not one of your cells is able to resist it. Alcohol causes dehydration, and this leads to hangovers. When alcohol breaks down, its products damage the liver directly, and as the liver struggles to metabolise away the poisons, many vital vitamins and minerals are used up, leaving the nervous system weak.

Heavy drinkers are more prone to become irritable and short tempered, suffer from memory loss and the peripheral nerves in their limbs are damaged, leading to loss of feeling.

The key here, as in many aspects of optimum health management, is moderation. The current UK guidelines advise limiting alcohol intake to 14 units a week for women and men. This is equivalent to drinking no more than six pints of average-strength beer (4% ABV) or seven medium-sized glasses of wine (175ml, 12% ABV) a week.

And it's not okay to reserve your whole weekly allowance and drink the lot in one or two sittings as this will damage the liver even more quickly!

Caffeine

Caffeine, which most of us consume in coffee, tea and fizzy drinks, is a mildly addictive stimulant. When too much caffeine has been consumed, people can become over-anxious, restless and unable to concentrate. Some may also notice stomach pains, persistent headaches and sleeping problems.

High doses of caffeine are toxic and can cause high blood pressure, heart palpitations and vomiting. All this occurs because the caffeine buzz puts us into fight or flight response, where our brain and muscles work at the expense of our digestion and immunity. We become less able to achieve any decent nourishment from our food – and we get acid stomachs to boot.

WORKING WITH YOUR BODY

You are responsible for what you put into your body. Whatever goes in has to be digested and then stored or purged in some way. When you become ill, your body immediately starts to try to cure it – this cure begins by eliminating toxins from the body. You eliminate toxins through urine and the bowel; you also get rid of toxins through the skin, the mouth and through the lungs.

The start of an illness can also be the start of the cure, provided you listen to, and work with, your body. Take cats, for example: as soon as they feel something is wrong they eat grass, and it makes them vomit. This is the beginning of the healing process, because they're getting rid of the toxins in their bodies. Humans are very similar; we have automatic responses for eliminating toxins, but these are frequently masked by taking medication, which may get rid of symptoms like sneezing, coughing or diarrhoea, and yet these are the very things which are actually getting rid of the poison and starting the healing process.

CANCER PREVENTION

More than one in three people will develop some form of cancer during their lifetime. Although there are more than 200 different types of cancers, it is lung, breast, prostate and bowel cancer which account for more than half of cases.

According to Cancer Research UK (www.cancerresearchuk.org) an unhealthy lifestyle is the root cause of about a third of all cancers. Smoking, for example, causes almost all lung cancer and poor diet has been linked to bowel, pancreatic and oesophageal cancer. While the healthy lifestyle changes that I talk about in this chapter can help prevent many cases of cancer, screening aims to drive down cancer cases even further.

APP ALERT!!

National screening programmes can identify cancer at an early stage when it's more treatable, so please make sure that you:

- know the key symptoms of cancer, starting with the excellent NHS *'Be Clear on Cancer'* campaign, at www.nhs.uk/be-clear-on-cancer

- take up the offer of cancer screening. Find out more about the NHS screening programmes at www.nhs.uk/conditions/nhs-screening

PREVENTING HEART DISEASE

Most cases of premature death from coronary (or ischaemic) heart disease are completely preventable.

Smoking, being overweight, having high blood pressure and/or high cholesterol, heavy drinking and physical inactivity are all key risk factors.

If you're over 40, ask your GP about the NHS Health Check, a free five-yearly mid-life MOT to look for things like blood pressure and cholesterol levels.

Exercise can reduce your risk of heart attack by 30%. Try to do more exercise, especially aerobic exercise like walking, swimming and cycling. You don't have to become a fitness freak, but a straightforward exercise plan for beginners combining aerobic, strength and flexibility exercises can easily be sought at a gym or via a link such as this one, again courtesy of the NHS: www.nhs.uk/live-well/exercise/12-week-fitness-plan

The NHS is also a great starting point to find out about managed weight loss plans, such as the Change4Life healthy eating campaign and 12-week weight loss plan. I'm advocating these NHS initiatives because they cost you nothing, removing the "it's bound to be expensive" objection from the get-go: www.nhs.uk/live-well/healthy-weight/start-the-nhs-weight-loss-plan

REDUCING YOUR RISK OF STROKE

Stroke is the third leading cause of death in England each year and the leading cause of disability.

More than 100,000 people suffer a stroke every year in the UK but, according to The Stroke Association (www.stroke.org.uk) up to 10,000 of these could be prevented if more people were aware of the symptoms and sought emergency treatment.

High blood pressure is the main cause of stroke. Almost one in three people in England have high blood pressure and nearly half of them aren't receiving any treatment for the condition, says the British Heart Foundation (www.bhf.org.uk). Go to their website to find out what lifestyle and preventative changes you can make such as reducing high blood pressure, cutting down on salt and having a healthy diet.

REDUCING YOUR RISK OF LUNG DISEASE

Respiratory disease covers a variety of conditions ranging from asthma to chronic obstructive pulmonary disease (COPD), one of the most common causes of death.

COPD is almost completely avoidable, states the NHS on its website. Most cases (around 85%) are caused by smoking. The other 15% of cases are triggered by exposure to fumes, chemicals and dusts at work or, very occasionally, because of a rare genetic tendency to develop COPD called alpha-1-antitrypsin deficiency.

- find out how the NHS can help you to stop smoking at www.nhs.uk/live-well/quit-smoking and you can also download the free NHS Smokefree app for daily tips and support.

REDUCING YOUR RISK OF LIVER DISEASE

Liver disease is on the rise in England with a 20% increase in cases over the last decade. The disease develops silently and many people have no idea there's anything wrong until they develop liver failure and it's too late.

The three main causes of liver disease are heavy drinking, obesity and viral infection of the liver (hepatitis). More than a third of men and over a quarter of women regularly exceed the recommended daily alcohol allowance. Practical insight and advice on how to take control of your drinking is available from the NHS Change4Life programme at www.nhs.uk/live-well/alcohol-support

A sound starting point to find out if you, or those you care for, are a healthy weight is to understand what your BMI (Body Mass Index) is and how you can calculate it at: www.nhs.uk/live-well/healthy-weight/bmi-calculator You can also read articles on how to sensibly and sustainably lose weight at home via: www.nhs.uk/live-well/healthy-weight/start-the-nhs-weight-loss-plan

The British Liver Trust has plenty of advice and information on maintaining liver health and preventing the causes of conditions such as hepatitis at www.britishlivertrust.org.uk

GUARDING AGAINST OBESITY

Halting the general obesity trend will require a shift in thinking and approach across the board in society – from government to education to business to communities to individual families. It means creating an environment that educates and encourages healthier eating and physical activity – but what it boils down to is eating less and moving more.

It's scary to think that the only country to have successfully reversed its obesity problem was Cuba – not through a calculated strategy, but as a by-product of an economic slump in the early 1990s. With severe food and fuel shortages, the average Cuban lost 5.5kg in weight over the course of the five-year economic crisis. What also dropped was the amount of cases and deaths due to cardiovascular diseases, Type 2 diabetes and some cancers.

In the UK, we can acknowledge various government and private sector initiatives around obesity such as:

- giving people advice on healthier food choices and physical activity through the NHS Change4Life programme

- improving labelling on food and drink to help people make healthy choices

- encouraging businesses on the high street to include calorie information on their menus

- giving people guidance on how much physical activity they should be doing

- Responsibility Deal pledges with UK businesses and the voluntary sector to improve public health

- Encouraging food manufacturers and retailers to cut down on the amount of fat, sugar and salt in popular food products

This is all good stuff, but it is you and I that are practically responsible for our own health and need to act as role models for our families and loved ones: your body, your sense of purpose. As Susan Jebb, Professor of Diet and Population Health at Oxford University, states,

"We've all got the potential to be fat. In the environment we live in, it's easy to overeat and be less active. Some people need to work harder than others at keeping weight gain in check."

GETTING ACTIVE & EXERCISING REGULARLY

The UK Chief Medical Officer's guidelines state that the general benefits of physical activity are improved health and sleep, maintenance of a healthy weight, stress management, and an improved quality of life.

More specifically, it can reduce your chances of suffering from Type 2 diabetes by up to 40%, cardio-vascular disease by 35%, falls, depression and dementia by 30%, joint and back pain by 25% and cancers (colon and breast cancer) by 20%.

So, what does a reasonable physical activity and fitness guideline look like, particularly for those who aren't necessarily schooled in the language and workings of the gym? I recommend the free NHS Live Well programme.

In addition to its 'lose weight' section which clearly gets to grips with healthy weight loss, including healthy snacks and breakfasts, speeding up your metabolism and food labels, its health and fitness section promotes down-to-earth ideas on getting more active whatever your starting point, including starter-friendly exercise plans, strength and flexibility workouts and 10-minute workouts.

It also has a digital apps library which allows you to download free apps which do everything from comparing supermarket ingredients to easing your stress and anxiety: www.nhs.uk/live-well

To summarise the LiveWell recommendations, in order to stay healthy, adults between the ages of 19-64 should be active daily and undertake:

- at least 150 minutes of moderate aerobic activity such as cycling or fast walking every week, and

- strength exercises two or more days a week that work all the major muscles: legs, hips, back, abdomen, chest, shoulders and arms.

OR

- 75 minutes of vigorous aerobic activity such as running or a game of singles tennis every week, and

- strength exercises on two or more days a week that work all the major muscles

OR

- A mix of moderate and vigorous aerobic activity every week. For example, two 30-minute runs plus 30 minutes of fast walking equates to 150 minutes of moderate aerobic activity, and

- strength exercises on two or more days a week that work all the major muscles

All adults should also break up long periods of sitting with light activity. Sitting for long periods is thought to slow the metabolism, which affects the body's ability to regulate blood sugar and blood pressure and break down body fat.

Many adults in the UK spend more than seven hours a day sitting or lying down, and this typically increases with age to ten hours or more. This includes watching TV, using a computer, reading, doing homework and travelling but does not include sleeping.

Activities that require moderate effort for most people include:

- walking fast
- water aerobics
- riding a bike on level ground or with few hills
- doubles tennis
- pushing a lawn mower
- hiking
- skateboarding
- rollerblading
- volleyball
- basketball

Moderate activity will raise your heart rate and make you breathe faster and feel warmer. One way to tell if you're working at a moderate level is if you can still talk, but you can't sing the words to a song.

There is good evidence that vigorous activity can bring health benefits over and above that of moderate activity.

Examples of activities that require vigorous effort for most people include:

- jogging or running
- swimming fast
- riding a bike fast or on hills
- singles tennis
- football
- rugby
- skipping rope
- hockey
- aerobics
- gymnastics
- martial arts

Vigorous activity makes you breathe hard and fast. If you're working at this level, you won't be able to say more than a few words without pausing for breath.

In general, 75 minutes of vigorous activity can give similar health benefits to 150 minutes of moderate activity.

Muscle strength is necessary for:

- all daily movement
- to build and maintain strong bones
- to regulate blood sugar and blood pressure
- to help maintain a healthy weight

Muscle-strengthening exercises are counted in repetitions and sets. A repetition is one complete movement of an activity, like a bicep curl or a sit-up. A set is a group of repetitions.

For each strength exercise, try to do:

- at least one set
- eight to 12 repetitions in each set

To get health benefits from strength exercises, you should do them to the point where you struggle to complete another repetition.

There are many ways you can strengthen your muscles, whether it's at home or in the gym. Examples of muscle-strengthening activities for most people include:

- lifting weights
- working with resistance bands
- doing exercises that use your own body weight, such as push-ups and sit-ups
- heavy gardening, such as digging and shovelling
- yoga

You can do activities that strengthen your muscles on the same day or on different days as your aerobic activity – whatever's best for you. Muscle-strengthening exercises are not an aerobic activity, so you'll need to do them in addition to your 150 minutes of aerobic activity.

Some vigorous activities count as both an aerobic activity and a muscle-strengthening activity, such as:

- circuit training
- running
- football
- rugby
- netball
- hockey

11

INSPIRATION AND FULFILMENT

*Getting inspired and
becoming fulfilled*

In the *'Why Do You Do That?'* chapter, we looked at Abraham Maslow's and Tony Robbins' 'human needs' models which chart the driving forces behind our behaviour. I'm a great fan of these models and use them a lot in my work because I firmly believe that by understanding our needs and acting positively to meet them, we will pretty much determine the direction our lives take and vastly increase our chances of untapping and fulfilling our potential.

The purpose of **You Can Raise Your Game!** is to share my lifetime's experience of the principles, materials and tools that I hope will inspire you TO TAKE ACTION towards fulfilling your needs and crafting an inspiring life for yourself, your loved ones and your community.

So, with the principles and tools now geared up for you to use, let's take some final glimpses at what inspiration and fulfilment look like through the eyes of people who have earned it for themselves and see what we can learn from their journeys.

WHAT DOES IT TAKE TO BE INSPIRATIONAL?

With the aim of *'mapping the world's most inspirational people throughout history'*, Raconteur – the British publisher of high quality current affairs and special reports on business, finance, tech and healthcare (www.raconteur.net) – canvassed over 2,000 of its international readers, followers, writers and contemporary figures and asked them *"who is the most inspirational person of all time?"*.

I like this approach because its main focus is upon the word 'inspirational' rather than 'powerful', 'wealthy', 'influential' etc... bucking the trend of many other such headline-seeking surveys. What I also like is that the list is ethnically, culturally, sexually, geographically and historically diverse AND many of the respondents voted for their own mothers, fathers or children – so much so that these categories occupied three spaces in the Top 50 inspirational people of all time.

The other 47 places were occupied by figures from all eras and all walks of life, including scientists, religious figures, artists and authors, political personas, business people, sports heroes, and public figures.

I've included overleaf the infographic of the survey's results (For a closer look visit www. raconteur.net/infographics/ the-worlds-most-inspirational- people). You may not fully agree with the cast of characters, and I'm sure you can think of other people who should make the list.

Just asking a few of my friends and colleagues led to answers such as Muhammad Ali, Bill Gates, Mark Zuckerberg, William Shakespeare, J.K. Rowling, Pablo Picasso, Buddha, John Lennon, Joan of Arc, Mo Farah, Princess Diana, Stephen Covey and Tom Cruise (plus various Bournemouth Athletic Football Club legends, of course!). Either way, it's a fun and informative exercise, and a worthy reminder that we could all benefit from a few more real-life contemporary inspirers in our midst.

"Whatever the role each person on the map has played, it's been worthy of inspiring others to succeed and achieve... it's certainly a testament to the breadth of inspiring people and the exemplars of humanity",

the Raconteur team correctly concludes.

Reading this Top 50 prompted me to look for some common attitudinal and behavioural denominators between the people on the list. What gave them all the strength of mind to pursue their beliefs with such courage and conviction, creating a legacy of inspiration? What traits do Margaret Thatcher and Mother Teresa share? Or Bob Marley and Stephen Hawking? Isaac Newton and Steve Jobs (apart from the significance of 'apple' in their lives, of course!)?

Obviously we can't all possess the scientific or mathematical brilliance of Albert Einstein, Hawking, Newton, Nikola Tesler and Alan Turing, or the artistic creativity and imagination of Leonardo da Vinci, Walt Disney, Coco Chanel, Estée Lauder and George Lucas. But is there something within these people that we all have the capacity to capture and shape to fulfil our potential, or to 'self-actualize' as Maslow describes it?

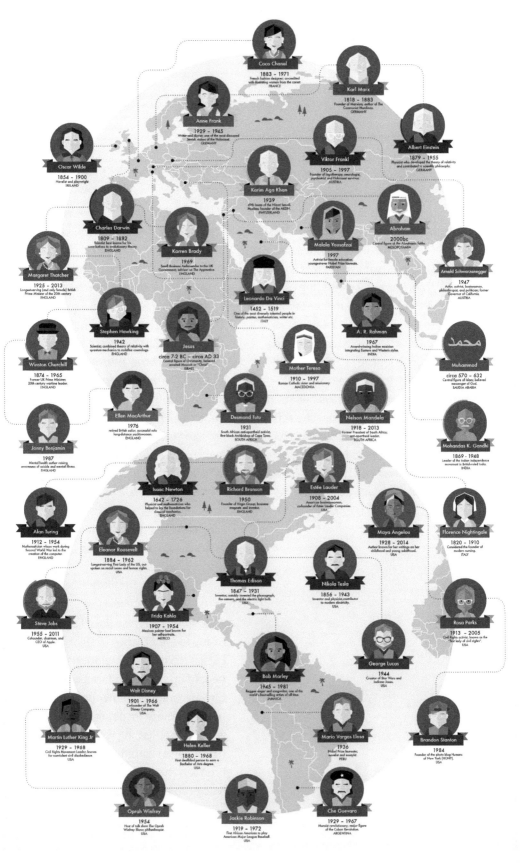

FAITH

Looking at the list, there are some instant headline observations that we can make. Apart from the obvious religious icons many of the top 50 hold a strong religious belief, across a variety of faiths. This is what links Margaret Thatcher (who was a Methodist lay preacher before entering politics) to Bob Marley (a militant follower and advocate of Rastafarianism) to Oscar Wilde (who had a long intense journey to Catholicism) to Rosa Parks (the civil rights campaigner who says her strength came from God when she refused to give up her bus seat to a white man in 1955) to Eleanor Roosevelt, who in her 1932 speech – titled *What Religion Means to Me'* defined her beliefs in this way:

"To me religion has nothing to do with any specific creed or dogma. It means that belief and that faith in the heart of a man which makes him try to live his life according to the highest standard which he is able to visualize... in all cases the thing which counts is the striving of the human soul to achieve spiritually the best that it is capable of and to care unselfishly not only for personal good but for the good of all those who toil with them upon the earth."

(You can read the speech in full at www.gwu.edu/~erpapers/ documents/articles/ whatreligionmeans.cfm)

A religious faith also links Karren Brady to Walt Disney to George Lucas... to the vast majority of people on the list, in fact. Such an obvious and potent denominator between these inspiring people is clearly something we cannot ignore, and I would like to broaden this out slightly without being too evangelistic about it.

I will always remember the day when I ran an employee engagement seminar for a well-known British retailer and I was addressing a room of around 250 store managers and their shop floor colleagues. We were discussing how to identify the needs of your fellow colleagues and customers and how to take these needs into account when communicating effectively with each other. Our outcome was to draw up a list of 'fundamental principles' that the store colleagues could implement in their relationships with each other and with their customers.

During the discussions, the subject of religious belief was brought up by one of the participants. She thought that it was important for her colleagues to take her beliefs into account when working with her and vice versa.

APP ALERT!!

We then discovered that we had followers of every major religion in the room on that day – Christians, Jews, Sikhs, Buddhists, Hindus, Muslims and also Spiritualists.

We therefore thought that it would be pertinent for them to talk about their respective religious principles and to see if we could distil some of them into a 'shared' set of principles that would be appropriate to use within the day-to-day running of their workplaces. The principles or 'fundamentals' we agreed upon were:

- *'The Golden Rule' – treat others as you wish to be treated*

- *Give more to the team than you wish to receive*

- *Compassion and respect for everyone*

- *Seek to understand before being understood, as Stephen Covey said. Be on 'receive' rather than 'transmit'.*

- *Look for the good in yourself and others*

And, as a Stalkie bonus, *'Love the day'* was also included.

These fundamentals were made visible on wallcharts and posters within their stores, as a collective conscience for everybody, regardless of their status within the store and their individual beliefs. And, to cut a long story short, when this was backed up by a further set of simple rules, processes and behaviours to bring the principles alive on a daily basis, it proved to be a breakthrough for stores where harmony had previously been lacking.

Just as many on our list of inspirers have been guided by a faith in someone or something greater than themselves, and have utilised the principles and 'rules' of that faith to achieve a higher potential, so have our 400 store colleagues. It may seem mundane – unlike our inspirers, they haven't broken any world records, invented a life-changing product or theory, or created a universally adored work of art or literature – BUT they have made a positive step-change in their own lives, the working lives of those around them and of their customers.

The knock-on effect was actually enormous and improved the quality of their daily existence *in line with their values* (the meaning of which we have already explored in *'Let the Real You Shine Through'* chapter of this book). If you can wake up every morning and look forward to making a positive difference in your own daily circle of influence, then it can only be a good thing.

Having faith is undoubtedly a means of enhancing your capability, and achieving your higher potential. We may not all be wired to believe in a God or a higher power, but we are all social beings who have an evolutionary need to feel connected to the world and others within it. Having faith, religious or otherwise, provides channels and opportunities for us to make such meaningful connections.

I have experienced much change and fulfilment in my own life and I have coached thousands of others to do the same, with faith being at the core. If you have faith that you can overcome an obstacle, conquer a fear, become an expert, learn a concept, hone a passion, complete a tricky task, or manage an awkward conversation, then it is likely that you will succeed.

You will find some robust tips on how to achieve this mindset in the *'An Attitude of Gratitude', 'Ignite Your Self-Belief'* and *'Praise Your Game Now!'* chapters of this book.

For a religious person it might be a faith in God that will assist them to succeed, for others it might be a faith in some other guiding force that regularly appears in their lives – but what's magical is that whenever you acknowledge and put your faith in that force it seems to appear more often. Our top 50 list has a great many inspirers who have gained an abnormal insight as a result of doing something greater than themselves. They have created meaning within themselves to give to others.

We all harbour a greater life than perhaps we are aware of.

APP ALERT!!

ADVERSITY AND ATTITUDE

Another undeniable connection between many of these inspirational people is their personal experience of adversity in their lives. Not only have they learned from their strength in coping with and, in many cases, conquering adversity, but they have also captured these learnings and passed them on for the benefit of others, many millions of others. By sharing their stories and passing on the principles and beliefs which gave them the strength of character to live through adversity, many of them have become role models in the process.

Some of these incidences of adversity are politically, eco-nomically or socially generated such as the pain and terror of Viktor Frankl and Anne Frank's experiences during the Holocaust, or the persecution and civil oppression that Martin Luther King Jr., Rosa Parks, Desmond Tutu, Nelson Mandela, Gandhi and Jackie Robinson all faced.

There is the sexual prejudice, victimisation or abuse that Maya Angelou, Oscar Wilde, Oprah Winfrey and Alan Turing stood firm in the face of. There are many fearless women represented on the list who have broken the historical barriers of gender equality through their words, deeds and leadership.

And there are those such as Stephen Hawking, Helen Keller and Frida Kahlo who have overcome debilitating physical circumstances to trail blaze within their respective fields.

Whatever the circumstances that brought these people into the public conscience, they are ultimate examples of how to use the principles that we have covered in the *'Fear into Power'* and *'Take the Power Back'* chapters of **You Can Raise Your Game!**

An understanding of their motivation, their faith and how they were able to stack up their self-belief (as we have investigated in our *'Ignite Your Self-Belief'* and *'Why Do You Do That?* chapters) can educate us all to look for and untap the potential within ourselves. Fortunately, by documenting their stories, we don't have to wait for our own brushes with adversity before we choose to explore how deep we can dig inside ourselves to excel.

THREE MODERN DAY INSPIRERS

I'm now going to illustrate some character traits shared by the majority of our inspirational icons by focusing in some detail on the biographies of three of the members of the list. I've chosen these three because they are people who have become viewed as 'extraordinary' after starting life in the most ordinary of circumstances. Their stories are from the here and now, they are products of our contemporary society and can be related to by all generations. My own children have heard about these people in their school studies or via social media. Amazingly, they also have much in common with the established and exulted historical figures on our list.

Jonny Benjamin MBE

Jonny Benjamin began having mental health problems at the age of 10 when he started experiencing auditory hallucinations. He later developed depression at 16 and was eventually diagnosed with schizoaffective disorder, a combination of schizophrenia and bipolar disorder, in his early 20s.

He had also been experiencing the delusion that he was living his own version of the film, *'The Truman Show'* (in this film, Truman is a man whose life is fake. The place he lives is in fact a big studio with hidden cameras everywhere, and all his friends and colleagues are actors who play their roles in the most popular TV-series in the world called *'The Truman Show'*. Truman thinks that he is an ordinary man with an ordinary life and has no idea about how he is exploited, until the day he finds out everything).

In 2008, Jonny was hospitalised as a result of his condition. He ran away from the hospital and decided to end his life by jumping off London's Waterloo Bridge. Seconds before leaping, a stranger intercepted him on the edge of the bridge and persuaded him not to jump. This talk was a game changer for Jonny, and for the stranger too.

Jonny's recovery was slow but he wanted to track down the stranger who saved him. He thought the man had been called 'Mike' and in 2014 he launched the #FindMike social media campaign. The campaign was supported by various high-profile people including Stephen Fry, Boy George, and British Prime Minister David Cameron.

Millions of people shared the story online and the hashtag trended in the United Kingdom, South Africa, Australia, and Canada. Eventually, the stranger's girlfriend saw the plea on Facebook and he came forward. Jonny found his good Samaritan, who was actually called Neil Laybourn.

Their reunion was turned into an award-winning Channel 4 documentary called *'The Stranger On the Bridge'* which you can find online at www.channel4.com

"It sounds very simple but Neil said he believed in me and thought I would get better. That changed my mind about what I was about to do," explains Jonny. *"I wanted to let people know that it's ok to have suicidal thoughts and feelings. I also hoped to show people that through talking about it, and by having someone else listen, it is possible to overcome the darkness that overwhelms a person when they feel helpless. This is something that I learned from my exchange with Neil, and a message that I've been trying to pass on to others."*

And 'pass it on' he most certainly has. Jonny's work is simply immense. He started vlogging about his experiences of mental health issues on YouTube in order *"to reach out to others with mental health difficulties"*. Hundreds of thousands of people from around the world have watched his vlogs and he was awarded the first annual Janey Antoniou award by the mental health charity, Rethink Mental Illness, for his mental health campaigning in 2013.

Of the motivation behind his work, Jonny says: *"I know that a lot of people are reluctant to get help, and a lot of that is because of stigma. But the only way we'll get rid of stigma is if we are more open and talk about mental illness. There is no shame or embarrassment in it. These are human experiences."*

In 2016 Jonny launched ThinkWell, an initiative to bring mental health education into schools. ThinkWell is designed to educate young people about mental health and break down the stigma surrounding mental illness and suicide through school workshops. Each session is delivered by a trained workshop leader and a qualified therapist.

As well as working in schools, he also gives talks in places such as prisons and hospitals to try to inspire others who may be struggling with a mental illness. He has carried out mental health work in India to change attitudes and reduce stigma and has written a book also called *'The Stranger on the Bridge'* about living with mental illness, which was published in 2018.

"When I was a teenager, I thought: 'It's just me, everyone else is having the time of their life'. And when I went to university, I thought I was the only person suffering," says Jonny. *"I was scared and embarrassed to talk about it. When you're young, you want to feel normal and like you fit in but I thought I'd be rejected. I just wish I'd opened up. I want to make sure people put as much priority on mental health as physical health. I don't know why we separate the two – it's just health."*

From that moment on Waterloo Bridge, Jonny Benjamin is now an award-winning mental health campaigner, film producer, public speaker, author and vlogger. In the Queen's 2017 New Year Honours List, he was awarded an MBE for his services to mental health and suicide prevention.

Upon receiving the award, Jonny said, *"I really couldn't do the work I do on my own. There are so many charities, organisations and individuals that I work together with that deserve recognition. I owe this award to all of them for their tireless efforts to raise awareness and reduce the stigma attached to mental health, as well as to my family and friends who have helped and supported me to where I am today. None of this would at all have been possible without my partner in crime, Neil Laybourn, who I feel forever indebted to. Whoever thought that the conversation we had on the bridge nine years ago when I was ready to take my own life would lead to all of this?*

"... I hope this accolade may give some hope to others who might be struggling that there is life after a diagnosis of mental illness and that such a diagnosis should never put limitations upon anyone. I will use this honour to push further for parity between physical and mental health in all areas of society, from healthcare to workplaces, and particularly within schools. It doesn't make sense why mental health education isn't compulsory on the school curriculum and yet physical education is.

"75% of all mental illness begins in adolescence and suicide is now the biggest killer of young people under 35 in this country. This is the area I want to particularly focus on during the next year. I won't rest until there is a change in the system."

Dame Ellen MacArthur DBE

Ellen MacArthur was born in Derbyshire in 1976. Both her parents were teachers. She acquired her early interest in sailing firstly by her desire to emulate her idol at the time, Sophie Burke, and secondly by reading Arthur Ransome's *'Swallows and Amazons'* series of books. She has since become the Patron of the Nancy Blackett Trust which owns and operates Ransome's yacht, *'Nancy Blackett'*.

Her first experience of sailing was on a boat owned by her aunt, which then prompted her to save her school dinner money for three years to buy her first boat, an eight-foot dinghy. While at school, she also worked at a sailing school in Hull.

When she was 17, MacArthur bought a Corribee (a sailing yacht) and named it Iduna; she described the moment she first saw it as "love at first sight". In 1995 she sailed Iduna single-handed on a circumnavigation of Great Britain.

Ellen first came to general prominence in 2001 when she came second in the Vendée Globe yacht race, setting the world record for a single-handed, non-stop, mono-hull circumnavigation by a woman and earning her an MBE for services to sport. At 24, she was the youngest competitor to complete the voyage.

In 2003, she set up the Ellen MacArthur Cancer Trust to take young people, aged between 8-24, sailing to help them regain their confidence on their way to recovery from cancer, leukaemia and other serious illnesses.

Having failed in her first attempt at a round-the-world record for a crewed yacht when her mast broke, she had a 23m trimaran built, tailored to her small height, which was named B&Q/Castorama (after two companies in the Kingfisher Group who sponsored her) and used it to break the solo record for sailing non-stop around the world.

During her circumnavigation, Ellen set records for the fastest solo voyage to the equator, past the Cape of Good Hope, past Cape Horn and back to the equator again. She crossed the finishing line near the French coast at Ushant on 7 February 2005, 71 days after setting out. She beat the previous record set by 1 day, 8 hours, 36 minutes, at an average speed of 15.9 knots (29.4 km/h). She had no more than 20 minutes' sleep at a time during the voyage, having to be on constant lookout day and night, and her video diaries became famous online and on TV.

Following Ellen's return to England, she was made a Dame Commander of the Order of the British Empire (DBE), the youngest ever recipient of this honour. Her many other sailing records include a world record for a transatlantic crossing by women, beating the previous crewed record as well as the singlehanded version.

After heading up her own sailing team, BT Team Ellen, in October 2009 MacArthur announced her retirement from competitive racing to concentrate on her Ellen MacArthur Foundation dedicated to educating students and businesses on the subject of resource and energy use in the global economy.

Please do read more about her magnificent exploits in her books, *'Taking on the World!', 'Full Circle'* and *'Race Against Time',* or via www.ellenmacarthur.com

Malala Yousafzai

Malala Yousafzai was born in July 1997 in Mingora, Pakistan, located in the country's Swat Valley. For the first few years of her life, her home town remained a popular tourist spot that was known for its summer festivals. However, the area began to change as the Taliban tried to take control.

Yousafzai attended a school that her father, Ziauddin Yousafzai, had founded. After the Taliban began attacking girls' schools in Swat, and refused to let girls attend them, Malala gave a speech in Peshawar, Pakistan, in September 2008. The title of her talk was, *"How dare the Taliban take away my basic right to education?".*

In early 2009, Malala began blogging for the BBC about living under the Taliban's threats to deny her an education. In order to hide her identity, she used the name Gul Makai. Her activism resulted in a nomination for the International Children's Peace Prize in 2011.

That same year, she was awarded Pakistan's National Youth Peace Prize, citing her role model as Benazir Bhutto, twice Prime Minister of Pakistan, who was the first woman to head a democratic government in a Muslim majority nation before being assassinated in 2007 by a suicide bomber. The militant Islamist group al-Qaeda claimed responsibility, although the involvement of the Pakistani Taliban was widely suspected.

Bhutto was a controversial figure and faced much opposition from Pakistan's Islamist lobby for her secularist and modernising agenda. She nevertheless remained domestically popular and also attracted support from Western nations, for whom she was a champion of democracy and women's rights.

Malala's prominence resulted in the Taliban issuing a death threat against her and in October 2012, when 15-year-old Malala was on her way home from school, a gunman boarded the bus and fired at her, hitting Malala in the left side of her head; the bullet also travelled down her neck. In a critical condition, she was flown to a military hospital in Peshawar.

A portion of her skull was removed to treat her swelling brain. To receive further care, she was transferred to Birmingham, England. Once in the UK, Malala was taken out of a medically induced coma, but still required multiple surgeries to repair nerves which had paralysed the left side of her face.

In March 2013, she was able to begin attending school in Birmingham, and she gave a speech at the United Nations on her 16th birthday. She has also written a beautiful autobiography, *"I Am Malala: The Girl Who Stood Up for Education and Was Shot by the Taliban"*.

In spite of still being a named Taliban target, Malala remains a high profile advocate for the power of education for girls around the world. She has been twice nominated for a Nobel Peace Prize, winning in 2014 – the youngest person ever to receive the accolade. United Nations Secretary-General Ban Ki-Moon described her as "a brave and gentle advocate of peace who through the simple act of going to school became a global teacher."

Before winning the award Malala said *"If I win a Nobel Peace Prize, it would be a great opportunity for me, but if I don't get it, it's not important because my goal is not to get a Nobel Peace Prize, my goal is to get peace and my goal is to see the education of every child."*

For her 18th birthday in 2015, also called Malala Day, the young activist continued to take action on global education by opening a school for 200 Syrian refugee girls aged 14-18 in Lebanon. All expenses are covered by the Malala Fund, set up in 2013 to champion girls' rights to free education (www.malala. org). Upon opening the school she declared, *"Today on my first day as an adult, on behalf of the world's children, I demand of leaders we must invest in books instead of bullets."*

That day, she also urged her supporters on The Malala Fund website: *"Post a photo of yourself holding up your favourite book and share why YOU choose #BooksNotBullets – and tell world leaders to fund the real weapon for change, education! The shocking truth is that world leaders have the money to fully fund primary AND secondary education around the world – but they are choosing to spend it on other things, like their military budgets.*

APP ALERT!!

"In fact, if the whole world stopped spending money on the military for just 8 days, we could have the $39 billion still needed to provide 12 years of free, quality education to every child on the planet."

In April 2017, United Nations Secretary-General António Guterres appointed Malala as a UN Messenger of Peace to promote girls' education. The appointment is the highest honour given by the United Nations. Malala went on to study philosophy, politics and economics at Lady Margaret Hall College, Oxford, following in the footsteps of her heroine, the former Pakistani president Benazir Bhutto.

EDUCATION AND LEARNING

In Jonny, Ellen and Malala, we have three role models from three generations. The first connection to note? A desire for education.

In addition to her schooling, Ellen was committed to educating herself and becoming an expert in sailing – her biggest passion in life – from an early age. Malala's desire for an education was so strong that it took her into dangerously political territory, fronting up against the Taliban, and later, dovetailing her commitment to global campaigning with taking a degree at Oxford.

Jonny has learnt to become an eloquent and compassionate expert in the field of mental health which has not only given him the coping mechanisms to handle his own mental health challenges but also to conduct high level discussions with government agencies and to compose educational pieces that he delivers to schools and businesses.

Throughout the list of inspirational people, education is a key binding factor. In some instances, this refers to 'academic' education – all those inspirers who have made an impact in the world of science, technology, psychology, philosophy and the life sciences tend to have pursued the highest possible academic route, for example.

However, the word education is derived from the Latin word 'educare' which means to bring up. Another Latin word 'educere', means to bring forth. It's therefore not just about academic achievement, it also refers to the desire to want to improve, develop and build up knowledge in a passion, a venture, a pastime or in oneself: exactly what you are doing now by taking on board this information.

A lot of great entrepreneurs had issues with formal education; among those without college degrees are Steve Jobs, Richard Branson, Thomas Edison and Walt Disney.

Says Richard Branson , *"Looking back, I believe that the qualities that make for a great entrepreneur – such as boundless energy, a curious nature and, sometimes, an obstinate streak – are not often attributes demonstrated by top students in the classroom. So it should not be very surprising that many of the world's great entrepreneurs and business leaders had difficulties with formal education...*

"... Often, their frustration in the classroom was a result of impatience: The greats were eager to get out and build their businesses, which pushed them to drop out of high school or forgo college in order to follow their dreams. For instance, Walt Disney famously dropped out of school at age 16 to found his animation company, while the great American tycoons of the late 19th century – Andrew Carnegie, Cornelius Vanderbilt and Thomas Edison – had little or no formal education before they set out to seek their fortunes. Some entrepreneurs, including Carnegie and Henry Ford, the 20th century industrialist, came from impoverished backgrounds and did not have the support at home to start – let alone complete – their formal educations. Rather, they set up businesses to make ends meet and eventually flourished."

APP ALERT!!

Branson was not the perfect student himself: *"I was no exception, and I have written in previous columns that I was not great at school. I constantly pushed against rules and authority, and I liked to challenge the way that things were 'always' done. My curiosity often got me into trouble with teachers.*

"But it was not just my attitude that was different – I had dyslexia. When I was a young student, this learning disability was poorly researched and was often mistaken for laziness or a poor ability to learn. At school I was thought to be slow, and indeed I struggled to keep up. I initially channelled my youthful energy into sport, then I got into early business ventures." I can certainly relate to that myself!

"But my learning disability has never been a setback – it actually gave me a great advantage in business, since I have been able to bring a different perspective to problems and challenges, which often enables me to see solutions more clearly.

"For example, I have always hated jargon, and I am confused by long and wordy drafts of plans. So in Virgin's early days, I would ask simple questions that others did not. Over the years, asking the simple questions and striving to answer them have become some of Virgin's most important characteristics.

"So in many ways, my education has been my career. For almost 50 years, Virgin's varied collection of businesses and non-profits means that I have studied and come to understand many sectors – aviation, banking, media, hospitality and the fitness industry, to name a few. More recently, my career has also given me interesting new perspectives on many significant issues such as climate change, conflict resolution and global health care. In the end, solutions to big problems such as these won't come from doing school reports, but by getting out there, asking questions, seeing things differently and finding the answers ourselves." (This interview material is published at www. virgin.com/entrepreneur/richard-branson-why-entrepreneurs-struggle-with-formal-education)

ROLE MODELS AND MENTORS

Many of our most inspiring sportspeople don't boast of a formal education, but they have become true experts in their field, not just as a result of their talent but because of their desire to fulfil their potential, their commitment to practice and the coaching they have received. Usain Bolt, for example, never hesitates to praise his long-term coach and mentor Glen Mills, Head Coach at Racers Track Club in Kingston, Jamaica.

After a disappointing showing at the Athens Olympics, crashing out of the heats in the 200 metres, Bolt hired Mills to take him to the next level and finally fulfil his youthful promise. Mills appreciated Bolt's natural ability, but recognised his poor technique – a backwards running style and lack of core strength, triggering a series of hamstring problems.

Together, they undertook a two year project of tearing down Bolt's technique, breaking his bad habits, and then reconstructing it all into world-beating form. It was a repetitive and challenging process, supplemented by hours of video analysis to help correct every metre of Bolt's individual race stages. The rest is golden history.

This leads me to my next observation: the natural propensity of our inspirers to value role models in their lives and to seek out and surround themselves with mentors and influencers or peers who share similar purpose and values. Let's look again briefly at our three modern day heroes.

From becoming a loner, Jonny Benjamin fortuitously found his ideal mentor in Neil Laybourn, who Jonny describes as his *'partner in crime'*. Theirs is a relationship that not only saved a life, but created a united purpose which has resulted in them collaborating on many projects including their joint founding in 2019 of Beyond Shame Beyond Stigma, a mental health education charity supporting young people, their families and teachers. Read more at www.jonnybenjamin.co.uk

Ellen MacArthur has always stated that one of her motivating factors to becoming the best yachtswoman in the world was her desire to emulate her idol Sophie Burke. At every step of her illustrious career, Ellen has engaged the foremost sailing tutors, yacht designers and crew to deliver her dreams. It's a facet that she has now taken into her new life with The Ellen MacArthur Foundation where the roll call of experts and partners (Google, Nike, Philips, Unilever) is phenomenal. She proudly admits that she is the figurehead, they are the stars.

Malala is treading a similar path, hailing Benazir Bhutto as her role model and connecting herself not just to the finest academic tutors in philosophy, politics and economics but also working alongside an impressive leadership team within her Malala Fund and travelling the world meeting, lobbying and learning from political and business leaders at the highest level.

Throughout our list, we can trace abundant examples of our inspirers learning from the best practitioners in their respective fields and attaching themselves to peer groups and collaborators who share similar values, talents and passions: from Charles Darwin who enjoyed active membership of groups such as the Plinian Society and the Geological Society; to Karl Marx who idolised the philosopher Hegel, had a lengthy collaboration and founded Marxist theory with Friedrich Engels; and to Coco Chanel who mixed with the elite in the arts such as Stravinsky, Nijinsky, and Sam Goldwyn amongst a host of others.

The politicians amongst the group obviously share manifestos and doctrines with their fellow party members, the religious leaders share their faith with their God and their fellow worshippers, and the business leaders run their businesses with trusted colleagues who share a common aim for (hopefully) great customer service and sustained growth.

I highly commend the need for idols and role models in your life. Your role models don't have to be the stuff of fantasy or beyond reach. I was determined enough to meet some of my heroes such as Sir Charles Dunstone, Julian Richer and Randy Gage, but I have also gained role models from much more humble sources such as The Boys' Brigade, my local church, business contacts, people I have met socially and clients who have wowed me with their insight into life experiences that we all encounter.

It's for this reason that I run my 'Mastermind Groups' (which you can get a flavour of by looking at the video footage on www.paulstalker.com) where entrepreneurs and business leaders of all types come together on a monthly basis to share their personal and business-related challenges, opportunities and successes, and to mentor and be mentored by like-minded individuals.

These groups are not only very dear to me, our members and our personal development, but they are also great fun and produce many mutually rewarding friendships. They are living proof that the more accessible your mentors are to you, and the more you can find out about them and discover the ingredients of their success, then the more you can model their behaviours and call upon their wisdom to reach your own goals.

If your goal is to be a great parent or to have flourishing personal relationships, who do you know who has achieved this in their lives? If you wish to start a business, who has done the same? Who has overcome an obstacle similar to one that you're currently encountering in your life? Who do you know that has turned their health around, or maybe grasped an opportunity to travel, or to perform on stage, or turned their hand to something creative? If these are things you aspire to, who can inspire you to walk in their shoes?

Perhaps it could be a neighbour, somebody in your sports team, social or hobby group, or a local business person? Or, of course, a coach such as myself or a member of my talented Raise Your Game team. Remember also that three places in the inspirational top 50 list were reserved for 'family members' (who were voted for by Raconteur's readers) – if you view your parents, grandparents, sisters and brothers, aunts and uncles as solid role models in your life, do you regularly tap into their knowledge and advice?

APP ALERT!!

SHARED VALUES AND COLLABORATORS

Due to the series of events that have occurred in their lives – some random, some thrust upon them, some through their own design and control – the list of top 50 inspirers is jam-packed with people who have each identified a purpose in their life and have achieved their iconic status by being true to their mission and values – the importance of which was covered in depth in *'Let the Real You Shine Through'* chapter of **You Can Raise Your Game!**

In addition to your role models, who do you know that shares a similar purpose or values and beliefs as you? The majority of inspirers on our list have all benefited significantly from the company they have kept and the involvement that their special allies have had in supporting them in their lives.

We've discovered in the *'Fear into Power'* and *'Take the Power Back'* chapters how we all default or gravitate towards people who help us meet our needs at any given time.

We have also learned in the *'Why Do You Do That?'* chapter that we all have the gift to choose whether to meet our needs positively or negatively. Remember the near terminal downward spiral that Ade's life took when he conspired to keep the company of fellow drug dealers and addicts? These were allies who helped him to meet his needs negatively.

When circumstances dictated that he was cared for by people who helped him to meet his needs positively, Ade's life was dramatically turned around.

A similar transformation happened to me when I was supported through my cancer by health and nutritional experts such as Dr. Rosy Daniel and I built my faith, my emotional and spiritual health, through learning from my mentors.

Have you thought hard about the company you're keeping and whether your current peers and friends are the ideal collaborators to support your growth and personal development, and vice versa?

Do they help you to play to your strengths and manage your weaknesses? Do they have a similar curiosity and appetite to learn and be educated in the types of skills and pursuits that you are interested in?

Are they inspiring? Just what can they bring to your table, and you to theirs? Of all the people you know, or wish to know, who are the ones that could serve you best in achieving your goals?

Overleaf, in the final 'workout' of this book, we will take a closer look at the qualities you should be seeking in your personal 'board of directors'.

Stalkie's
'COLLABORATORS' WORKOUT

*On the page opposite, list in the first
column the goals you wish to achieve.
In the next column list the people you
will look to collaborate with to help
you fulfil each goal.*

*These are some top tips towards
choosing your dream team:*

- *Do they share the same goals and
  values as you?*

- *Do they share the same thirst for
  knowledge and education?*

- *Do they have previous experience
  or access to the tools and
  knowledge you require?*

- *Do you respect, trust and admire
  them?*

- *Do they walk the walk as well as
  talk the talk?*

- *Are they emotionally and
  practically resourceful?*

- *Are they influencers (able to follow
  through with other decision makers
  or to draw upon or recruit other
  like-minded people)?*

- *Are their strengths and weaknesses
  compatible with yours?*

- *Do they have energy, enthusiasm
  and are they fun?*

- *Will they look for the good and
  Praise Your Game, and vice versa?*

- *Are they creative and do they think
  outside the box?*

- *Are they credible and task
  completers?*

- *Are they open to challenges and
  to change, rather than set in their
  ways?*

- *Will they encourage and promote
  two-way feedback?*

- *Can you envisage forming a long-
  term bond with them?*

- *If you were to set up and market
  YOU Ltd, would you employ them
  to sit on your board of directors
  and to be a perfect ambassador
  for your brand?*

GOALS TO ACHIEVE

PEOPLE TO HELP ACHIEVE THEM

_____   _____

_____   _____

_____   _____

_____   _____

_____   _____

_____   _____

_____   _____

_____   _____

_____   _____

_____   _____

_____   _____

_____   _____

_____   _____

_____   _____

_____   _____

_____   _____

PHILANTHROPY

It's of no great surprise that the majority of inspirational people, particularly those who have mined the depths of their inner strength and surfaced wiser and stronger, develop an appetite for philanthropy – the practice of helping people less well off than themselves.

Because their accomplishments have put them firmly in the public eye, this has obviously given them a blessed opening to leverage their prominence and attract the expertise and investment required to set up a charity or foundation for example – to create a positive legacy around their passions, their areas of knowledge and their skills.

We can follow this thread not only through the heroes of our three case studies, but also through multiple members of our top 50 inspirers list: examples include The Bob Marley Foundation. Marley once said *"The greatness of a man is not in how much wealth he acquires, but in his integrity and his ability to affect those around him positively"*.

His family-run foundation aligns with charities and causes that support education, commit to protecting the earth, and invest time and resources into the well-being of humanity.

Arnold Schwarzenegger's incredible dedication to his various charitable organisations include his 'After-School All-Stars' project which provides comprehensive programmes that keep children safe and help them succeed in school and in life. In 2011 he co-founded 'R20', a global non-profit of sub-national governments and regional leaders working together to address climate change and build a green economy.

In 2012 he partnered with the University of Southern California to launch the USC Schwarzenegger Institute to continue his work on the many humanistic policy initiatives he championed during his two terms as Governor of California.

Whilst Governor, he did not accept his salary of $175,000 per year, and instead donated it to charities. After witnessing the violent clashes between white supremacists and anti-racism campaigners in Charlottesville, Virginia in 2017, Schwarzenegger donated $100,000 to the Simon Wiesenthal Center, an anti-hate organisation which has the mission of expanding tolerance through education and fighting hate all over America – in the streets and online. Arnie explained;

"While these so-called 'white nationalists' are lucky to live in a country that defends their right to voice their awful, incorrect, hateful opinions, the rest of us must use our voices and resources to condemn hate and teach tolerance at every opportunity. My message to them is simple: you will not win. Our voices are louder and stronger. There is no white America, there is only the United States of America. You were not born with these hateful views, you can change, grow, and evolve, and I suggest you start immediately." Arnie also has affiliations to at least 17 other charities.

One final example, to prove that philanthropy is not necessarily a matter of ego; in his lifetime, Steve Jobs received criticism for seemingly not donating enough money to worthy causes.

Jobs simply chose not to disclose his philanthropic endeavours and refused to discuss the subject even with his biographer, Walter Isaacson. It surfaced recently that the founder of Apple Inc. donated $50 million of his own money to hospitals in California and funded HIV and AIDS research. Steve Jobs' widow has now founded the 'Emerson Collective' which makes anonymous donations to various causes, from grants to political campaigns.

I have highlighted some pretty major league examples here because our list is full of major league players, but what I want to emphasise is that philanthropy exists at various levels, many of which we can instigate in our daily lives, without the need for wodges of cash, or without becoming a publicly recognised figure.

APP ALERT!!

GRATITUDE AND PASSING IT FORWARD

APP ALERT!!

When I researched these inspiring people, it was clear that one of the motivating pillars behind their amazing personal journeys and behind their subsequent philanthropy was gratitude. Whatever the reason for these people to reach their position of high standing in our society, they are (with few exceptions) highly grateful for their life experiences and grateful for the opportunity to make a difference to others who may relate to their challenges.

When they were faced with difficult situations (stimulus), they were ultimately able to choose their response – Jonny could have jumped off the bridge; Ellen could have given up after her failed world record attempts; and Malala could have chosen not to challenge the persecuting Taliban regime.

Instead, they all reframed the situations in front of them, put them into a new perspective and took action, just as we describe in the *'An Attitude of Gratitude'* chapter of **You Can Raise Your Game!**

Philanthropy affords the opportunity to pay your gratitude forward, to pass it on. To be inspiring in your everyday life, within your family, social group, workplace or community does not require big sweeping gestures. You may remember that one of my tips in the *'An Attitude of Gratitude'* chapter is to "Make someone's day more pleasant and rewarding without any thought of repayment".

It might be something as simple as chatting with them, thanking them, listening to them with interest. It may be by sending a card, a letter, flowers, helping with the shopping, giving them a lift, or a hug.

In the *'Praise Your Game Now!'* chapter, I insist that you should play to your strengths and manage your weaknesses – *"do more of what you love and what you're good at, rather than burn up belief, time and energy in what you're not good at. The aim is to relegate your weaknesses... so your strengths are free to develop"*. This is something else that our inspirers have in common with each other.

You may have a signature strength which you often receive compliments about – it could be your parenting skills, you might be good with words, or patient and kind, an astute business person, an expert at a hobby or skill, have a lovely singing voice, cook a great cake; organise cracking social events and parties, understand people and relationships well; maybe you're green-fingered, or IT and computer proficient – then please look for every opportunity to hone your strengths further and to pass your knowledge on to others.

"Being a force for good can be as small or big as you wish it to be depending upon your personal goals."

– Paul Stalker

You could start with your family, friends, colleagues and leave it there. You could venture further out to embrace a wider audience through giving talks, seminars and exhibitions with community, social and business groups.

I know so many people of an older generation who take enormous pleasure from being members of their local U3A (University of the Third Age) group where retired and semi-retired people come together to continue their educational, social and creative interests in a friendly and informal environment.

At its heart, the U3A believes that continuing to learn, develop your interests, make friends and try something new, is a life-long passion. Members of local U3As draw upon their knowledge and experience to teach and learn from each other. It's all voluntary, and covers hundreds of different subjects. It's a great vehicle to pass your knowledge on to a welcoming, attentive audience (www.u3a.org.uk)

APP ALERT!!

COMPELLING COMMUNICATION

Online and social media platforms now give us all access to communicate with a wide audience. And it's a genuine two-way process. Not only is it possible to learn from so many authoritative sources, subscribe to specialist forums and prompt an exchange of dialogue and ideas, but it also gives us a shop window to exhibit and express our own significant messages. It can prove a lucrative avenue to raise awareness and money for various philanthropic exploits.

This is also evidenced by the presence of Brandon Stanton in our inspirers list. Brandon was essentially a photographer/ blogger until his photojournalism book *'Humans of New York'*, (www. humansofnewyork.com) which contained hundreds of portraits of people living and working in New York, accompanied by snippets of conversations about their lives, went viral, with over 20 million followers on social media.

In 2013, Stanton was named one of Time Magazine's '30 Under-30 People Changing The World'. He has since travelled to the Middle East, to Pakistan and Iran to photograph people under the auspices of the United Nations. At the conclusion of his trip to Pakistan, Stanton crowd funded $2.3 million to help end bonded labour there.

In January 2015, Stanton was invited to the Oval Office to interview President Barack Obama. The trip concluded a two-week crowd funding campaign on Humans of New York in which $1.4 million was raised. In March 2016, Stanton opposed Donald Trump's presidential campaign, criticising Trump on social media for hateful speech. A day after his Facebook post, it had over 1.6 million likes and was shared nearly one million times.

Subsequently, Stanton posted stories and photos from the Paediatrics Department of Memorial Sloan Kettering Cancer Center in New York City. As he did for his other projects, Stanton created a fundraising campaign, and raised over $3.8 million for paediatric cancer research.

Again, we can detect some of the conclusive character traits of a truly inspiring person in Stanton, but what excites me, and I hope excites you too, is the organic, word of mouth (virtual mouth!) way in which he has come to prominence through the open source communication platforms he has used to attract his neighbourhood of followers and establish himself as a role model for the millennial generation.

We are in an era where celebrities such as Beyoncé, Kim Kardashian, Taylor Swift, Cristiano Ronaldo and Ariana Grande have over 250 million Instagram followers each (at the time of writing). We can all now create, disseminate and share messages with more people than ever before – the opportunities to inspire and be inspired, to fulfil and be fulfilled have, in theory, never been greater!

APP ALERT!!

But every person has their own view of what fulfilment looks like and means to them. Your quest is personal to you and to those whom you wish to involve. First you must learn what fulfilment means for you, then you must plot your growth path and take action towards it.

Using my **You Can Raise Your Game!** principles, materials and tools with faith, pig-headed determination, discipline, fun and celebration will get you there.

Love the journey.

Pass on the message and inspire others every step of the way.

TOP 10 TIPS TOWARDS BEING INSPIRATIONAL AND FULFILLED

1. Have faith. Using the examples of the inspirational people we have discussed in this chapter, you can see just how many of them have been guided by a faith in someone or something greater than themselves. Having faith is undoubtedly a means of enhancing your capability, and achieving your higher potential. We may not all be wired to believe in God or a higher power, but we are all social beings who have an evolutionary need to feel connected to the world and others within it. Having faith, religious or otherwise, provides channels and opportunities to make these meaningful connections.

2. Back your faith with a set of simple rules, processes and behaviours which keep it alive on a daily basis, such as:

   - *Treat others as you wish to be treated*

   - *Give more to the team than you wish to receive*

   - *Compassion and respect for everyone*

   - *Seek to understand before being understood*

   - *Look for the good*

3. You will become stronger through coping with and conquering adversity in your life – no matter the scale of the adversity. Capture your learnings and pass them on for the benefit of others. By sharing your stories and passing on the principles and beliefs that gave you the strength of character to deal with your challenges, you will become a role model to your family, friends, colleagues and community.

4. Throughout the list of inspirational people, education is a key binding factor. The word 'education' is derived from the Latin word 'educare' which means 'to bring up' or 'to bring forth'. It's therefore not just about academic achievement, it also refers to the desire to improve, develop and build knowledge in a passion, a venture, a pastime or in oneself (exactly what you are doing now by taking on board this information).

5. Seek out role models/mentors/ influencers in your life who share a similar purpose and values. Have you thought hard about the company you keep and if your peers and friends are the ideal collaborators to support your growth and personal development, and vice versa?

Do they have a curiosity and appetite to learn and be educated in similar skills or pursuits? Are they inspiring? Just what can they bring to your table, and you to theirs?

APP ALERT!!

6. Develop an appetite for philanthropy – helping people less well off than yourself. Philanthropy exists at various levels, many of which we can instigate in our daily lives, without loads of cash or becoming a publicly recognised figure.

7. Play to your strengths and manage your weaknesses – do more of what you love and what you're good at, rather than burn up belief, time and energy in what you're not. The aim is to relegate your weaknesses... so your strengths are free to develop.

8. One motivating pillar behind the amazing personal journeys of so many inspiring people is gratitude. Whatever the reason they reach their elevated standing in our society, they tend to be highly grateful for their life experiences and for the opportunity to make a difference to others who may relate to their challenges.

9. Communicate openly, through whatever channel suits you best. Online and social media platforms give us all access to communicate with a wide audience. As well as learning from so many authoritative sources and specialist forums, prompting an exchange of dialogue and ideas, they give us a shop window to exhibit and express our own significant messages. If the spoken word suits you better, and you only wish for a small, private audience (your family, for example), speak with them!

10. No prizes for guessing my final tip... yes, TAKE ACTION! You know by now that in Stalkie World, action supersedes everything. This chapter should provide you with the final proof of how taking action shaped the destiny and fulfilment of some of the world's most inspired and inspiring people. Now it's your turn to take action and Raise YOUR Game!

AN INDEX OF MAJOR TERMS, PRINCIPLES, PEOPLE AND PLACES IN YOU CAN RAISE YOUR GAME!

RAISE AR App

How to use, 12

View videos via the app on the
following pages –

Stalkie's Top 10 Tips

Stalkie's Workouts